Women Creating Indonesia

Women Creating Indonesia
The First Fifty Years

edited by
Jean Gelman Taylor

Published by

MONASH
ASIA
INSTITUTE

First published by
Monash Asia Institute
Centre of Southeast Asian Studies
Monash University
Clayton, VIC 3168

National Library of Australia Cataloguing-in-Publication Data:

Women creating Indonesia: the first fifty years

Includes index
ISBN 0 7326 1156 3
ISSN 0727 6680

1. Women - Indonesia - history. 2. Women - employment - Indonesia. 3. Women - Indonesia - social conditions. I. Taylor, Jean Gelman, 1944-. II. Monash University. Monash Asia Institute. (Series: Monash Papers on Southeast Asia; no.44)

305.4209598

For information on this and other publications from the Centre, write to:

The Publications Officer
Monash Asia Institute
Monash University
Clayton, VIC 3168
Australia
Email: monash.asia.institute@arts.monash.edu.au

Contents

Contributors

Susan Blackburn received her PhD in Political Science at Monash University in 1972. She teaches Southeast Asian Politics, Gender in Asian Politics and the Politics of Development at Monash University. She is the author of *Jakarta: A History* (under her former surname Abeyasekere) and *Practical Revolutionaries: A Study of Community Aid Abroad*.

Charles A. Coppel received his PhD in Politics at Monash University in 1976. He teaches modern Indonesian History at the University of Melbourne. He is the author of *Indonesian Chinese in Crisis* and 'From Christian Mission to Confucian Religion: The Nederlandsche Zendingsvereeniging and the Chinese of West Java, 1870–1910' in D.P. Chandler and M.C. Ricklefs (eds), *Nineteenth and Twentieth Century Indonesia: Essays in Honour of Professor J.D. Legge*.

Janet Elliot is a candidate for her PhD in History at the University of New South Wales. She is the author of 'Labour Legislation and Gender in Indonesia', *Asian Studies Review*.

Anton Lucas received his PhD in Southeast Asian History at the Australian National University in 1980. He teaches Indonesian Studies (language, history and musical culture) at Flinders University. He is the author of *One Soul, One Struggle: Region and Rebellion in Indonesia* and 'The Communist Anti-fascist Movement in Java' in A. Lucas (ed) *Local Opposition and Underground Resistance to the Japanese in Java 1942–45*.

Jean Gelman Taylor received her PhD in History at the University of Wisconsin-Madison in 1978. She teaches Southeast Asian History at the University of New South Wales. She is the author of *The Social World of Batavia: European and*

Eurasion in Dutch Asia and of 'Kartini in her Historical Context' in *Bijdragen tot de Taal-, Land- en Volkenkunde.*

Ailsa Thomson Zainu'ddin received her PhD in History of Education at Monash University, Melbourne in 1983. She taught History of Education, including History of Education in Southeast Asia and History of Education for Women, in the Faculty of Education, Monash University from 1965 to 1992. She is the author of *A Short History of Indonesia* and has also written a number of articles and papers on R. A. Kartini.

Glossary

Chinese

empeh	elderly, paternal, male relative
engkong	paternal grandfather; old man
she	family name
singkeh	China-born Chinese

Dutch

fröbelschool	kindergarten
hoogeschool	high school
Hoogere Burgerschool (HBS)	high school
Meester (Mr)	law graduate title
Mevrouw (Mevr)	Mrs
Meer Uitgebreid Lager Onderwijs (MULO)	middle school
raadsheer	justice, judge

Indonesian

adat	custom; customary law
asrama	dormitory
bupati	head of a region
camat	sub-district head
ibu	term of address, Mrs; mother
isteri/istri	wife
kabupaten	administrative unit below a province; residence of a *bupati*
kain	wrapped skirt
kampung	urban residential quarter; village
kaum kuno	conservative people
kaum santri	orthodox (Muslim) community
kebaya	long-sleeved blouse
kewajiban	duty
kerudung	woman's hairstyle
kretek	clove cigarette

kromo	level of Javanese language
lurah	village head
mas	term of address, e.g. by wife to husband
mbok/embok	term of address; older sister
nyai	term of address for secondary wife or mistress
nyonya (ny.)	Mrs
pak/bapak	Mr; father
pangreh praja	civil service
pedjonggo/pujangga	poet, classical poet
pemuda	youth; young man
peranakan	person of mixed race
pesantren	Islamic school
pici	fez-style man's hat
pinggitan	seclusion (of unmarried girls)
pryayi	Javanese upper class
sarong/sarung	sewn skirt
sinjo/sinyo	term of address; Eurasian man
slendang/selendang	woman's decorative scarf; cloth used for carrying baby or goods
totok	immigrant
wayang	theatre; shadow puppet
wedana	district head

Japanese

hoko	service to the state
jugun ianfu	comfort women, camp followers
kempeitai/kenpeitei	Japanese secret police
ken	administrative region
kumicho	hamlet head
messhiboko	selflessness
mompe	pants suit for women
romusha	conscripted labourer; coolie
si	municipality

List of Organisations

Chinese

Chung Hwa Hui	Association of Chinese Students
Chung Hwa Hui Tsa Chi	Association of Chinese Students in the Netherlands
Tiong Hoa Kwee Koan	Chinese Association

Dutch Titles

Bond van Vereenigingen van Jong Chineezen in Indonesie	Union of Associations of Chinese Youth in Indonesia
Jong Islamieten Bond	Islamic Youth Union
Vereeniging voor Vrouwen kiesrecht	Organisation for Women's Suffrage
Vereenigde Oost-Indische Compagnie	United East Indies Trading Company
Volksraad	People's Council

Indonesian Titles

Balai Poestaka	Publishing House
Barisan Buruh Indonesia	Indonesian Workers' Alliance
Barisan Buruh Wanita	Female Workers' Alliance
Barisan Poeteri Djakarta Tokubetsu Si Fujinkai	Jakarta Municipality Girls' Brigade of the Women's Association
Barisan Srikandi	Srikandi Alliance
Golkar	Association of Functional Organisations
Istri Indonesia	Indonesian Wives
Madjlis Islam A'laa Indonesia	Indonesian Muslim Supreme Council
Partindo	Party of Indonesia
Perikatan Perempuan Indonesia	Indonesian Women's Association
Poeteri Mardika	Independent Young Ladies
Putera (Pusat Tenaga Rakjat)	Centre of the People's Forces

Japanese Titles

Fujinkai	Women's Association
Huzinhokokai	Women's Section of Java Service Association
Jawa Hokokai Honbu	Java Service Association
Joshi Sendenbu	Young Women of the Information Service
Keibodan	Vigilance Corps
Seinendan	Youth Corps

Introduction

Jean Gelman Taylor

A glance at the table of contents suggests diversity of topic in this little volume. Here collected in five essays are the impressions of a Dutch visitor to the Indies in 1912, debates over the new Chinese woman, analysis of an occupation-era magazine, reflections on photography and costume, and a review of post-war labour legislation. These essays range over half a century. They begin in the newly created Netherlands East Indies and end in the first years of the Republic of Indonesia. Closing this monograph is a memoir of Kurnianingrat Ali Sastroamijoyo, whose personal and professional life was intimately connected with the creation of Indonesia. Her story has been reconstructed from a draft manuscript and a correspondence spanning 40 years.

An underlying unity is revealed in the titles of these essays. Five carry a variant of 'woman'. This common focus is to be expected, for the essays were first conceived as papers presented at the Asian Studies Association of Australia's Fourth Conference on Women in Asia in October 1993. That conference prodded participants to return to materials already mined in order to bring the female half of society into the story of the making of Indonesia. These essays show how rich are the written sources; the memoir illustrates how a friendship sustained through correspondence generates material for constructing the social history of an era.

Writing women into history does not end with adding a few more pieces to the jigsaw puzzle. Each essay in this volume, if read alone, does add to our knowledge of Indonesia in the first half of this century. Read together, the essays modify standard accounts of a new nation in the making. Out of these very different essays I find a congruence of themes. I will briefly summarise the papers, and then show how they produce new perspectives and suggest new areas for research.

First in this monograph is Susan Blackburn's 'Western Feminists Observe Asian Women: An Example from the Dutch East Indies'. We have for the years 1899–1904 the view from the aristocratic household of Java in the letters of R.A. Kartini. We also have biographies of lettered women who followed her. Examples are the lives of widely known figures such as Dewi Sartika and Maria Ulfah, as well as biographies of heroines with regional reputations, such as Walanda Maramis and Rahma El Junusiyah. We have also the institutional history of women's organisations. What is known is what a select group of Indonesian women thought, felt and argued.

Susan Blackburn asks: to whom were Indonesian women talking? What were their companions in dialogue saying? The Abendanon family preserved all Kartini's letters; the Sosroningrat family, it seems, did not preserve any of Rosa Abendanon's letters to Kartini. Susan Blackburn, therefore, looks to the published correspondence of Dr Aletta Jacobs to help fill the gap. Aletta Jacobs was the first female physician in Holland and a campaigner for the vote for women. She toured Java and Sumatra in 1912. Kartini had already died, but her letters had been published the previous year in Holland. Dr. Jacobs's status and interests ensured that she was introduced to women of Kartini's class and education. Women's issues were on the agenda of the Dutch press. Aletta Jacobs was commissioned by an Amsterdam newspaper to write a regular column on her immediate impressions as she met representatives of women in travels through Asia and Africa.

We find that Aletta Jacobs saw the problems for women in the same way as did Kartini. She, too, lamented the plight of the aristocratic woman, urged reform of marriage laws, argued there was a relationship between education of girls and motherhood, and discussed the benefits to society to be expected from vocational training for girls. These observations and goals formed the platform of all the Indonesian women's organisations of the 1920s and 1930s. So Susan Blackburn discovers a community of analysis; she establishes how quickly ideas could run around the world. The concerns of those Indonesian women who met in congresses were in line with those of women in Europe and the United States. There was more than an international consensus; there was an international sensibility.

An end to polygamy was the catchword of the times. Kartini said it, Aletta Jacobs said it, Poetri Mardika said it, and so did spokeswomen for the Indonesian Chinese community. The social history of that community tends to be overlooked. Yet it seems to have mirrored trends in the larger society. The Yap sisters, who are the subject of Charles Coppel's essay, 'Emancipation of the Indonesian Chinese Woman', realised Kartini's ambition to live and study in the Netherlands. They spoke and wrote in Dutch on topics of interest to the colonisers. Like Kartini, they received favourable reports in the Dutch-language press, and enjoyed patronage in the highest levels of the colonial service. On one occasion at least, the audience addressed by the Yap sisters included J.H. Abendanon, ex-director of native education, mentor of Kartini and collector of her letters. Our topics are as intertwined as was the colonial elite.

Speeches made by the two sisters to the association of Indies Chinese students in the Netherlands form the starting point for Charles Coppel's essay. Like Susan Blackburn, he looks for the partner in dialogue, and finds it for the Yap sisters in the serialised novels published by the Chinese-owned, Malay-language press. He selects from a wide reading two such novels for detailed study. Their leading female characters are the Dutch-educated, Sino-Indonesian girl who is looking for a marriage partner. When the Yap sisters addressed public forums on new roles for Sino-Indonesian women, they were wives and mothers. Married woman and mother are absent from the novels. The novelists look at the path to womanhood proposed by the Yap sisters (and by Kartini, Aletta Jacobs, Poetri Mardika and the rest), and declare it to be undesirable. The partner in dialogue asserts that a Dutch education corrupts because it brings a girl into the public domain. Far from being equipped as ideal mother, she is rendered unmarriageable to any man of honour.

What is striking in the speeches and in the novels is that the model held up for emulation is China. The older Yap sister rested her argument for women's rights on the assertion that equality between men and women existed in pre-Confucian China. For their part, the novels idealise China's family and social system. On the one hand, then, we have utopia identified as a society 2600 years in the past, and on the other, praise for a social system that produced mass impoverishment and no solution save male emigration. The model for the Sino-Indonesian community is a China that never existed.

Rules of conduct for the new Asian woman came from many quarters. Anton Lucas looks at those generated by the militarist society of Japan in 'Images of the Indonesian Woman During the Japanese Occupation, 1942–45'. His essay takes up a phase in Indonesia's history as yet little studied. For three years, Indonesia, along with many other countries of Asia, was absorbed within an empire at war. New models for Indonesia's women were imposed by a country that in 1925 had given all adult Japanese men the vote (called universal suffrage by many historians), whilst banning all adult Japanese women not only from joining political parties, but from listening to political speeches and reading political pamphlets.

Japanese military administrators on Java directed their messages through the women's organisation, Fujinkai and through *Djawa Baroe*, a fortnightly Malay language magazine published in Batavia. What was the Japanese part of this dialogue? Above all, Indonesian women were exhorted to enter the workforce. Here Japan's military administrators showed themselves as blind as most historians of Indonesia in failing to note what Aletta Jacobs reported to her Amsterdam readers: the great majority of women in Indonesia worked outside the home. Equality of situation was not offered, but Fujinkai and *Djawa Baroe* alike urged Indonesian women to become equal participants with men in combatting western imperialism.

Indonesian women were also told to serve husband and nation by adopting Japanese-inspired hairstyles, clothes, perfumes and standards of beauty. Anton Lucas reviews the magazine covers, advertisements and cartoons which convey the model born of Japan's encounter with the west in the Meiji era. In Japan the daughters of impoverished peasants were drafted into factory labour or sent into brothel prostitution. We do not yet know if the middle class Indonesian ladies who joined Fujinkai and read *Djawa Baroe* altered their hairstyles and renounced the goals of their pre-war organisations which called for reform of marriage laws, education for girls, independence from foreign rule for Indonesians, and equality of rights for citizens. Histories of the Indonesian women's movement and of the revolution are silent on Fujinkai. They also omit from examination the wartime experience of Indonesian women as factory labourers and prostitutes for the Japanese army.

Fifty years have passed since the declaration of Indonesia's independence on 17 August, 1945. Most Indonesians alive today have never known colonial rule. Indonesia's government offers these inheritors of a free Indonesia a vision of their country's past that makes the ending of Dutch rule the defining moment. Whilst the period of Dutch rule was one brief moment in a much longer history, the declaration of independence allowed nationalist historians to gather up many diverse and parallel histories into one. Holland's role, in nationalist historiography, was to be the agent of disruption, fracturing old unities. For personal experience is substituted official history and official photography. The technology of printing and photography that the Dutch introduced to Indonesia is now used to fix and make permanent a particular view of the past.

In my essay, 'Official Photography, Costume and the Indonesian Revolution', I examine photographs recording the historic proclamation of independence in 1945. I trace aspects of Java's history that led to the western suit becoming the costume of men holding political power. I also discuss the invention of a costume dubbed 'traditional' that made women representatives of the nation's past. Official photography also preserves a record of women's involvement in the struggle for independence through militia, Red Cross and government agencies. The printed text is silent on women working for their country's independence. The photographic record says they did, and its evidence is that such women saw themselves as linked to the future, not the past. Like the men, women in action wore western costume.

In 1949, the world recognised Indonesia as an independent state. The Republic's government and unions adopted as policy equality of access to education and jobs for men and women. Republican cabinets of 1947 and 1948 had written into law the goals formulated by the pre-war women's associations. Here we see the concrete influence of the first generations of Dutch-educated women and of their congresses, whose activities are consigned (if noted at all) to sections on education in general histories of Indonesia.

Implementation of policy was altogether different, as Janet Elliot shows in 'Equality? The Influence of Legislation and Notions of Gender on the Position of Women Wage Workers in the Economy: Indonesia 1950–1958'. She demonstrates that the relevant context for considering problems in implementing labour laws is not the history of the Indonesian Women's Congress, but a colonial past of unequal pay and restricting women workers to the lowest level of jobs. We might add that the era of Japanese rule proves to be a continuity as far as the history of women workers is concerned.

In their time, Kartini and the Yap sisters called for vocational training and public careers for women. Their class interests did not inspire them to reflect on the problems of women already working, for example, the servants in their households and the tenants on their family fields. Nor did Kartini and the Yap sisters offer solutions (or thought) for the majority of women in the paid workforce, those down mines, on plantations, in factories or working from home on piece-rates. Janet Elliot shows that cultural notions of gender in colonial and independent Indonesia produced tasks labelled 'women's work' that were equated with low pay, and divorced from job training and security of tenure. The power of received ideas affected all workers adversely. Working class women provided a huge reserve of cheap labour to keep everyone's wages down.

Having introduced the essays as snapshots of discrete moments in a half-century of dramatic change, I will now suggest how attention to women members of society can alter the narrative of the whole. In their several ways, these essays confirm, but also challenge, interpretations in the current literature. The big picture is reinforced, on some essential points, with the addition of data on women. On other points a rethinking is called for by data showing that the impact of specific events differed according to an individual's gender as well as class. Such conclusions are common to all social histories that focus on women and gender.

Takashi Shiraishi (1990) has argued that a nationalist discourse was created in the early decades of the 20th century by countless individuals. His study focusses exclusively on men. Apart from the now obligatory mention of Kartini's name (which is different than considering her intellectual contributions to Indies life), there is not a single reference to the women who were editors, party leaders, writers, educators, or social workers in his period. The men of the Shiraishi study were bent on questions of identity. We must turn to other sources if we wish to add women into the intellectual ferment of Shiraishi's period. Insofar as women were included in, or contributed to, this discourse, it was in the following manner. Women of the well-to-do classes were urged to acquire a western education in order to be supportive wives to modern men, exemplary mothers of future leaders, and channels of useful information to the mass of the poor. In this latter role they would actively promote the welfare of the state.

Kartini's name is linked in the standard histories with this aspect of the new discourse. Susan Blackburn's paper reminds us that the Indies context included European women. We know about the European men who contributed to the early union movement. Names such as Hendrik Sneevliet and E.F.E. Douwes Dekker are well known to students of the 'awakening' or nationalist movement. The same is true for the European men associated with the Ethical Movement such as D. van Hinloopen Labberton, J.H. Abendanon and C. Th. van Deventer. Now we learn that European women also contributed to the debates of the day.

Susan Blackburn focusses on a visitor to the Indies in Dr Aletta Jacobs. Jacobs's main purpose was not meeting Indonesian women, although that was on her agenda. Her chief object was to elicit support amongst European women who were living temporarily in the Indies for the right of Dutch women to vote in representative institutions in Holland. Accordingly, in any narrative of the evolution of political life and parties in the Indies there should be reference to the Indies branch of the Organisation for Women's Suffrage. It has bearing on the course of Indies history that the Dutch women who mixed socially with members of Indonesian women's organisations were themselves the target of political agitation.

Dutch women attained full citizenship in Holland in 1919. Proponents of women's rights then turned their attention to elective bodies in the Indies, the city governments and the Volksraad (People's Council). Because these were multi-racial bodies, the issue of female suffrage included Indonesian women as well as Europeans from the beginning. The rights of women were being discussed, therefore, by Dutch and Indonesian women who had none.

Charles Coppel produces evidence that women also contributed to the discourse provoked within the Sino-Indonesian community by political revolution within China itself. Sons of Chinese families whose history in the Indies stretched back over several generations attempted to reformulate an identity as Chinese that was modern and focussed on the new China of Sun Yat-sen. They demanded parity with Europeans at law, cut off their queues, put on the suit, demanded Dutch and Mandarin Chinese in the school curriculum. All this is familiar territory to the student of the Tiong Hoa Hwee Koan. The influence of immigrants from China after 1911, the importing of tutors for schools, the sale of books in Chinese, all that is well enough understood.

Women were amongst those early 20th century immigrants from China. As yet their story is untold. Only the poorest of the poor, purchased in the Singapore transit auctions for brothels, have received much attention from scholars (e.g., Ingleson 1986, Warren 1990). Research needs to be done on another segment of the Chinese female immigrant group: the imported wife. Not all immigrant men in the 20th century maintained two households, with a village wife in China and a local wife in Indonesia. Men with money sought a wife from China. She was emphatically not a farm girl, but the daughter of the China-based partner in a commercial firm. Photographic records and memoirs (Nieuwenhuys 1988: p.124; Chang 1981) tell us that this bride was usually a woman with bound feet. She was the one who demonstrated family status and connections, the one who would rule a household made up of numerous women collected in the Indies.

So it is that some girls of the Indies, the daughters of Indonesian women in Chinese households, came under the rule of women of old China. One possible future for them was as wife to a connection of their father, a business partner who might be based anywhere in the Indies, in Southeast Asia, or in China itself. These Sino-Indonesian girls were just starting to attend schools alongside Europeans and the well-off Javanese. They, too, began to speak and think in Dutch, and they espoused deals we associate with Kartini and her disciples.

Kartini's world held in it the polygamous household of the bureaucratic elite. The world of the rich Sino-Indonesian girl held within it old China. As part of a re-sinicising community, therefore, women used the new forums of Indies Chinese associations to condemn two evils of old China: polygamy and footbinding. This is why so much of the content of the speeches Charles Coppel has unearthed is devoted to a country which most of the Sino-Indonesian community, and certainly the great majority of its women, had never seen. This is why the Yap sisters railed against footbinding.

It could be argued that the practice of footbinding had no relevance to the communities of Java where Sino-Indonesians lived. This marker of female status seems never to have been introduced into Indonesia. Attention to women in history explains why this is so. The history of Chinese migration to Indonesia is the history of male migrants until the 20th century. In China, footbinding was associated with region and class; it was a practice of northern China and characteristic of women attached to upper class men as wives, daughters, concubines and prostitutes. Most migrants to Southeast Asia, however, were men and they came from southern China.

Another layer of explanation lies in identifying who in Chinese society bound feet. In China, men were admirers of small feet, but those who reshaped the feet of little girls were women. Evidence has not been uncovered that men, after they had grown wealthy in Indonesia, imported women from China who could perform such a task on girls in their households. When women with bound feet did arrive in Indonesia from China as wives this century, it was too late to establish the custom for their daughters. For it was after 1911, and the practice was becoming condemned in China itself.

Histories of the overseas Chinese stress the trade diaspora (e.g., Fitzgerald 1972; Wang 1981). That was made up of a constant movement of men buying and selling from fellow countrymen who had settled permanently in ports along the trade network. Essential to that diaspora, though little remarked, was intermarriage with women from the host community and the creation over generations of permanent mixed communities. I will return to this aspect below. A feature of the well-established trade diaspora now appears to be the movement of women both into and out of China. The Yap sisters indirectly tell us this in their speeches demanding that women in Sino-Indonesian households be protected from polygamy and bound feet, and associated with the ideals of 1911.

At this point it is useful to note that the Yap sisters were proposing a foreign model for women like themselves. They were born in the Indies; their first language was Malay; they could not read Chinese. The Yap sisters, in fact, seem very like Kartini and the women Aletta Jacobs met. But they did not urge young Sino-Indonesian girls to become Kartinis. Here, again, attention to women produces layers of explanation to what we think we already know. The Chinese of Indonesia made an effort to re-sinicise themselves, to recover a speaking knowledge of Chinese, to attain literacy and to learn the literature and history of China. 1911 was a turning point for Chinese Indonesians. After the revolution, China became paramount to Chinese living overseas. The Coppel essay adds to our information: Chinese women were a part of this trend too. They also wanted to shake off the Indonesian part of their heritage and become more

Chinese. The communications networks of the colonial power enabled women to do so, alongside the more publicised activities of their brothers.

I think that the Yap sisters and those hostile to their aspirations from within the Sino-Indonesian community tell us something more. Somewhere within the history of the Sino-Indonesian community lies the history of Indonesian women. We are used to the single reference in histories of the *peranakan* Chinese to 'local women' who obligingly married all those immigrants (e.g., Reid, 1992; Bouquet-Siek, 1981; Skinner, 1960). Frequently, there is the assertion that local wives must have been helpful in promoting the businesses of their Chinese husbands: they could sell trade goods because they spoke the local language. The clichéd high status of the Southeast Asian woman, unhesitatingly contrasted with the oppressed status of women in China, is the reason why local women are thought to have filled a commercial role.

Along the way, Indonesian women bore children and saw to it that their babies grew into adults who spoke no Chinese. In the Indies, colonial law, Confucian traditions and Muslim prescription all discouraged women from crossing boundaries of race and religion through marriage. When it occurred, all three agreed that the woman ceased to be a member of her community of birth and joined that of her husband. This is why Indonesian women were counted as Europeans if they married Dutch men, and why Indonesian women were Foreign Orientals if they married Chinese men.

We can now make a guess at the social origins of women who did cross boundaries of race and religion. They were not the Kartinis in their *kabupatens* of privilege, nor the daughters of the *kaum santri*. Arranged marriage and privilege assigned such girls to men of their own group. And where the family itself functioned, when not prey to depredations from the local *bupati*, or dispersed by poverty, then, too, daughters tended to marry within their own group.

Jan Breman and E.V. Daniel (1992) have argued that the colonial world contained numbers of men no longer attached to their birth communities. They trace a pre-colonial history for wandering men. They were the ones who would be targeted by labour recruiters for work on the plantations of Sumatra. Recruiters did not go into the village and lure the sons of prosperous families away from their paddy fields. They took men already landless, men who denied family responsibility, who appeared to be 'free'.

Breman and Daniel focussed on men who, after all, made up most of the coolies. But we can hazard a guess, whilst waiting for the detailed research, that there were similarly women detached from their birth communities, and that they were the ones recruited for coolie labour and for work in the households of Europeans and Chinese as housekeeper-concubines. We have the dim outlines of a pre-colonial history for detached women too. For the trade networks flowed with slaves. Three thousand Chinese merchants had temporary wives in Banten in 1596 (Reid, 1992: 205); about 50,000 foreign traders in Malacca in 1511 apparently also had temporary wives (Thomasz, 1993: 71).

In the 19th century slavery died out in the archipelago. Batavia's slave market had closed in 1816. Chinese and European men thereafter took into their households 'free' women, those whose families could not provide an arranged marriage and a secure place in the local community. The influence of those local mothers can be discerned in food, language, unbound feet. Such women, the rejects of their own society, did not urge their Sino-Indonesian daughters to model themselves on the aristocratic lady of Javanese culture. The maternal side did not have Kartinis in it. Javanese women who ended up in Chinese households were the servants of Kartini's class, women who had been exploited, sold, driven off the land, without protection or patron. Western-educated daughters in Sino-Indonesian households needed roots and role models. There was nothing in their mothers' heritage on which they could wish to draw. The speeches of the Yap sisters thus lead us into the history of Indonesian women from the poorest classes as well as into the history of the modernising Chinese.

Emphasis on women leads into another set of explanations too. These have to do with polygamy, role models, poverty and work. Polygamy is usually seen as the issue par excellence of the upper class woman. This is because they were the ones who commanded the latest technology. Print fixed the ideas of Kartini and the Yap sisters. We know what they thought, and more broadly we know the history of their class. Kartini and the Yap sisters were married women. Polygamy became, in the nationalist discourse, something that all modern folks rejected, men as well as women. It was not the rights of women so much, perhaps, as the demands of modernity that made polygamy become at first shameful and then deemed an outmoded custom amongst men of the colony who mixed much with the Dutch and hoped for promotion in the colonial world. We can signal here the influence of Dutch women from Holland in fostering a mentality that equated polygamy with backwardness, inferiority and being Asian.

Polygamy was not just a problem for the Javanese and Sino-Indonesian lady. It was also a problem for the other woman, the secondary wife, the concubine, the servant to the chief wife and male head of household. Such women were not sent to Dutch schools. They did not visit European ladies and discuss with them the rights of women. They did not attend meetings of the Indies Chinese Students Association or study law in Holland. They had no rights to their own children, not even to be addressed as 'mother'. Even Kartini exercised her superior rights in the polygamous household in speaking of 'my children', and she worked to detach her husband's children from their birth mothers.

Once polygamy became rarer, the candidates for jobs as concubines and secondary wives had now to seek new forms of employment. One alternative was the factory. Janet Elliot shows us that women factory workers experienced the same problems as concubine and secondary wife: long hours, no protection under the law, harrassment from employers, sudden dismissal, status of servant not worker. Janet Elliot sees a link to colonial capitalist forms of employment in the 1950s view of women as cheap, expendable labour. Employers in independent Indonesia, according to this reasoning, had their attitudes formed in the colonial Indies, and this is why they continued to treat their female employees as the lowest on the ladder. I see another continuity, that is a history of men and women detached from social supports, pushed out of village and landownership, lacking tenants' rights. The history of employment in Indonesia from colonial and pre-colonial times does not contain the concept of workers' rights.

It is curious that costume is cause for comment in all of the essays. We are used to the notion that status is demonstrated by clothing, through quality of materials, superior design and construction, and degree of restriction to physical movement. Clothing in Europe had evolved in the age of mass production to demonstrate the political rights of the middle class male, and the decorative role of the woman. Upper class men in the colonised world and upper class men in societies in contact with the colonising world cut their hair and adopted the western suit. This was characteristic of men in Meiji Japan and in Siam, for example, and they did so around the same time that Mangkunagoro VI of Java cut his own hair and ordered his suite to follow him. I quote Sukarno rejecting the *sarung* as the costume of servants. He promoted *kain* and *kebaya* for women. Janet Elliot's photographs of women in the unhygienic factories of the 1950s show them in *kain* and *kebaya*. The lowest paid and the unskilled wear tattered versions of the clothing style launched as national costume for women, the servants of the nation. The new nation was committed to the goals of the ladies; but it asked women workers in *kain* and *kebaya* to wait until the country could afford to give them the same rights and pay as men.

All our essays raise issues of identity, language and print technology. The general connections between language and identity are well understood. Kartini and her class wrote in Dutch to analyse, disseminate and create ideas. So did the educated Sino-Indonesian woman. Men were quicker to grasp that they must communicate in a language of the people, not of the rulers. Neither Dutch nor Japanese could ever become the new *kromo* of Java. Because the key feature of *kromo* is that it is the language inferiors use to address their superiors. Dutch and Japanese were the languages elite Javanese men and women used to address their foreign rulers. They were never the languages of the majority.

The Chinese of Indonesia were early users of Malay. Their elite was in far off China. In Indonesia they had only the language of their maternal heritage. Some did use Malay to argue for learning Chinese. But it is Malay that brings Indonesian Chinese into literature, that is the literature of printing press and book. Sino-Indonesians did not introduce or debate their ideas in the Chinese language. They urged the learning of Chinese on a readership that spoke and read Malay. That readership was both male and female. The Yap sisters derived their notions of China from the Malay-language press.

It is this fact that helps us put the immigration from China into its Indonesian context. The immigrant or *totok* experience was a brief moment in a much longer history. That history is the transformation from a society of trade diasporas into local communities, detached from Chinese language because of the influence of the women of the household who raised generations of Sino-Indonesian children to speak the local vernacular. Chinese language in Indonesia is the history of an introduced language, the attempt of self-conscious Chinese organisations. The real language of the Chinese of Indonesia was Malay. Male immigrants were absorbed into the host community through its female members. The descendants of male immigrants wrote in the language of the host community, not because they picked it up in the market place and pawnshop, but because it was their mother's tongue. It is the male ordered view of history that obscures this fundamental point.

The history of Japan's rule of Indonesia represents a major discontinuity when focus is on the relations between immigrant men and local women. In Indonesia's history, women follow men. Indonesian wives of Chinese men were Chinese; Indonesian wives of Dutch men were Dutch. But Indonesian wives of Japanese men were not Japanese. This long Indonesian tradition led those women who lived with Japanese officers to perceive themselves as wives. Recent research (Amsakasasi 1992) shows they expected to be called to Japan by their Japanese husbands after the war, once the repatriated soldiers were resettled in their homeland. This cultural expectation of Indonesian women tells us something about Japanese values and Japan's history as a colonial ruler. Japanese concern for racial homogeneity was so powerful it denied the privilege of cross-racial and cross-religious marriage to men as well as to women. Societies, such as the Dutch, that permitted men to marry outside the racial group made the foreign women insiders. Japanese society stressed racial purity; it allowed Japanese men to exploit foreign women sexually, whilst preventing incorporation of foreign women into Japanese society through marriage.

We can deduce from Anton Lucas's research that mass organisations, such as the Jawa Hokokai, created in Indonesia by the Japanese, were really associations for men, with very small women's sections, and there were also separate women's organisations altogether. Single sex membership was a feature of party organisation in Japan. It was also characteristic of all pre-war nationalist parties in Indonesia.

One legacy is the continuing excision of women from their socio-economic class. Janet Elliot shows this in labour legislation specifically designed for women. As a group, women's morals were to be protected. (Why is it that Indonesia's political leaders did not worry over the morals of male workers?) Detaching women from class removes them from legal protections in terms of equality of earnings and promotion. The history of political organisation in Indonesia is one that defines men by ideological allegiance, and defines women by gender, divorced from ideology. That history produced labour legislation that categorised female employees as women, rather than as workers deserving equal protection under the law.

Ailsa Thomson Zainu'ddin brings to this volume a contribution of a different order. A specialist in the history of education, Ailsa Zainu'ddin was also the intimate of Jo Kurnianingrat. Their friendship had its roots in the early years of the Republic of Indonesia, when Kurnianingrat was representative of the new Indonesian woman as careerist and Ailsa Zainu'ddin was recruited to assist in introducing the teaching of English to Indonesia's schools. Their professional and personal association took place within a circle of Indonesian and Australian scholars. On the urging of many, Jo Kurnianingrat began to write an account of her life and of Indonesian women in the pre-war nationalist movement and the revolution. By the time she set to rewriting Indonesia's history, it was almost too late. Kurnianingrat was ill and blind; death came before the life was written. Ailsa Zainu'ddin has undertaken, therefore, to connect fragments of the manuscript, personal memories and the private correspondence of Jo Kurnianingrat's circle, using, as far as possible, her subject's own words.

We learn details about Indonesian society that escape the general histories. Indonesia of the 1920s and 1930s has been characterised a society of 'apartheid' (Fasseur 1994: 31); yet we learn from this memoir that Indonesian men and women presided over classrooms in European first class schools to teach Dutch children, and that they were members of the teaching staff of the Dutch-Chinese schools. The corrosive hatred of Sino-Indonesians is apparent from this memoir, and also the deep-seated suspicion of the 'ningrat class'. Jo Kurnianingrat furthers our conception of the revolution as civil war. In every family there were individuals who fought for the revolution, others who worked for the Dutch and drew their pensions. Jo Kurnianingrat's happy recollections of growing up in a polygamous family differ markedly from the lonely childhood and sense of neglect experienced by others who have left a record in print (e.g., Hatta 1981; Partini Djajadiningrat 1986).

Published memoirs and biographies are still few for Indonesia as Andrew McIntyre points out in his introduction to *Indonesian Political Biography* (1993), which examines seven men's lives. They are even fewer for women. Yet the peculiar circumstances of women's lives—enforced leisure in the case of Kartini, or the habit of maintaining friendship through correspondence—may mean, as Ailsa Zain'uddin shows, that the sources exist. Social history lies in private correspondence. If brought to light it might well integrate women into the story of Indonesia's creation.

In the second half of the 20th century change has come to how we view the past. Contemporary historians do turn their attention to women in the societies they study, not as an undifferentiated group, but as individuals distributed amongst all classes, creeds and historical epochs, influenced by and influencing real events. These few essays are a part of that scholarly enterprise.

References

Amsakasasi et al. 1992, 'Screams from the Bamboo House', *Review of Indonesian and Malaysian Affairs*, 26(2), Summer.

Bouquet-Siek, Margaret 1981, 'The Peranakan Chinese Woman at a Crossroad', in Lenore Manderson (ed.), *Women's Work and Women's Economic Roles*, Australian National University Press, Canberra.

Breman, Jan and E. Valentine Daniel 1992, 'Conclusion: The Making of a Coolie', *Journal of Peasant Studies, Special Issue on Plantations, Proletarians and Peasants in Colonial Asia*, 19(3 & 4), April-July.

Chang, Queeny 1981, *Memories of a Nonya*, Eastern Universities Press, Singapore.

Djajadiningrat, B.R.A. Partini 1986, *Partini, Tulisan Kehidupan Seorang Putri Mangkunagaran*, as told to Roswitha Pamoentjak Singgih, Jakarta, Djambatan.

Fasseur, C. 1994, 'Cornerstone and Stumbling Block: Racial Classification and the Late Colonial State in Indonesia', in Robert Cribb (ed.), *The Late Colonial State in Indonesia*, KITLV Press, Leiden.

Fitzgerald, C.P. 1972, *The Southern Expansion of the Chinese People*, Australian National University Press, Canberra.

Hatta, Mohammad 1981, *Mohammad Hatta, Indonesian Patriot: Memoirs*, C.L.M. Penders (ed), Gunung Agung, Singapore.

Ingleson, John 1986, 'Prostitution in Colonial Java', in David P. Chandler and M.C. Ricklefs (eds.), *Nineteenth and Twentieth Century Indonesia: Essays in Honour of Professor J.D. Legge*, Monash Papers on Southeast Asia No.14, Centre of Southeast Asian Studies.

McIntyre, Andrew (ed.), 1993, *Indonesian Political Biography: In Search of Cross-Cultural Understanding*, Clayton, Monash

Papers on Southeast Asia No. 28, Centre of Southeast Asian Studies.

Nieuwenhuys, Rob 1988, *Met vreemde ogen: Tempo Doeloe- een verzonken wereld*, Querido, Amsterdam.

Reid, Anthony 1992, 'The Rise and Fall of Sino-Javanese Shipping' in V.J.H. Houben et al. (eds.), *Looking in Odd Mirrors: The Java Sea*, Leiden University, Leiden.

Shiraishi, Takashi 1990, *An Age in Motion: Popular Radicalism in Java, 1912–1926*, Cornell University Press, Ithaca.

Skinner, G.W. 1960, 'Change and Persistence in Chinese Culture Overseas: A Comparison of Thailand and Java', *Journal of the South Seas Society*, 16.

Thomasz, L.F.F.R. 1993, 'The Malay Sultanate of Melaka' in A. Reid (ed.) *Southeast Asia in the Early Modern Era. Trade, Power, and Belief*, Cornell University Press, Ithaca.

Wang Gungwu 1981, *Community and Nation: Essays on Southeast Asia and the Chinese*, Heinemann, Kuala Lumpur.

Warren, James Francis 1990, 'Prostitution and the Politics of Venereal Disease in Singapore, 1870–1898', *Journal of Southeast Asian Studies*, XXI(2), September.

Western Feminists Observe Asian Women: An Example from the Dutch East Indies

Susan Blackburn

Indonesian feminism is considered to date from the start of the 20th century, with the writings of Raden Adjeng Kartini (1879–1904), the daughter of a Javanese *priyayi* (traditional official). From Kartini's correspondence with a number of Dutch people, including feminists, it is clear that she was profoundly influenced by Western feminism.[1] At an impressionable age, she devoured a Dutch feminist novel of the time, entitled *Hilda van Suylenberg* (Goedkoop de Jong van Beek en Donk, 1897), whose message, that it was essential for women to be educated and enter the workforce rather than be destined purely for marriage, she endorsed wholeheartedly.

Reading Kartini's letters raises the question as to what Dutch feminists thought about Indonesian women. The colonial period witnessed interaction between these two groups, yet we know little about this dialogue and its effects. Feminists engaged in such exchanges today are beginning to be interested in the antecedents and lessons from the past of this frequently discomforting but stimulating relationship, as witness the burgeoning literature about the colonial feminist experience. India is especially rich in alliances and conflicts between colonial and colonised women.[2] As yet, however, there is very little

---

1 Kartini's letters have been published in different collections and in various translations. The most comprehensive collection in English is translated by Joost Coté, (Kartini, 1992). It contains a bibliography on Kartini, pp.557–83.
2 A good collection of studies on this subject is Chaudhuri and Strobel, 1992.

feminist writing about the colonial period in Indonesia, or the Dutch East Indies as it was then called.[3]

Some insight into early feminist encounters can be gained from the travel writings of Aletta H. Jacobs, including her description of travels in the Dutch East Indies in 1912. Jacobs (1854–1929) was the pioneering and most famous feminist in the Netherlands of the late 19th and early 20th centuries. Indeed, she could have provided the inspiration for Kartini's favourite novel, *Hilda van Suylenburg*: like one of the leading characters in the novel, Jacobs was a doctor and a tireless campaigner on behalf of poor women (for whom she provided, among other things, birth control advice) and of the value of education, training and socially-useful work for all women. From 1903 until Dutch women won the right to vote in 1919, Jacobs was president of the Vereeniging voor Vrouwenkiesrecht (VVVK or Organisation for Women's Suffrage).[4]

Jacobs published her travel letters, really a collection of articles for an Amsterdam daily paper, as *Reisbrieven uit Afrika en Azie* (Jacobs, 1913, Travel letters from Africa and Asia) in two volumes in 1913. Closer inspection of the circumstances of these writings reveals how unusual they were.[5] In 1911–12 Jacobs undertook a tour lasting 15 months along with the leading American suffragist, Carrie Chapman Catt (1859–1947), to spread the message of women's right to vote. Catt and Jacobs

---

3   Dutch feminists have begun to mine this field in the last few years. Examples of their writing can be found in some of the chapters in Locher-Scholten and Niehof, 1987. A useful survey article is van Bemmelen, 1989.

4   Surprisingly, there is no full-length biography of Aletta Jacobs. See the entries under her name in *Biografisch Woordenboek van Nederland*, 1979, pp.271–74; and by Inge de Wilde, in *Biografisch Woordenboek van het Socialisme en de Arbeidersbeweging*, 1988, pp. 83–88. Aletta Jacobs' memoirs have also been published: Jacobs, 1924.

5   In one way Jacobs' book can be seen as an example of the new travel journalism made possible from the late 19th century onwards as improved transport and the global spread of colonialism made it easier for Europeans to travel. J. van Goor (1992) has made a study of some Dutch travel writings contemporaneous with Jacobs. Of the writers he discusses, Jacobs bears most comparison with van Kol, the socialist parliamentarian, who reported on Indies affairs for his party.

were pioneers of the International Women's Suffrage Alliance (IWSA), which, since its formation in 1902, had held five international congresses, bringing together suffrage organisations (mainly from European and North American countries) to exchange experiences and ideas in their struggle to win the vote for women. Catt was president of the IWSA from 1906 to 1939 (Van Voris, 1987). The tour was intended to raise further support for women's suffrage and to learn about women's situation in parts of the world which as yet had no representation at IWSA congresses: it was an attempt to make feminism more truly international. For the two women concerned, it was also a chance to escape temporarily from the politicking in which they were constantly engaged, at a time when movement towards their goals was dishearteningly slow in their respective homelands: it was not until after the ordeal of the First World War that women gained the vote in 1919 in both the United States and the Netherlands.

What has to be remembered is firstly that at this time women had the vote in only a very few countries, and secondly that Jacobs and Catt were visiting primarily colonised countries, where virtually no democracy existed. Although travelling as part of the colonising world, they also saw themselves as belonging to an oppressed group which was fighting for its liberation and trying to construct an international sisterhood on behalf of a global campaign for justice for women.[6] The interest in reading Jacobs then, is to see how far she identified with women in the countries she visited and what she thought could be achieved in Asia and Africa for the cause of women generally and of women's suffrage in particular. It is a test case for feminism as a global movement. As we shall see, Jacobs' writing moved uneasily between support for colonialism and feminism.

Before examining Jacobs' writings in more detail, it is necessary to point out a few relevant aspects of these travel

---

6   It has been suggested to me by Jean Taylor that Aletta Jacobs was doubly marginalised by her Jewish ancestry. This may be the case, although her parents were assimilated Jews, meaning they did not practise their religion, and her memoirs never acknowledge any Jewish connection.

accounts. Both Jacobs and Catt kept records of their tour, but only Jacobs' have been published; Catt kept a personal diary, a few extracts of which have been published in biographies of her. The fact that Jacobs was writing for a newspaper audience means that her presentation was influenced by what she thought would interest liberal Dutch readers, and that she used the occasion to campaign for her concerns rather than always to reflect her personal impressions. The extracts from Catt's diary reflect more spontaneous reactions which were sometimes at variance with what Jacobs was recording.

For instance, after a meeting with daughters of the Paku Alam prince in Yogyakarta, Jacobs wrote for the newspaper that she rejoiced to have met such an interesting family who all spoke perfect Dutch; she regarded the young princesses as worthy examples of the modern Javanese woman, of the calibre of Kartini; she noted that they too were great admirers of *Hilda van Suylenberg* (Jacobs, 1913: 485). Catt, on the other hand, clearly found the visit more upsetting than inspiring:

> They are in revolt of mind but poor little prisoners, they do not know what to do. They went to a Dutch school but were taken away at about twelve, for after that it is wrong for a woman to be seen in public. Soon they will be married to some man they have never seen! If breaking windows could liberate our sex, we ought to smash every one in the world (Van Voris, 1987: 94).

From a leader who had disdained the methods of the British suffragettes, these were strong words.

The tour of the two suffragists covered South and East Africa, Egypt, the Middle East, India, Ceylon, Burma, Singapore, the Dutch East Indies, the Philippines, China, Korea and Japan. Both of them widows in their fifties, they appeared to relish the adventure and travelled by almost every known form of transport, not allowing heat or personal discomfort (exacerbated by the unsuitable European clothes of the time) to prevent them visiting out of the way locations which interested them. Wherever possible, they had arranged in advance contacts with local members of women's suffrage organisations who lined up meetings for them to publicise this cause. Their itineraries always included investigation of the sitation of local women and meetings with representatives of women's organisations. The sea voyage from one country to another provided time for preparation: both women obviously read as much as they could lay hands on about the countries visited.[7]

Since the focus of this paper is particularly on Indonesian women, it will concentrate on what Jacobs had to say about the Dutch East Indies, where the travellers spent about three months, from the end of March to the end of June 1912.[8] Almost all their time was spent in Sumatra and Java, where the vast majority of the population lived. This was the longest they spent in any single country and Jacobs' role there differed from the one she played in the other countries visited. For one thing, she was best informed about the Indies. Although she had never visited the colony before, she had longstanding family links with it. Four of her brothers and two sisters had worked there in various capacities (de Wilde, 1992b: 23). One brother, Julius Jacobs, was an army doctor who had published anthropological books about Aceh and Bali (Jacobs, 1883, 1894). Most significantly, her sister Charlotte had been working as an apothecary in Batavia (now Jakarta) for almost thirty years.[9] Aletta Jacobs also had excellent contacts in the colony through Dutch members of the VVVK. Her reknown in the Netherlands gave her easy access to highly placed colonial officials; the visit included an appointment with the governor-general, whom she lobbied for education and training for Javanese girls. What also marked her Indies visit as different was that her special mission there was to enlist support for and set up branches of the VVVK, to strengthen the movement at home.

---

7   The general ideas of Jacobs as revealed in the travel letters are discussed briefly in Claudia Vrieling.

8   Jacobs' observations on Egypt have been analysed by Harriet Feinberg, 1990. Feinberg usefully points to the distinction in Jacobs' discourse between 'encouraging our peers' and 'lifting up our native sisters'. Because I think the Indies situation was rather more complex than Egypt for Jacobs, my discussion tries to tease out some of the other strands in her encounters in that colony.

9   On Charlotte Jacobs, see Inge de Wilde, 1992a.

Jacobs was pursuing two aims which appeared to have very little connection between them. Like Catt, she sought information about the situation of Indonesian women and wherever possible tried to publicise where and how their position could be improved; but she was also active in the Dutch community in the Indies with an agenda aimed at politics back in the Netherlands. The search for women's suffrage had little to do with Indonesian women or the colonial situation in her eyes. She was clearly surprised (if gratified) when she noted Indonesians present at the public meetings she addressed in the Indies: she expected to discuss suffrage primarily with white people. Among Indonesians her concerns were prompted by genuine interest in their ways of life and a desire to 'uplift the natives', especially the women.

What is striking in Jacobs' account is the very sympathetic reception she encountered in the Indies when she raised both of these matters—women's suffrage and the interests of Indonesian women. Although it was doubtless in her interest to present the visit in this light, there is reason to believe that her ideas fell on fertile ground in the Indies.[10] Her visit was exceptionally well timed, for reasons that will be explained below.

In relation to the suffrage issue, the two women addressed thirteen public meetings in Java and Sumatra, leading to the formation of branches of the VVVK in Medan, Bogor, Padang, Bandung, Yogyakarta, Solo, Semarang and Surabaya (a branch already existed in Batavia, led by Charlotte Jacobs). From the good attendance at each location, it is obvious that much interest had been generated in the colony by publicity of the activities of women's suffrage organisations in the West, and in particular the militancy of British suffragettes. Opinion was swinging towards acceptance of votes for women in these countries. Jacobs noted that almost all (both women and men) who heard her and Catt, were sympathetic. At each meeting scores of new members of the VVVK were signed up, adding to those present who had already joined, and thus establishing that

---

10   Reports in *De Locomotief* of the suffragists' tour indicate considerable support at public meetings. The paper itself was sympathetic to the suffrage cause.

the Indies contained a sizeable pool of European feminists in the early twentieth century. Europeans in the Indies attended these meetings as part of their participation in homeland politics rather than in relation to Indies affairs. At only two meetings, in Buitenzorg (now Bogor) and Yogyakarta, did Jacobs note the attendance of a few Indonesians (of both sexes).

At this time in the Indies there were very few opportunities for anyone to exercise a vote. Decentralisation reforms in 1905 led to the introduction of some municipal councils, and Jacobs attended a congress in Bandung of organisations involved in municipal council activities. At this time voting for the councils was very restricted and indirect: Jacobs noted that in Bandung women members of the electoral organisation there could in fact participate in nominating candidates for the councils but they could not vote or stand as candidates. In 1912 the colonial government announced the formation of a national Volksraad (People's Council), to contain both nominated members and some elected by European and non-European men. The Volksraad did not sit until 1918, and women were not eligible to exercise a vote until 1941, although the government appointed a woman Volksraad member in 1935 and the first women were elected to municipal councils in 1938. In short, in 1912 any discussion of Indonesian women's suffrage appeared irrelevant, since there were virtually no democratic institutions. In a conversation with a Javanese official, Jacobs learnt that Javanese women who owned land (of whom there were few) could participate in the election of village heads. Her response reflected her own bias: 'Thus the Javanese woman is...in this respect ahead of her Dutch sisters! Is this not shaming?' (Jacobs, 1913: 482).

Jacobs had no apparent interest in advocating political reform in the Indies, where admittedly the pace of change had been accelerated since the start of the century: she seemed quite content with colonial authoritarianism, so long as it was exercised benevolently. Her views were in keeping with the Ethical Policy which had been the prevailing colonialist rhetoric of the Dutch since 1901 and which reached its apogee under Governor-General Idenburg, who gave Jacobs a sympathetic hearing in 1912. According to that ideology, colonialism should not aim to exploit 'the natives' but rather to improve their situation. In general Jacobs was patriotically proud of what the Dutch had achieved in the Indies in the way of 'protecting the natives' and at one point in her letters explicitly ruled out the notion that the Indies was ready for independence (Jacobs, 1913: 470). There is no doubt that Jacobs was steeped in the racist assumptions of her day, yet she was by no means unequivocal in her support for Dutch colonialism. Earlier in the century she had joined her brother Julius, who served as an army doctor in Aceh, in criticising the long and bloody war fought by the Dutch to subdue that territory: as a pacifist Aletta Jacobs had already seen the dilemmas of colonialism (Jacobs, 1913: 133). During her 1912 visit, what is interesting in her writing is the tension between the paternalistic and racist attitudes of colonialism, and her espousal of the ideals of international feminism.

Carrie Chapman Catt's views on colonialism were well in advance of Jacobs': in the Philippines she was sympathetic to the cause of independence (Van Voris, 1987: 94). The two women reflected the differences between Dutch and American responses to colonialism at this time: unlike all other colonial powers, the Americans had already begun to consider eventual independence for the Philippines.

Although the interest taken by Jacobs in Indonesian women fitted within the Ethical Policy concerns for 'uplift of the natives', she and Catt had their particularly feminist slant on welfare. Both felt strongly that women had a right to equal education and work opportunities which were essential to their self-respect and independence. Their concern about education fitted in well with the spirit of the time in the Indies, and Jacobs' observations coincided with those made by a number of enlightened Europeans at this time. It was their interest in work and in gender relations which differentiated them.

Private schools for girls were founded in the Indies from the beginning of the 20th century, starting in Minahasa in North Sulawesi, where Western impact was stronger and local tradition less resistant than in Java. Missionaries opened girls' schools in Minahasa from 1901 (Vreede de Stuers, 1960: 70). At the time of Kartini's death in 1904, a Sundanese woman, Dewi Sartika, founded a girls' school in Bandung; by 1912 she had started nine such schools in West Java. These were private initiatives: Kartini's supporters were attempting to engage government support. Girls were able to attend village schools started by the colonial government in accordance with Ethical Policy guidelines, but in Java in particular, parents were reluctant to allow girls to attend mixed schools once they entered puberty.

When Jacobs and Catt arrived in the Dutch East Indies in 1912, a strong campaign was under way, led by friends of Kartini, to persuade the government to fund girls' schools. In the same year as the suffragists' visit, a committee led by Kartini's Dutch champion, J.H. Abendanon, a former colonial director of education, was conducting a 15-month investigation into girls' education in the Indies, leading to a report that was released the following year. In 1912 Kartini sympathisers created the Kartini Foundation to raise money for girls' schools in Java. The first of these schools opened in 1913 in Semarang and received a government subsidy. Following on the heels of Abendanon's publication of the very popular selected letters of Kartini in 1911 (Kartini, 1912), the education campaign began to take off. In 1914, a government commission established some years before to investigate what was perceived to be the declining welfare of the Javanese, also received seven submissions from Javanese women about girls' education, including a spirited case put by Siti Soendari entitled 'The Javanese nation will not progress if the Javanese woman remains ignorant' (Onderzoek, 1914). In 1913 Siti Soendari had founded a Javanese periodical called *Wanito Sworo* (Voice of Women).

Jacobs and Catt sought out educational institutions and always commented on their access to girls. In visiting a government primary school for Indonesians in Buitenzorg, for instance, Jacobs remarked

> It is pitiful to see how few girls still take part in education; in all the schools that we have so far visited, in every class of about 20 or 25 pupils there are not more than one or two girls. In some of the lower classes there were three or four, but often these girls are taken away from school

by their parents as soon as they have had a couple of years' teaching (Jacobs, 1913: 426).

Although she was aware that this practice could be attributed to local custom, Jacobs was quick to condemn any signs of discrimination in government education policy. At a teachers' training school in Fort de Kock (Bukittinggi) in West Sumatra, she noted that although the school had grown rapidly and now had 120 students, there were only a few Indonesian women in training. Whereas the government paid for the board and lodging of male students as well as a monthly stipend, no assistance was available to female students, and furthermore at the last admission round, six girls who had performed outstandingly at the admission examination were refused entry because 'the class was too full'. Jacobs laid this squarely at the feet of the Ministry of Education in Batavia. She noted the same discrimination at a teacher training school in Yogyakarta (Jacobs, 1913: 448–49, 484–85). Interestingly, she also criticised the agricultural training school in Buitenzorg for not admitting women, and thus perpetrating Western notions that agriculture was unsuited to women (Jacobs, 1913: 460).

In Bandung Jacobs visited one of Dewi Sartika's schools. After recounting the pathbreaking work of this Sundanese woman in education for girls, she criticised the colonial government for failing to support these schools on the grounds that the Javanese women teachers did not have diplomas. The content of their schooling struck Jacobs as very practical (domestic sciences and basic literacy and numeracy of a kind which would prevent them from ever being cheated in the market) but she yearned for something that could extend these girls a little further. She was outraged at this school to observe the custom of school pupils 'crawling' before their teachers: a traditional sign of respect in Java. The 'feudal' behaviour at the courts of central Java also disgusted her (Jacobs, 1913: 475–77, 490). Although such reactions may be seen as ethnocentric, it is well to remember that a number of Western-educated Javanese were by then following in Kartini's footsteps in rejecting these customs.

Most of Jacobs' observations on girls' education probably did not differ much from those being made by a number of influential people at this time. Their value was the weight they added to the impetus for change, which was gaining momentum. Rather more radical and idiosyncratic were the suffragists' views on women's work in the Indies, which tied in with voices beginning to be heard from Indonesian women also. Most of the arguments put forward by the 'Ethici' in favour of education for girls were to the effect that it would help them to be better wives and mothers and, through their responsibilities for child-rearing, it would contribute to modernising and elevating the behaviour of Indonesians. Jacobs and Catt, on the other hand, valued education for girls as a means of making them more independent as individuals and able to play a public role in society. They linked education and work, viewing socially valuable and income-earning work as essential for women. To some extent these concerns derived from their own urban middle-class Western background, coming as they did from societies where higher education and paid work were not considered respectable for middle-class women, whose main aim in life should be to find and support a bread-winning husband. Similarity of experience enabled a ready identification between discontented upper-class Indonesian women like Kartini and European upper- and middle-class feminists on the issue of education and work. Both Jacobs and Catt displayed their sympathy with Javanese *priyayi* women in Kartini's situation. In their discussions with the governor-general about training for Javanese girls, they spoke of middle-class careers for these girls in teaching and medicine. It is important to remember, however, that they saw these positions not just in terms of personal advancement but as a means of working for other, poorer women: more female teachers were necessary to attract more girls to schools; female doctors were essential to treat female patients (Jacobs, 1913: 425).

Yet in Indonesian society, even more than in Dutch society, the vast majority of women worked for a living, joining the men in agriculture and dominating petty trade. Only a small minority were excluded from economic independence. Jacobs recognised this at once. It was the work of ordinary Indonesian women which she noted with interest and appreciation wherever she went. Although at first she had been inclined to write very patronisingly of Indonesians as in need of leadership from Europeans, the more she saw of ordinary Indonesian women the more respectful she became. In her view their hard work provided a lesson to many Western women: it earned them valuable independence and status in society. It was one of the reasons why she considered Indonesian women far in advance of those she had met in India, and why she was much more willing to accept Indonesian women as sisters and equals, compared with women in African and most other Asian countries whose position she regarded as much more backward.

What is particularly interesting is the way in which Jacobs sought to fit women's work into a broader understanding of the evolution of gender relations. Throughout their travels, the two suffragists appeared to be groping towards a framework which could accommodate the diversity they observed. For instance, contemplating women bringing in the rice harvest at Padang Panjang in West Sumatra, Jacobs commented:

> For us, the sight of these hardworking women was full of interest just because these cheerful, apparently happy people made such a wonderful contrast with the depressed, apparently dissatisfied women in Egypt and British India. If you wish to be convinced that women can only be happy if responsible work rests on their shoulders, that the nature of women entails them being usefully busy and that only under such circumstances can they feel contented, then take yourself to the Padang highlands and compare these active women with those in countries where the development of industry or prevailing manners and customs have taken all useful activity away from them. The whole women's movement, especially in the civilized world, which is apparently moving along different paths, in fact has no other cause and no other goal than the wish to win back the significance that woman in the original world had for the human race, to wish again to participate in work for the general good, again to be responsible for half of the work which must be done for the maintenance of the human race and the progress of mankind (Jacobs, 1913: 451).

These comments reflect Jacobs' thinking about the history of women's work, strongly influenced by two contemporary feminist writers whose books she had translated into Dutch. The two influential and popular works were Charlotte Perkins Gilman's *Women and Economics* (1888) and Olive Schreiner's *Woman and Labour* (1911). Part of the 19th century tradition which saw human history in evolutionary terms, these two authors argued for the importance of women's work for the future of the human race, while at the same time demonstrating how 'modern civilization' had 'tended to rob women, not merely in part but almost wholly, of the more valuable of her ancient domain of productive and social labour', thus reducing women to the position of parasites (Schreiner, 1911: 50). It was only through a determined campaign that women would be able to convince society that they needed to work, since ultimately where women decayed through lack of useful labour, so would society decay. Here the feminists clearly felt that the tide of progress thus far experienced was not in favour of women, who had actually been the economic equals of men in earlier forms of agricultural societies: industrialisation had eroded their economic position.[11] In this respect, colonialism as the bearer of progress to countries like the Indies was, at least temporarily, detrimental to women.

That these ideas were widespread in Jacobs' day is seen when her views are compared with those of some Indonesian women reflecting on work at around the same time. Raden Ajoe Mangkoedimedjo, a *priyayi* woman from Yogyakarta, wrote for a local journal in 1909 an article entitled 'Kemadjoean bangsa perempoean' (The advancement of women) which presented a history of the evolution of *priyayi* women (Mangkoedimedjo, 1977). Like Jacobs, she envisaged an 'original world' in which women's work was valued. She held Western influence

---

11   For modern readers the historical link between writers like Schreiner and Ester Boserup, 1970, is obvious. Boserup's classic book, which has sparked an avalanche of research on women and development, has just revived a debate begun among feminists in the late 19th century. I think that Claudia Vrieling (1992) has not sufficiently taken the influence of these feminist writers into account when analysing Aletta Jacobs' view of 'progress'.

responsible for destroying traditional handcrafts at which *priyayi* women had been skilled; ever since then 'We have fallen into second place', regarded by men as just useless ornaments. With an optimism similar to Jacobs', she expected that as women increased their knowledge, they would come to challenge their place in society:

> Individualism will increase and it will be rare for women to feel obliged to marry if the party does not appear suitable to them; they will then prefer to work and use their knowledge to earn their own livelihood.

Less visionary and more practical was the approach of Dewi Sartika, in her submission to the 1914 government commission on declining welfare:

> It is certain that the *kaum kuno* (old folks) take the education of girls into consideration, and there has never been question of neglecting it as my progressive compatriots often claim...The case is rather that school instruction for our girls is lacking...It would be desirable at the same time to train midwives, office-girls, typists, housekeepers, horticulturists, etc., in short, all the professions, which, according to conservative ideas, do not belong to women and have been up to now reserved for men. Let us not forget that there is a considerable number of female laborers who have no professional training whatsoever and have at present to earn their 'bowl of rice' in the factories and on the plantations (de Stuers, 1960: 58).

Like Jacobs, it seemed that Indonesian women were also thinking about the significance and future of their work. Education was a means to an end, and in the minds of some feminists the end was not just bringing up children and caring for husbands, but economic independence for women—and ultimately the welfare of the human race.

The lyrical outburst by Jacobs occasioned by watching women rice-harvesters occurred, significantly, in West Sumatra. This area had a particular fascination for both suffragists, because, like the agricultural work of women, it appeared to offer a key to the lost history of women. The Minangkabau of West Sumatra were famous for their matrilineal society, property being passed down through the female line. Jacobs and Catt spent two weeks there, trying to learn as much as possible about what they referred to, wrongly, as a 'matriarchal' system, where men were treated as guests in the houses of their wives' families. In their view, clearly, it was a chance to study a very different arrangement of gender relations, which offered a challenge to those accepted as normal in the West. Like Western feminists of later times, Jacobs and Catt looked hopefully to matrilineal societies for clues to a 'golden age' before patriarchy. Catt subsequently wrote two articles about West Sumatra (Van Voris, 1987: 94), and this section of the Indies tour was also of great interest to Jacobs.

The suffragists were shown around by Dutch officials and visited a number of matrilineal families. They were cautious in their judgements. Jacobs' main conclusion was that, given the social change occurring in West Sumatra, it was imperative that women anthropologists should record the situation there, because the understanding of Dutch male officials was inadequate. Jacobs noted that matriliny offered certain benefits for men as well as women. Because according to Islam men could have up to four wives, a man could live nearby and be treated like a king in the houses of his wives, all of whom paid to marry him. Jacobs and Catt visited a village head who seemed to find this a very satisfactory arrangement:

> Can any of my Dutch gentlemen readers imagine a more regal and peaceful life, than that of this village head and his fellow-men?...He is not bothered by teething children, or cantankerous women, and if he is not greeted with open arms and tasty dishes, then next time he will stay away longer so as to be sure of a heartier welcome (Jacobs, 1913: 411).

Jacobs did not idealise the Minangkabau way of life. In her view, women had to work extremely hard just to make a meagre living. Observing all the female labour that went into producing sugar, for instance, she concluded that subsistence living must give way to machine production because it was much more efficient.

> But so far as the current level of development of the Minangkabau Malays stands, women still have their hands full of work; from early in the morning until late at night you see them busy and you see also from their self-respecting appearance that they also feel very good about how important they are for the maintenance of their race. They bring the following generation into the world and at the same time do almost all the important and responsible work, that is worth performing for society and family. Only there, where the new times have shaped new activities, there men come to the forefront, considered by the 19th and 20th century spirit of the age as having the right to almost all the work outside the house and to what must be done in the office and in public affairs (Jacobs, 1913: 447).

Again, she was wrestling with nostalgia for a past which appeared to afford women greater respect while burdening them with heavy labour.[12]

Jacobs wrote that Sumatra's West Coast had made a deep and lasting impression on both women (Vrieling, 1992: 454). Catt also considered it a highlight of the trip, although like Jacobs she was not swept off her feet by the advantages of this alternative set of gender relations. In one of her articles about the Minangkabau she concluded: 'The Matriarchate is as onesided and abnormal as the Patriarchate and a compromise between the two is what we want' (Van Voris, 1987: 94). Clearly the modern world required change, and these two suffragists were still seeking a model for the kind of world they were trying to mould.

In this respect, they were no different from educated women in Minangkabau at the same period. Although Jacobs and Catt were unaware of them, Minangkabau women were beginning to form modern organisations and express their views in the press. For instance, Rohana Kudus was writing in the newspaper

---

12   Unlike Claudia Vrieling (1992, p.26), I do not interpret Jacobs' writing about West Sumatra as endorsing a return to 'matriarchy': her comments indicate some ambivalence.

Soenting Melajoe about the need for Minangkabau women to participate in the movement to modernise their region (Tamar Djaja, 1980), and others were establishing schools for girls. In West Sumatra both colonisers and the local elite were examining, reconstructing and questioning the nature of 'traditions' like matriliny.[13] Again, colonialism had thrown into question received notions about women which appeared incompatible with aspirations to modernity.

Throughout their travels, the two women were becoming more and more receptive to new impressions, less likely to prejudge situations and cultures. The climax of their tour came near the end, when they visited China in the immediate aftermath of the 1911 nationalist revolution. In the upheaval, they found places where nationalist women who had fought alongside men for the overthrow of the Manchu regime, had been able to win seats in regional legislatures. Jacobs and Catt were thrilled to be able to attend a sitting of one of these councils in Canton and see women making speeches. They interviewed these women later and in Shanghai and Nanking held public meetings on women's suffrage. In distress they recorded how the nationalist leaders of the revolution were abandoning the women's cause despite the sacrifices of women for the sake of the revolution. In Peking Catt met with 'an ideal suffragist', Captain Sheng, who impressed her with an inspired vision of equality of the sexes (Van Voris, 1987: 101).

On returning from their tour, the two suffragists presented their findings at the 1913 congress of the IWSA in Budapest. Carrie Chapman Catt summed it up this way:

> The main fact to understand is that there *is* a serious women's movement in Asia. On many a hill-top the beacon lights of the reformer are aflame. There are women physicians in many countries. Women have their own papers in India, Burma, and China. There is a greater demand for girls' schools than the authorities are able to

---

13   Joel Kahn (1993) has recently investigated at length the ambivalent images held by both 'insiders' and 'outsiders' of West Sumatran society in the early 20th century. Unfortunately he has had little to say about women's role in the changes of this period.

provide. They vote upon the same terms as men in the municipal government of Rangoon, Bombay, and other Indian cities...The women of East and West have a common cause. Liberation lies in their common rebellion against every influence which robs them of their liberty (Schreiber & Mathieson, 1955: 22–23).

At the congress, when the flags of all the nations represented were unfurled, Jacobs presented the banner prepared for the congress by women in Nanking. In Chinese characters it bore the slogan, 'Helping each other, all of one mind' (Schreiber & Mathieson, 1955: 20–21; Van Voris, 1987: 99). It was a high-point in the effort to create a global women's movement. The presence of Asian, African and Latin American women at subsequent congresses strengthened the solidarity of the women's suffrage struggle.

Back in the Indies, the visit of Jacobs and Catt contributed to the ferment of the times which saw a sudden upsurge of organisation by Indonesian women. In the year of their tour, the first modern Indonesian women's association, Poetri Mardika (The Independent Woman) was founded in Batavia to give financial assistance for the education of talented girls, and to encourage women to play a role in public life. In 1913 it began publishing its own journal which canvassed such issues as child marriage, polygamy and the IWSA congress in Paris. At about the same time a number of other women's groups sprang up in Java and Sumatra (Vreede de Stuers, 1960: 61–73). Although there was no direct connection between the Western suffragists and these organisations, they helped to provide the right climate for the flowering of early Indonesian feminism.

Jacobs' and Catt's tour of Africa and Asia offers unique insights into Western feminist views of 'other' women. Both women acknowledged that they had learned a great deal through their encounters with different cultures. As Carrie Chapman Catt, the product of country-town United States, cheerfully admitted, 'Once I was a regular jingo but that was before I had visited other countries. I had thought America had a monopoly on all that stands for progress, but I had a sad awakening'. She also referred to the tour as 'an experience so upsetting to all our preconceived notions that it is difficult to estimate its influence upon us' (Van Voris, 1987: 105). Compared with other Western travel accounts of the period, their focus was squarely on women, and for a country like the Indies where women had received little attention and were as yet scarcely organised, their insights are valuable. They added to the pressure in that colony for women's education and emancipation which led to an outburst of activity on behalf of women both by Europeans and by Indonesian women themselves.

Jacobs' and Catt's experience adds to the ambivalent history of Western feminist relations with Asian women. Certainly in a largely unself-conscious way these two suffragists brought their cultural baggage of Western superiority to the Indies, sometimes judged on flimsy evidence and saw much of what they expected to see. Jacobs' writings reveal at several points an unresolved tension between feminism and colonialism: colonialism is seen as the bearer of progress, yet there is an implicit admission that in less advanced societies women were more equal. As they travelled, the two women came to acknowledge that women in places like the Indies provided some lessons for Western feminists, and that observing Asian women could both broaden their own horizons and contribute to their own struggles in the West.

References

Biografisch Woordenboek van Nederland, 1979, vol. 1, Martinus Nijhoff, 's-Gravenhage.

Biografisch Woordenboek van het Socialisme en de Arbeidersbeweging, 1988, vol. 3, Nederlandse Vereeniging tot Beoefening van de Sociale Geschiedenis, Amsterdam.

Boserup, Ester, 1970, *Women's Role in Economic Development*, Allen and Unwin, London.

Chaudhuri, Napur and Strobel, Margaret (eds) 1992, *Western Women and Imperialism: Complicity and Resistance*, Indiana University Press, Bloomington.

de Wilde, Inge, 1992a, 'Minder opvallende dan haar "meer roerige zuster": over de apothekeres Charlotte Jacobs (1847–1916)', *Groniek*, 25.

—— 1992b, *Er is nog zooveel te doen op de wereld: Brieven van Aletta H. Jacobs aan de familie Broese van Groenou*, Walburg Pers, Zutphen.

Feinberg, Harriet, 1990, 'A Pioneering Dutch Feminist Views Egypt: Aletta Jacobs' Travel Letters', *Feminist Issues*, 10(2), Fall.

Gilman, Charlotte Perkins, 1888, *Women and Economics*, Harper and Ron, New York.

Goedkoop de Jong van Beek en Donk, C., 1897, *Hilda van Suylenburg*, Scheltema en Holkema, Amsterdam.

Jacobs, Aletta, 1913, *Reisbrieven uit Afrika en Azie*, Hilarius Almelo, Amsterdam.

—— 1924, *Herinneringen*, Van Holkema en Warendorf, Amsterdam.

Jacobs, Julius, 1883, *Eenige Tijd onder de Baliers*, Batavia, G. Kolff & Co.,

—— 1894, *Het Familie- en Kampongleven op Groot-Atjeh*, E.J. Brill, Leiden

Kahn, Joel, 1993, *Constituting the Minangkabau: Peasants, Culture and Modernity in Colonial Indonesia*, Providence, Berg.

Kartini, Raden Adjeng, 1912, *Door Duisternis tot Licht: Gedachten van Raden Adjeng Kartini*, 's-Gravenhage, N.V. Electrische Drukkerij 'Luctor et Energo', 2nd printing.

—— 1992, *Letters from Kartini: An Indonesian Feminist, 1900–04*, translated by Joost Coté, Monash Asia Institute, Monash University, Melbourne.

Locher-Scholten, E. and Niehof, A. (eds) 1987, *Indonesian Women in Focus*, Foris, Dordrecht.

Mangkoedimodjo, Raden Ajoe, 1977, 'Kemadjoean bangsa perempoean', translated by Claudine Salmon, *Archipel*, 13.

Onderzoek naar de Mindere Welvaart der Inlandsche Bevolking op Java en Madoera, IXb3: Verheffing van de Inlandsche Vrouw, 1914, Drukkerij Papyrus, Batavia.

Schreiber, Anne and Mathieson, Margaret, 1955, *Journey Towards Freedom,* International Alliance of Women, Copenhagen.

Schreiner, Olive, 1911, *Woman and Labour*, T. Fisher Unwin, London.

Tamar Djaja, 1980, *Rohana Kudus*, Mutiara, Jakarta.

van Bemmelen, Sita, 1989, 'Zwart-wit versus kleur: Geschiedschrijving over Indonesische vrouwen in de koloniale periode', in F. de Haan et al (eds), *Het Raadsel Vrouwengeschiedenis: Tiende Jaarboek voor Vrouwengeschiedenis*, SUN, Amsterdam.

—— et al (eds) 1992, *Women and Mediation in Indonesia*, KITLV Press, Leiden.

van Goor, J., 1992, 'Indische reizen in de negentiende en twintigste eeuw:van verkenning tot journalistiek tourisme', *Tijdschrift voor Geschiedenis*, 105.

van Voris, Jacqueline, 1987, *Carrie Chapman Catt: A Public Life*, The Feminist Press, New York.

Vreede-de Stuers, Cora, 1960, *The Indonesian Woman*, Mouton & Co., 's-Gravenhage.

Vrieling, Claudia, 1992, 'Voortgang der menschheid: Aletta Jacobs' visie op beschaving' in M. van Tilburg et al (eds), *'Op Mij Rusten Grooter en Ernstiger Plichten': Dr Aletta Jacobs' Zorg Voor de Wereld*, Groningen, Rijksuniversiteit.

Emancipation of the Indonesian Chinese Woman[*]

Charles A. Coppel

The first number of the journal of the association of Chinese students in the Netherlands, the *Chung Hwa Hui Tsa Chih*, featured an address given to a General Meeting of the association in The Hague on 23 December 1916 by Mevr. Yap Hong Tjoen on 'The Chinese Woman' (Yap Hong Tjoen, 1917a). As was the case with most of the articles published in the early numbers of the journal, we are given the text in Malay as well as in the original Dutch. This contribution is unusual, however, in being graced by a two page photograph of the speaker and her audience in the sumptuous surroundings of the Hotel Paulez, where the meeting was held *(see illustration)*.

Standing at the lectern on the far left is our speaker, Mrs Yap Hong Tjoen. Her audience of about 50 people is seated beneath the chandeliers. Those in the first two rows (some 14 individuals) are identified in the caption. This is not just an audience of students: important people are present. In the front row at the extreme left sits *Meester* Ph. H. Fromberg, the former raadsheer in the High Court of Justice in the Netherlands Indies. Next to him is His Excellency T'ang Tsai Fou, the

*   I wish to acknowledge the financial support of the Australian Research Council for a wider project of which the present paper forms a small part. My period as Fellow-in-Residence at the Netherlands Institute for Advanced Study in the Humanities and Social Sciences (NIAS), at Wassenaar, the Netherlands in 1995–96 gave me the opportunity to discuss the paper and the two Mrs Yaps with Elisabeth Winarta and Ming Govaars (whose contributions are acknowledged below as are those of Myra Sidharta). I am also most grateful for the assistance of Helen Pausacker (whose careful reading of the "histories" has been invaluable in preparing the paper). Responsibility for any remaining deficiencies is of course mine.

Chinese ambassador, and His Excellency Oudendijk, formerly Netherlands ambassador in Teheran, with Mrs Oudendijk. Next we have Mrs Fromberg, who is seated beside Mr Shen Tchong Huin, first secretary of the Chinese Legation, and Mr Ezerman, adviser for Chinese affairs in the Netherlands Indies. In the second row, again from left to right, we find Mr Tan Pang Ie, Dr Yap Hong Tjoen (husband of the speaker), and a Mrs Rappard with her husband, who is an assistant resident on leave. Beyond him sits *Meester* Abendanon, former director of education in the Indies (and, we may recall, the patron of R.A. Kartini and the editor of her letters when they were first published five years earlier). The others identified are Mr Be Tiat Tjong and Mr Meyer, a former resident.

The speaker, like her husband, was born into the *peranakan* Chinese aristocracy of Java. She was born Tan Souw Lian (Léonie), the second daughter of Tan Thouw Soen and Liem Hiang Nio. Tan Bian Ing, her paternal grandfather, was *majoor* (Major) of the Chinese in Bangkalan, Madura; Liem Liong Hien, her maternal grandfather, was *majoor* of the Chinese in Semarang.[2]

---

2   I am indebted to Elisabeth Winarta (personal communication) for this information, which she obtained from Liem May Hua, daughter of Dr Yap Hong Tjoen and his second wife Tan Souw Lien (Caroline Valentine). They plan to write an extended piece on Mrs Liem's mother and her family. When this paper was presented in 1993, I was unaware that Dr Yap had remarried, and knew very little about the speaker. According to Myra Sidharta, the lecturer was the author of a letter which appeared in the Batavia daily *Sin Po* on 7 October 1914 under the pseudonym 'Y' or 'Miss Y'. Sidharta says the letter advocated school education for girls, because to deprive them of education would mean that the (Chinese?) nation 'was trying to achieve progress while limping on one leg' (Sidharta, 1992: 69, 74, 76).

Lecture by Mrs Yap Hong Tjoen on 'The Chinese Woman' for the
Chung Hwa Hui held on 23 December, 1916 in the Hotel Paulez, The
Hague. Insert: Committee of the Chung Hwa Hui, 1916–17

Source: *Chung Hwa Hui Tsa Chih* 1(1), April 1917, p.48. Koninklijk
Instituut voor Taal-, Land- en Volkenkunde, Documentatie Geschiedenis
Indonesie (DGI).

Her husband and their son were both to become famous eye specialists. The son, Dr Yap Kie Tiong (1915–69), born in Leiden in the previous year, was 21 months old at the time of her address. Her husband, Dr Yap Hong Tjoen (1885–1952), son of Yap Ping Lien, *kapitein* (Captain) of the Chinese in Yogyakarta, had been one of the founders of the Chung Hwa Hui in 1911, was its second president, and was given honorary life membership in 1919 (Han Tiauw Tjong 1919).[3] After their return to the Indies, he became engaged in a polemic with Tjoe Bou San, the editor of *Sin Po*, to such an extent that Kwee Hing Tjiat entitled his book *Doea Kapala Batoe* (*Two Stubborn Men*) in their honour (Kwee Hing Tjiat 1924; Yap Hong Tjoen 1918). After helping to found the Indies-based Chung Hwa Hui in 1928, Dr Yap's organisational activity was mainly in social welfare associations (e.g. youth, unemployed, the poor, rehabilitation, scholarships) which were not confined to the Chinese (Tan Hong Boen, 1935: 78–79).

In the conference paper upon which the present paper is based, I examined what I thought were the ideas of Mrs Yap Hong Tjoen as expressed not only in the address delivered in The Hague in December 1916, but also in two other articles published in 1917 and 1928. I have since discovered that, although the author of the 1928 article was indeed married to Dr Yap Hong Tjoen, she was not the same Mrs Yap. The author of this article was the younger sister of the first Mrs Yap. This was Tan Souw Lien (Caroline Valentine), the third daughter of the same parents, who was born in September 1889. She graduated in law at the University of Utrecht in 1923, and may have been the first *peranakan* Chinese woman to qualify as a lawyer. In that same year, the first Mrs Yap (Léonie) died in a car accident. In the following year, Dr Yap married Caroline, her younger sister

---

3   Information about Dr Yap Hong Tjoen's father from Winarta (personal communication). The pamphlet containing the address given by the president of the Chung Hwa Hui, Han Tiauw Tjong, in honour of Dr Yap Hong Tjoen on this occasion is dedicated to Mrs Yap. He expressed the gratitude of all members for the hospitality of the Yaps, and concluded the pamphlet by saying that Dr Yap owed his life membership primarily to her and by expressing the wish that she might be 'a fine example for our younger sisters in the Indies' (Han Tiauw Tjong 1919).

(a practice known as *turun ranjang*).[4] This second Mrs Yap, the author of the 1928 article, brought up her sister's children and never practised law. She died on 24 March 1991 in the Netherlands, in her 102nd year.

In this paper, therefore, I examine the ideas of the two Mrs Yaps (or should we say the Tan sisters?) on the emancipation of the Indonesian Chinese woman and compare them with more conservative positions taken in contemporary colloquial Malay 'histories' or novels. Although the authorship of the 1928 article is different, the remarkable similarity in its ideas and style with the earlier pieces is understandable in the light of the double relationship between the two authors.

---

4   Myra Sidharta (personal communication) first alerted me to the existence of the two Mrs Yaps. The further family details about the two sisters comes from Winarta (personal communication), see footnote 2 above. This information helped to clear up two mysteries. One mystery was the title 'Mr' (*Meester in de Rechten:* law graduate) attached to the author of the 1928 article; the other was a 1926 publication (which I had subsequently mislaid) in which the editors referred to 'the late Mrs Yap' (*wijlen Mevr. Yap*) having 'broken a lance for the moral uplifting of women in a documented address in December 1917 (sic)' (Phoa Liong Gie et al, 1926: 11). Although their husband and son /stepson both appear in Leo Suryadinata's *Prominent Indonesian Chinese: Biographical Sketches* (Suryadinata, 1995: 132, 233–34), neither of the Mrs Yaps (the Tan sisters) themselves are mentioned. Caroline Tan's claim to be the first *peranakan* Chinese woman to graduate in law is not certain. Ming Govaars (personal communication) has drawn my attention to an article in *De Chineesche Onderwijzer* 6(1), (1 January 1932) p.26, in which it appears that there was a 'Miss D. Tan' who was 'the first meester in de rechten' from the Rechtshoogeschool (RHS) in Batavia. The same article states that 'Mrs Yap Hong Tjoen is also a *Meester* but has not gone into practice'. Ming Govaars also referred me to Kwee Kek Beng, *Overzicht Chineesche Geschiedenis* (1925), p.234 which states: '...some years ago Miss C. Tan obtained the degree "meester in de rechten"; she was the first Chinese young woman from Java with an academic degree'. It is tempting to speculate that the 'Miss D. Tan' referred to might be the eldest of the Tan sisters, Tan Souw Liam (Desirée), who died in 1927 (Winarta, personal communication) but further research is obviously needed.

The First Mrs Yap Hong Tjoen on 'The Chinese Woman'

I start with the address by the first Mrs Yap Hong Tjoen to the Chung Hwa Hui on 'The Chinese Woman'. In the time of Confucius, she said, women and men in China were equal in status and rights. It was only later, after the fall of the Chin dynasty, that the position of Chinese women deteriorated. Where Chinese women had previously been able to mix freely with men, they were now segregated, and kept secluded in their rooms. The morality of the state was bought at the price of women's freedom. Seclusion undermined their capacity to educate their children, and this in turn meant that China lost its high place among the world's peoples.

Closely related to seclusion of women was the system of marriages being arranged by parents without the consent of those concerned. Unlike European marriages, which were like a contract between husband and wife, the Chinese wife incurred obligations to her husband's parents as well as her husband. The younger generation of the Chinese Republic had now recognised by law that marriages should only be valid if entered into voluntarily.

After condemning the practice of footbinding,[5] Mrs Yap next criticised polygamy and the practice of concubinage, which she saw as excesses arising from the institution of ancestor worship. Because only men were supposed to worship the ancestors, they would look elsewhere if their wives did not produce a son. But such a view demeaned women, if it meant that a wife was no more than a means to producing a son. Because the size of the male and female populations was roughly equal, monogamy was thus in accord with the laws of nature. Refusal to follow the laws of nature was to contravene the *tao*, and thus was contrary to the true spirit of China, the spirit of Confucius. The Chinese Republic had now placed family law on the basis of monogamy, and there were voices in the Parliament calling for concubinage to be outlawed. Would the administration of the Netherlands Indies, where the Indies-born Chinese were Dutch subjects, be left behind in this, she demanded?

---

5   It is not suggested here that footbinding of women was commonly practised in the Netherlands Indies. Mrs Yap was speaking of China.

She welcomed the part being played by women in the national awakening in China, which showed that the classical Chinese concept of equality of men and women (this *truly Chinese idea* —emphasis in original) had pushed to the surface again. So too, if the position of the Chinese in the Indies was to be improved, the female half of the population should not be ignored or its energies dissipated in the struggle against the bigotry of conservatives who were not in full agreement with the abolition of *'pingittan'*, or marriage which was through free choice, or the introduction of a family and inheritance law by which the wife was an equal party to the marriage contract and the daughter an equally valued child of her parents.

If education was to be for boys alone, it would be of little use; education for girls was essential for rearing children. In the present turning of the tide between the old and the new China, it was all too easy for women to blame men for their self-interest and tyranny. But, said Mrs Yap, it was better for them to ask what they had done to help their sisters. Lack of education led some women to fear criticism, some to apathy and some, albeit unconsciously, to hold their own sex in low esteem.

In conclusion, she appealed to 'the gentlemen members of the Chung Hwa Hui' to use the opportunity while they were in the West to study the women's question. As Mr Fromberg had rightly observed, since the War began this had undergone great change; women in the countries at war were now fully mobilised and were showing what they could do. The members of the Chung Hwa Hui should remember that in the hands of the Chinese woman rested the future of a nation which comprised one third of the human race.

Mrs Yap Hong Tjoen on 'The Chinese Girl and Employment'

The first Mrs Yap Hong Tjoen makes a second appearance in the first volume of the *Chung Hwa Hui Tsa Chih*. This was a short article on 'The Chinese young woman and employment', written in response to a recent article in the Chinese Malay press in Java by someone who signed himself 'Heer Vis à Vis' (Yap Hong Tjoen, 1917b). Mr Vis à Vis, it seems, disapproved equally of European education for Chinese girls and of their working in offices. Some occupations could be accepted, such as teaching or nursing (of women patients), jobs which involved little contact with men and were not in the public eye. But young women who worked as telephonists or postal clerks, for example, were at risk.

Mrs Yap replied that for a poor girl there was less danger if she got a good income by working hard, even in a post office. To those who might say there was no danger in their staying at home, she answered that girls who were kept at home (*terkoeroeng*) would encounter there the deadly poisonous flowers of boredom and dissatisfaction. In this connection, she quoted from C. de Jong van Beek en Donk's *Hilda van Suylenburg* (which was, we may recall, the novel which had such a great influence on Kartini and was, in turn, inspired by the feminist Aletta H. Jacobs).[6] She also pointed to the dangers incurred by women who lacked money, who had no education and were unfortunate in marriage, who had to live like beggars or, worse, fell into brothels. She would rather see a Chinese girl working hard behind a ticket window than have her brooding in her room like a doll in a glass cupboard waiting for a good proposal.

On the positive side she agreed with what Anna Polak had written in 'De Vrouw, de Vrouwenbeweging en het Vrouwenvraagstuk', namely that methodical work would better fit a girl for her tasks in marriage. Her household would be managed more practically, her children brought up more wisely. So too education which a girl received before she became a mother would not only benefit her, but her husband and children as well. She had the same right as her brother to schooling and preparation for the struggle for existence, both of course within the limits of their parents' means.

The Second Mrs Yap Hong Tjoen on 'The Revolution in the World of Women'

The second Mrs Yap Hong Tjoen makes her appearance for me in the February 1928 Congress number of the *Orgaan der*

---

6   See Susan Blackburn's paper in this volume.

Centrale Chung Hsioh, the journal of the Union of Associations of Young Chinese in Indonesia (*Bond van Vereenigingen van Jong-Chineezen in Indonesië*),[7] with an article on 'The revolution in the world of women' (Yap, Mr Dr Mevr., 1928).

A decade has passed since her sister's earlier writings, the decade following what was then called the Great War. Mrs Yap, living in the Indies, can point to dramatic advances in the position of women in the West, China and even in the Indies. But the situation was different in the Indies, where most of the Chinese were not free of the influence of native society, indeed the Indies Chinese woman 'differs little in customs, practices and pleasures from her brown sister'.

A small proportion, mostly the well-off, follows the Western path, however:

> For example, the auditorium in which I speak contains a mixture of women and men. The sight of it would make our grandparents turn in their graves. Similarly, stage performances with men and women on stage together. Pageboy haircuts, bobbed hair, modern dancing, games of tennis, etc. have all made their mark on our women's world.

Many think they go too far in their emancipation, but for Mrs Yap it is only understandable that the newly awakened young woman casts off the yoke of the old with both hands and seizes on an ideal of freedom which they think they can see on the Western horizon; and that they will have their fling and break loose from the bonds of convention and tradition. The Indies Chinese woman is awake. She no longer sits locked up and carefully supervised, waiting for a 'good party', with her hands in her lap. We now see her as dentist, pharmacist, schoolteacher, postmistress, etc, seizing an independent position.

---

7   Attention is drawn to the surprisingly early use of the word 'Indonesië' in the title of this journal. The first extant issue which uses the word in the title is June 1927; the last extant issue before this is October 1926, which used 'Nederlandsch-Indié'. No explanation survives for the change of name, but the content of the journal does not suggest either a positive identification with Indonesian nationalism or a doctrinaire opposition to it.

Since the introduction of the 1917 family and inheritance law, her legal position has improved. True, as Mr Phoa Liong Gie has written, concubinage still flourishes in practice notwithstanding the 1917 law, but his pessimism is premature. You can't expect to overthrow in ten years something which has been deeply rooted in the society for centuries. The old 'Enkongs' and 'Empehs' are still alive, the conservatives with their harems, but official statistics now show a very small percentage of polygamous marriages. Of course clandestine polygamy is not included in these figures, but the fact that men don't openly acknowledge themselves as polygamists itself marks an advance.

The growth in the numbers of girls attending schools in the space of ten years shows what a transformation is going on in the Indies Chinese community. In 1927 we even have two female law students enrolled. But there is much more to be done. Whereas among the Europeans the ratio of boys to girls in these schools is 1:1, among the Chinese it is 4:1. This must change. 'It is the struggle of every Indies Chinese Mother and every Indies Chinese Woman to raise the ratio to 1:1 from the Fröbelschool up to the Hoogeschool'.[8]

Finally, Mrs Yap returns to the concluding theme of her sister's 1916 address. All around us we can see businesses collapsing. This is because the Chinese community is only using half the forces which comprise it. Modern men should extend a helping hand to the new modern women, here as in our country of origin, so that the revolution of awakened sisters may grow and expand in their struggle against obsolete, conservative ideas, customs, traditions and laws.

Colloquial Malay Histories

I want to contrast the writings of the two Mrs Yap Hong Tjoen (which may be seen as an expression of the emancipatory project of Dutch-educated Indonesian Chinese women) with two colloquial Malay stories or 'histories' written in the same period (apparently by Indonesian Chinese men). What I am calling 'colloquial Malay histories' is a genre of colloquial Malay writing

---

8   i.e. from kindergarten up to higher education.

(very common in the early 20th century) which used a formulaic subtitle such as 'A Story which really happened in the year...in ...'[9]

For instance, one of these stories, *Rasia Bandoeng*, by Chabanneau (a pseudonym) is said to have 'really happened in Bandung and ended in 1917' (*Satoe Tjerita jang benar terdjadi di kota Bandoeng dan berachir pada tahon 1917*), the year before the publication of the book. The realism of the story is heightened by the use of precise dates and times, purported photographs of some of the characters and of places where the events in the story are said to have occurred. Letters are allegedly reproduced or summarised, and, more significantly, details are given of newspaper reports (including the date and issue number) which are said to refer to the characters. Occasionally, the author says that he has been able to find out certain information, and he presents himself as an authority on the story by people in Bandung. It is not only in the title and through such devices as these that Chabanneau asserts that his story is authentic. At the beginning of the book he declares (in verse):

> *Tjerita ini betoel terdjadi boekannja djoesta,*
> *Boewat pendoedoek di Bandoeng kota,*
> *Samoewa taoe benarnja ini tjerita.*

> *This story really happened, it's not a lie,*
> *For the people of the city of Bandung,*
> *Everyone knows the truth of this story.*

Only the names have been changed, he says:

---

9   These 'histories' seem to have been addressed to an audience of both women and men, although in some cases they contain a warning against young people or women reading them. Similarly, the readership does not seem to have been confined to ethnic Chinese, although it is unlikely that *totok* Chinese read them. Some 'histories' were written by Indonesians and (Eurasian) Indos, and members of these groups would also have been among the readers. I am working on a larger project which I hope will appear as a book with the proposed title *Colloquial Malay Histories: Between Fact and Fiction in Colonial Java*.

Tapi soepaja tida langgar atoeran,
Nama orang saja sengadja bikin penoekaran,
Sebab kaloe taoe, wet poenja keangkaran,
Pembatja tantoe mengarti, apa jang djadi lantaran. (...)

Sebabnja samoewa nama jang saja karang,
Antero masih hidoep sampe sekarang,
Kaloe ditoelis namanja dengan berterang,
Selainnja wet, hati sendiri djoega melarang. (Chabanneau,
1918: 2)

But to avoid breaking the rules,
I've deliberately made changes in people's names,
Because as you know, the law is severe,
Readers will know what the consequences are. (...)

Because all the names which I'm writing about,
Are all still living to this day,
To write their names openly,
Apart from the law, my own heart would forbid it.

If the genre of 'colloquial Malay histories' can be represented
as a continuum stretching from the most factual to the most
fictional, *Rasia Bandoeng* seems, on the face of it, to be at the
factual end. Without making an extratextual investigation of the
story (for example, by checking the cited contemporary
newspaper reports) one cannot exclude the possibility that this is
a case (perhaps an extreme one) of an author using
'authenticity' as a discursive effect (Ruthven 1991).
Such effects are, of course, part of the art of the novelist. On
the opening page of *Roxana, The Fortunate Mistress*, Daniel
Defoe's relator/narrator tells us that its foundation 'is laid in
truth of fact, and so the work is not a story, but a history' (cited
in Davis, 1983: 14). Rather than early 18th century England,
the two stories or 'histories' I refer to here were written in the
early 20th century in colonial Java. Like the early English
novels of which Davis was writing, however, the genre to which
these texted representations of the past belong explicitly claim
that they are true while at the same time, in most cases, they
have been read as works of fiction.

At the time of the conference when the previous version of this paper was delivered, I had not tried to check the historicity of these stories outside their text. My belief that *Rasia Bandoeng* was at the factual end of the continuum of 'colloquial Malay histories' has since been confirmed, however. Myra Sidharta has kindly sent me a copy of a chapter from an unpublished memoir by a friend of hers called William Paramita (Tjia Bing Lie). In this chapter (entitled *La cause célèbre*), he acknowledged that *Rasia Bandoeng* was the story of his grandfather and aunt, and supplied the correct names of his relatives (which were very thinly disguised by Chabanneau). Indeed, as Paramita points out, the six stanza verse which prefaces Chabanneau's story 'was composed in such a way, that when people read the emphasised first letter of each line, they could know the real names of my grandfather and his daughter'. The solution to the acrostic to which he refers reads 'TAN TJENG HOE DAN HERMINE TAN' (Chabanneau 1918: 3). 'Hilda Tan' thus turns out to have been Paramita's aunt, Hermine Tan.

Further research identified a 'history' by another author on the same subject.[10]

Whether fact or fiction, the two (hi)stories discussed here share an antagonism to Western education for Indonesian Chinese girls. To limit my choice to two examples was not easy, since there were several other strong contenders for inclusion. I will indulge myself briefly by quoting from one of these also-rans, the 'history' by Quo Vadis? (the question mark is part of the author's pseudonym) with the title *Kemerdikahan jang membawa binasa atawa Resianja Gadis dari familie Ong (Satoe tjerita betoel terdjadi dalem tahon 1923 di Weltevreden)* (Freedom which brings disaster, or The secret of the girl from the Ong family (A story which really happened in 1923 in

---

10   See K.Kh. Liong (Kwee Kheng Liong) 1918. On the other hand, so far I have been unable to trace any reference to the affair in the contemporary press. Tineke Hellwig is writing an article about *Rasia Bandoeng* and its historical foundations, which will include family photographs which she has obtained from descendants of the protagonists who are living in the Netherlands (personal communication).

Weltevreden) (Quo Vadis? 1923). In the introduction, the author sets out his purpose in writing the book. It is to show 'how Western education and intercourse (*pergaoelan*) which are the basis of the extensive freedoms which have been given to Chinese girls are really not an improvement and not a true way for Chinese girls to hold more firmly to their honour and their family name (*nama toeroenan*)' (Chabanneau 1918: 3). The author cites the authority of a Dutch friend, educated at HBS,[11] for the statement that 'Chinese girls with a Dutch education are actually just delicious food for the *sinjo-sinjo*!'. The same Dutch friend claimed to have taken the virginity of ten Chinese girls, he said (Chabanneau 1918: 5).

Rasia Bandoeng

The primary title of the book by Chabanneau referred to earlier, *Rasia Bandoeng, atawa satoe pertjintaan jang melanggar peradatan 'Bangsa Tiong Hoa'* (The Secret of Bandung, or a love which transgressed the customs of the 'Chinese Nation) (Chabanneau 1918), gives early warning of its content. The protagonists, Tan Tjin Hiauw and Tan Gong Nio (Hilda), shock traditional Chinese ideas by marrying although they have the same *she* (family name). Hilda studies for a year at a HBS in Batavia, and continues with private lessons in Bandung. She wears European clothes and rides a bicycle (which is said to be unusual for a Chinese girl). She behaves outrageously by conservative standards, walking around the streets of Bandung with Tan Tjin Hiauw, deceiving her father by saying that she is seeing girl friends from school. Tjin Hiauw tries to persuade his family that this behaviour is acceptable because

> firstly, most people these days are in favour of progress, so if they see the two of us together, just say that I'm copying European *adat*; and secondly, because Hilda and I have the same *she* (family name) (Chabanneau 1918: 27).

Tjin Hiauw is also Europeanised, though less highly educated

---

11   HBS (Hoogere Burgerschool) was the prestigious Dutch secondary school.

in formal schooling. He attends a Malay primary school, but through hard work became fluent in Dutch and obtains a diploma of bookkeeping, taking private lessons in English, French and German. He and his friends use European expressions like 'Allright', 'Hallo' and 'Goeden middag' in conversation, and when Tjin Hiauw says goodbye to the members of his organisation, they shake hands in European style.

Hilda corresponds secretly with him, until her father discovers one of his letters. Her father (Tan Djia Goan, a rich *singkeh*, who is also a Christian, as it happens) beats her brutally, removes her from lessons, and keeps her at home. (So much for Tjin Hiauw's hope that because Djia Gwan was a Christian, he might agree to ignore the rule forbidding marriage between members of the same *she*, on the basis that it was 'a rotten, old-fashioned custom!') As might be expected, this is not the end of it. To cut a long and complicated story short, the lovers elope and make their way to Makassar, where they discover Hilda is pregnant. They return to Java by way of Singapore (where they marry) and Hilda gives birth to a daughter in Bandung. Tjin Hiauw gets a job with good wages with an English firm in Batavia, and the three move there in March 1918.

It almost sounds like a happy ending, but Hilda's father has cut her out of his will and legally disowned her after attempting without success to prevent the marriage. The author presents the moral of the story very explicitly, in verse:

> *Bagimana bingoeng pikirannja, orang jang djadi Bapa,*
> *Jang pikirin anak-anaknja haroes dapat peladjaran apa,*
> *Sebab toekar agama, peladjaran bangsa sendiri djadi di loepa,*
> *Lantas tetap ingatan, ambil fihak peladjaran Europa.*
> (Chabanneau 1918: 30).

How confused his thoughts, a man who was a father,
Who should consider what sort of education his children must have,
Because he changed religion, forgot the education of his own nation,
Then decided to choose the side of European education.

Hilda is compared very unfavourably with her elder sister Tan Kaij Nio (Helena), who although educated at a Dutch primary school, was attracted at the age of 14 to 'her own language' and took evening lessons in Mandarin and Chinese script at the THHK building in Bandung, in addition to her French, piano and English lessons. Helena was engaged to marry Tjia Sioe Loei (Peter) when both were about 20 years old, and their wedding was blessed by a Christian priest.

The moral of the story is summarised thus:

> *Satoe djedjaka pintar dan tjoekoep peladjaran,*
> *Lantaran satoe waktoe, dapat salah pikiran,*
> *Hendak robah bangsa Tiong Hoa poenja atoeran,*
> *Penghidoepan jang bagoes, ampir djadi kapiran.*
>
> *Satoe Tiong Hoa Siotjia jang dapat pendidikan Europa*
> *Pada peradatan bangsa sendiri, ija djadi loepa,*
> *Hingga brani membantah, kahendaknja ija poenja bapa,*
> *Kerna toeroet perasaannja, hal itoe tida djadi apa.*
>
> *Daritoe baiklah semoewa iboe-bapa berati-ati,*
> *Djangan teledor, misti ingat di hari nanti,*
> *Kerna maskipoen kita ada harta berketi,*
> *Sesalan dan maloe tida datang berganti.* (Chabanneau 1918: 4).

A clever bachelor with a good enough education,
Because at some point his thinking went astray,
He wanted to change the rules of the Chinese,
A fine life almost became a mess.

A Chinese girl who received a European schooling,
Forgot the customs of her own people,
So she dared to oppose the will of her father,
Because she followed her feelings, that didn't matter to her.

So from this all mothers and fathers take care,
Don't neglect your duty, remember the future,
Because even if we are millionaires,
Regret and shame cannot be exchanged.

Valentine Chan

My second example of a story or 'history' with an agenda in opposition to Dutch education for Chinese girls is Liem Hian Bing, *Valentine Chan atawa Rahasia Semarang* (Valentine Chan, or The Secret of Semarang) (Liem 1926).[12] Valentine Chan, apparently still attending the MULO,[13] is an only child who lives with her widowed father in a Bodjong (Semarang) house, but sleeps in a *pavillion*, which has its own entrance, at the rear. The name Valentine was chosen by her teacher. She and William Ong are introduced at the Stadstuin dance hall by a Dutch woman, and at once engage in conversation in Dutch. Their clothes are as European as their names, and they are both from wealthy families. Among the crowd of mostly Dutch people, they dance the foxtrot, two-step, and tango (less enthusiastically in William's case) to the music of a jazz band, and they drink champagne.

William, who lives with his widowed mother, recently graduated from the HBS, and plans to do a law degree in the Netherlands. Powerfully attracted to each other, they are inseparable in the few weeks before William departs for the Netherlands and they become informally engaged.

In his absence, however, she goes to dances and movies and meets other men. One of these is Tan Hok-bie, who rescues her from a runaway vehicle, and they start going to dances together. In his absence through serious illness, another dancing companion, an Indo called De Geert takes her to a hotel and seduces her. Her father receives an anonymous letter informing him that his daughter is longer a virgin, and threatening further action if he does not take steps to keep his daughter under control. A few days later an article appears in a Semarang newspaper about Valentine, with the names (initials) of all concerned. Valentine, who has by now learned from a doctor that she is pregnant, calms her father's fears. Meanwhile she

---

12   This is, strictly speaking, a story rather than a 'history' in that there is no subtitle with the 'really happened' formula. The discursive effects of 'authenticity' used in it are, however, very similar.

13   MULO (*Meer Uitgebreid Lager Onderwijs*) was a Dutch junior high school.

brings about a miscarriage by eating a lot of unripe pineapple, but she becomes very ill and bleeds, again requiring the attention of the doctor. Another anonymous letter informs her father that Valentine has aborted her baby. He abuses her verbally, threatens to disown her, and beats her with a cane until the servants intervene.

A few months later, Tan Hok-bie, evidently somewhat recovered, invites Valentine to go swimming with him at Tjandi. He orders a room for them at a hotel, where they can eat and leave their belongings. Hok-bie then seduces Valentine after their swim but, discovering she was not a virgin, wants nothing more to do with her.

Meanwhile, the faithful William Ong has been forced to return from the Netherlands because of illness (lovesickness?). His uncle tells him of Valentine's shame and shows him the newspaper reports. William gains confirmation of his uncle's view that she is no longer suitable to be his wife by observing her at the dance hall the next Saturday evening. Angrily he writes her a letter breaking off their unofficial engagement, saying that he is going to leave Semarang.

Embittered, Valentine stays at home reading books until one day she reads a newspaper article about a young man in Surabaya who has killed himself because he was crossed in love. She realises that the article is about William. The next morning Valentine hangs herself.

The intended moral of this book is clear. Chinese people should not adopt Western customs, particularly dancing, which leads to sex and a loss of virginity, making a Chinese girl unmarriable. As the author comments:

> Those methods of dancing performed by a group of young people are far from decent, (and) can only be called an art (*kunst*) as an activity to arouse lust (*boeat bangoenken napsoe birahi*)...' (Liem Hian Bing, 1926: 108, 41)

Parents should also keep close watch over their children. The author sums this up in the final paragraph:

> The story set out in this book is like a looking glass for
> our Chinese girls and a source of knowledge for parents who
> have a mania for the West (*gila barat*). (Liem Hian Bing,
> 1926: 124)

The author of *Valentine Chan* recognises that there has been rapid progress in the Chinese world, and that now is not the time for conservatism (*kekolotan*). 'The world has changed and people's lives must flow with the current of the age (*aliran djeman*)' (Liem Hian Bing, 1926: 40). But there are blemishes in the forms of that 'modern' way of life now enjoyed by the Chinese in Java which he believes must be removed. Not all Western morality (*kesopanan*) is bad, but the Chinese have transplanted rotten elements of it and 'people can see how many girls have become victims of that kind of morality' (Liem Hian Bing, 1926: 41).

Valentine Chan's family, in adjusting to the current of the age, has abandoned Chinese morality completely. Her father has gone over completely to the Western system, and worst of all he has given his daughter excessive freedom. Freedom is only acceptable where it is balanced and within bounds for the safety of the weaker (female) party. Valentine had free access to the car every day, could go out in the evenings on her own or with her male friends (*kontjo-kontjo*) and return home in the middle of the night. Her father allowed her to mix freely with the young men she met, and she didn't have the maturity (*ia masi terlaloe idjo*) to know about the temptations of life and love.

To judge by some of the advertisements which appear in the book, we must entertain some doubt about the purity of the publisher's motives, whatever the claims of the author. Immediately after the description of Valentine's seduction by De Geert, there appears an advertisement for the book *Akal resia: Orang lelaki aken mendapet perhatian dan katjintahan dari orang prempoean* (Secret knowledge: How men can attract the attention and love of women) (Liem Hian Bing, 1926: 69). Opposite the author's highminded final paragraph is the first of two advertisements for the two volume book *Boekoe pengatahoean tentang anggota Rasia dari orang prempoean berbagi bangsa terhias dengen gambar jang eilok-eilok menoeroet tjatetannja dokter-dokter* (Textbook about the secret parts of women of various nations illustrated with beautiful pictures according to notes by doctors) (125–6). (It is interesting to note the number of colloquial Malay books from this period which appear, at least from their titles, to broach the subject of women or of sexuality by purporting to uncover a 'secret'. The word *rahasia* (or its variants *rasia* or *resia*) crops up in many titles.)[14]

Henk Maier has drawn attention to the role of the Balai Poestaka in marginalising Chinese Malay literature and specifically in categorising it as *Schund literatur* (trashy literature):

> a derogatory reference to a corpus of texts that must have been at least fifty times larger than the production of Balai Poestaka: immoral, sensual, and, therefore, malignant and dangerous. Some mildly pornographic texts were indeed published by Chinese enterprises (the publication of *Perhoeboengan Rasia* in Semarang in 1937 comes to mind) but such books were rare, and it is, therefore, an inappropriate term for the corpus as a whole. (Maier, 1991: 79–80)

I agree, but I think Maier may have overstated his case. Unlike the Balai Poestaka, whose links were with education and uplift and was heavily subsidised by government, the colloquial Malay 'histories' and their authors were an extension of Indies journalism and were dependent on the marketplace for their readers. We can all think of examples of journalism which, under the cloak of proclaimed morality, make their sales pitch to the sensational and salacious. The colloquial Malay 'histories' too sometimes hovered between the highminded and the meretricious.

---

14   Apart from those already mentioned, see Butatuli & Hemeling 1913; Djie Kiat Gie 1930; Gouw Peng Liang 1923; Juvenile Kuo 1928a; Juvenile Kuo 1928b; Juvenile Kuo 1930; Pat Kwah Yong 1919; Probitas 1916; Sin Gan Peng 1919; Tan 1923; Tan Boen Kim 1914; Tan Boen Kim 1915; Tjermin 1918.

Some Tentative Conclusions

It is time to try to draw together a few threads. It is clear that the position of the Indonesian Chinese woman was already contested ground in the second decade of this century. The debates went on vigorously for the rest of the colonial period.[15] Considering their early date and the vigour of their expression, I believe that the ideas of the two Mrs Yaps deserve more attention than they have hitherto received. I cannot make any great claims for the tentative conclusions and points I highlight here. They are organised under three heads: (1) intellectual origins and context of the ideas of the two Mrs Yap Hong Tjoens about emancipation of the Indonesian Chinese woman; (2) the place of China and Chineseness in the debate; and (3) the fears and double standards expressed in the conservative (*kolot*) reaction to the changing position of Indonesian Chinese women.

Intellectual Origins and Context

The first Mrs Yap's address to the Chung Hwa Hui on 'The Chinese Woman' did not take place in a vacuum. Only eight months earlier, Mr Fromberg himself had delivered a lengthy address to the Chung Hwa Hui in Amsterdam on the subject of 'The Indies Chinese family and legislation' (Fromberg, 1926: 567–84), and it is clear from her address that she was familiar with it. Fromberg argued that Chinese personal law in the Indies, particularly with regard to marriage, adoption and inheritance, was in disarray and that new legislation was necessary:

> Civilized peoples have written laws. These written laws give *certainty of law*, in that people can read from them what their rights and obligations are, the nature of their relationship with their family, with their fellow-men in the community, to the State. (Fromberg, 1926: 569)

---

15   For later examples, see Bocquet-Siek 1983; Sidharta 1992. See also Chan 1995 for a valuable discussion of emancipationist positions expressed in the *peranakan* journals *Panorama* and *Maandblad Istri* in the late 1920s and 1930s.

The Regeeringsreglement, the constitution of the Indies, said that such matters were to be governed by 'their religious laws, institutions and customs', which, he said, merely meant 'by their *adat*, their customary law'. But this *adat* was unwritten. Where could it be found? The courts had first looked to a classical Chinese text, the *Ta Tsing Lu Li*, but for various reasons this was inappropriate in the modern Indies context. The next step had been to discover a specifically Indies Chinese customary law but this only gave rise to enormous uncertainty. That led him at once to the conclusion that the European law, as set out in the Indische Burgelijk Wetboek, should be applied to the Chinese, as indeed was now being proposed. What else could or should be done? In China itself, since 1911, the law was moving toward Western models, for example by accepting monogamy as the basis of the marriage law. The same address was directly referred to by the second Mrs Yap in her 1928 speech, when she repeated the comparison made by Fromberg of the position before and after the 1917 family and inheritance law (Fromberg, 1926: 576–77; Yap, Mr Dr Mevr. 1928: 43).

The Fromberg connection can be traced earlier. On 19 November 1912, he gave a lecture to the Indisch Genootschap in The Hague on 'The Chinese Movement in Java' (*De Chineesche beweging op Java*) (Fromberg, 1926: 449–70. This lecture should be distinguished from the longer booklet of the same name which he published in 1911, and is reproduced in Fromberg, 1926: 405–47.) Space and time don't permit me to develop this here, but a number of the ideas used by the first Mrs Yap in her address to the Chung Hwa Hui come directly from this lecture. My mind races to the hypothetical possibility of a correspondence between Mrs Yap and Mr Fromberg (not to mention his wife, sitting there in the front row of the picture with which I began) which might parallel that between Kartini and the Abendanons. We have noted the presence of Mr Abendanon at the first Mrs Yap's address. Were the Frombergs (or the Abendanons) sometimes guests at the 'open house' of the Yaps in the Netherlands? But of course there is no evidence for any of these things. We have already seen that she was familiar with the writing of Anna Polak. Was she in touch with Dutch feminists in the Netherlands?

We should also remember that there were other possible sources than European ones for the feminist ideas of the first Mrs Yap. We know that she read the Malay language press in Java, and indeed once contributed a letter to the editor of *Sin Po* (footnote 2). Could she have been a reader of the women's section of the *Tiong Hoa Wi Sien Po*, edited by Lim Titie Nio of Bogor, which commenced publication as early as 1906? Claudine Salmon links this publication with the reformist Confucian movement which gave birth to the Tiong Hoa Hwe Koan— Batavia in 1900, and notes that teaching for girls in THHK schools was important from their inception (Salmon, 1977: 160). That source would not only take us back to reformist Confucianism under Kang You-wei in China,[16] but also to the experience of THHK founders as students of Dutch missionaries in West Java (Coppel 1986). But Chinese sources are also evident in the writing of the sisters, who both cite Dr Chen Huan Chang (also known in Java as Tan Hwan Tjiang), author of *Economic Principles of Confucius and his School*, as their authority for the equality of men and women in Confucius' time (Yap, 1917a: 48; Yap, 1928: 44). This same man, a disciple of Kang You-wei with a Ph.D. from Columbia University, was highly regarded by conservative Confucianists in Java (Coppel 1989b). However, it seems clear that neither sister had direct access to Chinese sources in the original; like many *peranakan* Chinese, they were dependent upon translations into Western languages or Malay.

China and Chineseness

It is noteworthy that both Mrs Yaps and the conservatives they attacked invoked the authority of China and Chineseness in their arguments about the emancipation of the Indies Chinese woman. Both Mrs Yaps argued that equality of women with men was justified both because that principle had applied in

---

16   See the charming picture of Kang You-wei with the peranakan Chinese girls attending the THHK-Batavia school in 1903 (reproduced from Nio Joe Lan's history of the THHK-Batavia by Bocquet-Siek 1983: 36).

Confucius' time and because that was the principle adopted in the recently established Chinese Republic. They argued that the education of women, and their involvement in the working world, were essential if China and the Indies Chinese were to develop and be strong in the modern world. The first Mrs Yap was not opposed to Chinese customs, indeed she lamented that she could not read the great Chinese *poedjonggo* in the original. But to be true to China was, for her, also to be open to Europe. Many Chinese women were leaving China itself to gain skills in Europe, America and Japan. The Chinese women in the Indies should not be left behind their compatriots in China itself. Women who fought for the revolution in China were no less Chinese for that; neither were women in the Indies deserting Chinese customs, even though they might be failing to follow the narrow *adat* of Chinese peranakans in the Indies (*specifiek Indo-Chineesche zeden*).

It is interesting in this connection to note the remarks by the Chinese diplomats in response to the first Mrs Yap's 1916 address. The ambassador specifically approved what she had said about recent change in China and said that 'because of the increasing application of Western educational methods, the roles which women will be called upon to play can only become more important'. The first secretary of the Chinese Legation similarly called for increasing numbers of 'our sons and our daughters' to be sent to study in the high schools and universities of Europe. Although there had been some advances in the emancipation of women in China, and they still fell far short of the ideal, even these seemed to have made little impression on 'the majority of our compatriots in the Indies'.

The anonymous letter received by Valentine Chan's father contained the statement 'I cannot remain silent about an action which transgresses the customs (*adat-istiadat*) of our own nation' (Liem Hian Bing, 1926: 79). This remark may be better understood if we recall that in September 1924 a conference had been held in Bandung under the auspices of the Khong Kauw Tjong Hwee (a conservative Confucian organisation) to establish uniform Chinese customs for the Indies. One of the decisions of the conference had been to prohibit a young woman from going out or being alone with a man other than her brother, husband or father, unless an older relative was present, even if the man was her fiancé (Coppel, 1989b and 1996).

One of the concerns of the conservatives may have been the fear that Chinese girls would be defiled by sexual relations with non-Chinese. For example, in *Valentine Chan* Chinese girls seem to be regarded as less available sexually than girls of other ethnicity, and the Chinese youths are very disapproving of Valentine dancing with De Geert, an Indo (Liem Bian Hing, 1926: 58, 63). Sidharta suggests that 'Especially marriages to Eurasians (Indo-Europeans) became controversial' (Sidharta, 1992: 64) and we have already noted the statement in the book by Quo Vadis? that 'Chinese girls with a Dutch education are actually just delicious food for the *sinjo-sinjo*!'

The Kolot Reaction

If the *bête noire* of the first Mrs Yap was what (following Fromberg) she called 'bigot conservatism' of the 'kaoem kolot', the core of the conservatives' opposition to the mania for the West (*gila barat*) was its permissiveness, particularly with regard to Chinese girls. We have already noted the revulsion of the author of *Valentine Chan* toward Western dancing. At the point in the report of the second Mrs Yap's 1928 speech where she summarises the revolutionary social changes which have occurred since the Great War, her reference to 'modern dancing' attracts a comment from the editor of the *Orgaan der Centrale Chung Hsioh*:

> Our point of view about modern dancing is already known to you all: a strong stand needs to be taken against these delights of dubious quality. It is unbecoming of Mrs Yap to encourage our sisters to dance, just as if it was a report in one of the Chinese Malay papers. (Ed)

In the same piece, the editor interpolates another comment: 'The speaker seems to find the position of the Western woman so enviable and ideal (almost perfect). With all respect, we do not! (Ed)'.

Implicit in the conservative position was a defence of older practices in the Indies Chinese community such as confining adolescent girls to their homes, and parent-arranged marriages. They feared the loss of their daughters' virginity before they were safely married to a husband of their choosing. The double standards in this stance have been noted by others (Sidharta, 1992; Bocquet-Siek, 1983). They are very evident in the 'histories', where the Chinese boys frequent the brothels without evident disapproval of the authors.

Finally, one other element embedded in the conservative position portrayed in the two 'histories' we have considered is that of physical violence by father against daughter because she has deviated from the traditional sexual morality. In *Rasia Bandoeng*, when Hilda's father discovers the letter from Tan Tjin Hiauw, he beats her brutally with a *kimotjeng* (*roti pandjang*), until her mother, sister and brother-in-law stop him (Chabanneau, 1918: 78–79). In *Valentine Chan,*, when her father finds out that she is pregnant, he canes her until the servants intervene on her behalf (Liem Bian Hing, 1926: 93). In the latter case at least, the author seems to be remarkably tolerant of it.[17]

References
Bocquet-Siek, Margaret, 1983, 'The Peranakan Chinese Woman at a crossroad' in Manderson, L. (ed), *Women's Work and Women's Roles: Economics and Everyday Life in Indonesia, Malaysia and Singapore*, Australian National University Development Studies Centre Monograph No.32, Canberra.

Butatuli & Hemeling, 1913, *Boekoe wet dan rasia tentang perhoeboengan antara prampoean dan lelaki atawa pengetahoean hal bagi kamanoesiaan (jang haroes manoesia moesti taoe). Tersalin dari roepa-roepa boekoe ilmoe tabib bangsa Europa jang ternama. Terhias dengan 66 gambar-gambar dari bagian-bagian toeboe manoesia*, Tjiong Koen Bie, Batavia.

---

17   I am grateful to Helen Pausacker for drawing my attention to the similarities between these two incidents.

Chabanneau, 1918, *Rasia Bandoeng, atawa satoe pertjintaan jang melanggar peradatan 'Bangsa Tiong Hoa': Satoe Tjerita jang benar terdjadi di kota Bandoeng dan berachir pada tahon 1917*, Drukkerij Kho Tjeng Bie & Co., 2 vol., Batavia.

Chan, Faye Yik-Wei, 1995, 'Chinese Women's Emancipation as Reflected in Two Peranakan Journals (c.1927–1942)', *Archipel*, 49.

Chandler, David P. and Ricklefs, M.C. (eds) 1986, *Nineteenth and Twentieth Century Indonesia: Essays in honour of Professor J.D.Legge*, Monash Papers on Southeast Asia No.14, Centre of Southeast Asian Studies, Monash University, Clayton.

Coppel, Charles A., 1986, 'From Christian Mission to Confucian Religion: The Nederlandsche Zendingsvereeniging and the Chinese of West Java, 1870–1910' in Chandler and Ricklefs, *Nineteenth and Twentieth Century Indonesia: Essays in honour of Professor J.D.Legge*, Monash Papers on Southeast Asia No.14, Centre of Southeast Asian Studies, Monash University, Clayton.

—— 1989a, 'Culture Change by Conference: Bandung 1924', in May, R.J. and O'Malley, W.J. (eds) *Observing Change in Asia: Essays in Honour of J.A.C. Mackie*, Crawfurd House Press, Bathurst.

—— 1989b, 'Is Confucianism a Religion? A 1923 Debate in Java', *Archipel*, 38.

—— 1996, 'Peranakan Construction of Chinese Customs in Late Colonial Java' in Douw and Post, *South China: State, Culture and Social Change during the 20th Century*, Koninklijke Nederlandse Akademie van Wetenschappen, Verhandelingen, Afd. Letterkunde, Nieuwe Reeks, deel 169, Amsterdam.

Davis, Lennard J. 1983, *Factual Fictions: The Origins of the English Novel*, Columbia University Press, New York.

Djie Kiat Gie, 1930, *Resia Tangerang, Gadis oedik kepengen tinggal dikota atawa sasoedanja menjesel baroe djadi baek*. 2nd. ed., Kwee Seng Tjoan, Batavia.

Douw, L.M. and Post, P. (eds), 1996, *South China: State, Culture and Social Change during the 20th Century*, Koninklijke Nederlandse Akademie van Wetenschappen, Verhandelingen, Afd. Letterkunde, Nieuwe Reeks, deel 169, Amsterdam.

Fromberg, Mr P.H. Sr. 1926, *Verspreide Geschriften verzameld door Chung Hwa Hui*, Leidsche Uitgevers Maatschappij, Leiden.

Gouw Peng Liang, 1923, *Resia Pelatjoeran prampoean atawa nasehat jang bergoena besar aken tjega bahaja dari perkara djina, menoeroet karangannja satoe thabib jang kesohor di Berlin*, Weltevreden, (Favoriet?).

Han Tiauw Tjong, 1919, *Toespraak bij het aanbieden van het diploma en het insigne van het eere-lidmaatschap van 'Chung Hwa Hui' aan Dr Yap Hong Tjoen, op de algemeene vergadering te Den Haag, den 26sten Januari 1919, door den President: Han Tiauw Tjong*, Druk van D. Prooper, Delft.

Juvenile Kuo, 1928a, *Resia nona Hermine waktoe di Singapore, jaitoe tjerita pentjoerian dari sepasang giwang berharga 2000 dollars, dan tjerita Pembalesan toean Oey. Samboengan dari tjerita Resianja Njonja djanda Oeij*, Kwee Seng Tjoan, Batavia.

—— 1928b, *Resia toean Tangerang tentang polygamie, atau nona Hermine dengan ia poenja soedara prempoean*, Kwee Seng Tjoan, Batavia.

—— 1930, *Resia Tangerang, gadis oedik kepengen tinggal di kota atawa sesoedanja menjesel baroe djadi baek*, Kwee Seng Tjoan, Batavia.

K.Kh. Liong (Kwee Kheng Liong), 1918, *Tjerita Nona Tan Seng Nio alias Hermine T**** atawa tjara bagimana orang toea haroes didik sama anaknja. Satoe tjerita jang betoel soedah kedjadian die kota Bandoeng dalem tahoen 1912 dan berachier tahoen 1917*.

—— 1924, *Doea kapala batoe*, Maurer & Dimmick, Berlin.

Liem Hian Bing, 1926, *Valentine Chan atawa Rahasia Semarang*, Boekhandel 'Patkwah', Semarang.

Locher-Scholten, Elsbeth and Anke Niehof, (eds.) 1992, *Indonesian Women in Focus: Past and Present Notions.* KITLV Press, Leiden.

Maier, Hendrik M.J. 1991, 'Forms of Censorship in the Dutch Indies: The Marginalization of Chinese-Malay Literature', *Indonesia,* 56, October (Special issue on The Role of the Indonesian Chinese in Shaping Modern Indonesian Life).

Manderson, Lenore, (ed), 1983, *Women's Work and Women's Roles: Economics and Everyday Life in Indonesia, Malaysia and Singapore*, Australian National University Development Studies Centre Monograph No.32, Canberra.

May, R.J. and O'Malley, W.J. (eds), 1989, *Observing Change in Asia: Essays in Honour of J.A.C. Mackie*, Crawfurd House Press, Bathurst.

Pat Kwah Yong, 1919, *Rasia Djember atawa hasilnja katjintaan*, Pek Pang Eng, Grissee.

Phoa Liong Gie, Sim Ki Ay and Thung Tjeng Hiang (eds), 1926, *Gedenkboek Chung Hua Hui 15 April 1911–1926*, Chung Hua Hui, n.pl. (Leiden?).

Probitas, 1916, *Toedjoe belas tahon dalem resia: Satoe tjerita bagoes aken djadi satoe katja bagi gadis-gadis Tionghoa jang dapet pladjaran Europa*, Han Po, Batavia.

Quo Vadis? 1923, *Kemerdikahan jang membawa binasa atawa Resianja Gadis dari familie Ong (Satoe tjerita betoel terdjadi dalem tahon 1923 di Weltevreden*, N.V. Kong Hwee Po., Batavia.

Ruthven, Ken, 1991, '"Authenticity" as a Discursive Effect', Paper presented at the Conference on Histories in Cultural Systems, held at the University of Melbourne, 30 September– 3 October 1991, by the Humanities Research Centre, Australian National University.

Salmon, Claudine, 1977, 'Presse Féminine ou Féministe?', in *Archipel,* 13.

Sidharta, Myra, 1992, 'The Making of the Indonesian Chinese Woman', in Locher-Scholten, E. and Niehof, A. (eds) *Indonesian Women in Focus: Past and Present Notions,* KITLV Press, Leiden.

Sin Gan Peng, 1919, *Rasia Soerabaja atawa katjentilannja gadis hartawan jang dapet didikan adat Europa (benar soeda kedjadian dalem taon 1918)*, Pek Pang Eng, Grissee.

Suryadinata, Leo, 1995, *Prominent Indonesian Chinese: Biographical Sketches*, Institute of Southeast Asian Studies, (3rd edition), Singapore.

Tan, 1923, *Pertoenangan dalem resia atawa pertjintaan jang soetji*, Tan Thian Soe, Batavia.

Tan Boen Kim, 1914, *Tjerita Nona Gan Jan Nio atawa 'pertjinta'an dalem rasia'*, soeatoe tjerita jang belon sebrapa lama sasoenggoenja telah terjadi dalem kota Betawi, Tjiong Koen Bie, Batavia.

―――― 1915, *Njai Aisah atawa djadi korban dari rasia. Soeatoe tjerita jang betoel soeda terdjadi di Betawi pada achirnja taon 1914, samboengan tjerita Nona Fientje de Feniks*, Tjiong Koen Bie, Batavia.

―――― 1935, *Orang-orang Tionghoa jang Terkemoeka di Java*, The Biographical Publishing Centre, Solo.

Tjermin, 1918, *Rasianja satoe gadis hartawan atawa perdjalanan Nona Tan, satoe gadis Tionghoa di Weltevreden jang terpeladjar tinggi, achirnja mengandoeng baji rasia, lantaran kamerdika'an dan banjak dibitjarakan dalam taon 1917*, The Teng Hoeij, Buitenzorg.

Yap Hong Tjoen, 1918, 'Satoe penglihatan dari politiek program bangsa Tionghwa di Hindia (Contra s.k. 'Perniagaan' tersalin dalem bahasa Melajoe rendah), *Chung Hwa Hui Tsa Chih*, 2, 1–2 October.

Yap Hong Tjoen, Mrs 1917a, 'De Chineesche vrouw', in *Chung Hwa Hui Tsa Chih*, 1(1), April.

―――― 1917b, 'Het Chineesche Meisje en de Arbeid', in *Chung Hwa Hui Tsa Chih*, 1(1), April.

Yap (Hong Tjoen?) Mr Dr Mevr, 1928, 'De revolutie in de vrouwenwereld', *Orgaan der Centrale Chung Hsioh*, 4, February, (Congres Nummer).

Images of the Indonesian Woman During the Japanese Occupation 1942–1945[*]

Anton Lucas

'First of all, we must rescue the Indonesians from the habit of laziness. We must teach them diligence, effort, perseverance and devotion' (a Japanese military source quoted in Sato 1990)

The Japanese came to occupy Indonesia in March 1942 with a political ideology which aimed to mobilise all sections of the population to support their war effort. While the Occupation proved a disaster in economic terms, some Indonesians living in both rural but particularly urban areas, gained new skills and experiences in a range of wartime occupations and organisations as a result of the Japanese presence. Women had new roles to play as well as the traditional old ones, using family resources more efficiently, making a virtue of the necessity of coping with the brunt of shortages of foodstuffs, clothing and essential daily necessities.

Foremost in this new ideology by which the Japanese 16th Army ruled Java was the spirit of *hoko* or obligatory service to the state, and the spirit of *messhiboko* or selflessness. In wartime Japan, the main thrust of this political and semi-religious ideology justified and intensified the mobilisation of every Japanese subject for the war effort. However according to Sato, the closest the Japanese could get to the spirit of *hoko* in Java was obligation or duty (*kewajiban*), which in practice for rural women included learning how to plant and harvest castor oil plants, and new ways of planting rice. For urban women it meant

---

[*]   I would like to thank Keith Foulcher and Jean Taylor for their valuable comments and suggestions on earlier drafts of this paper.

having to work in a variety of wartime industry, and learning air raid and fire drills. The worst 'obligatory service' for women however was being forced to become comfort women (*jugun ianfu*). On the pretext of various kinds of employment or even further education, young women left home for attractive sounding new jobs, only to find themselves in brothel prisons working as sex slaves for the Japanese.

In the spirit of obligatory service to the state, the new colonisers thrust women into new social and cultural roles, as well as reinforced old ones. The Japanese military administration wanted to create a new economic order, by means of a regulated economic system based on public interest and selfless service, guided by the spirit of *hoko*. While this ideology and economic system proved acceptable to social conditions in wartime Japan, the same polices were, Sato argues, disastrous in Java, because of different economic and social conditions there (Sato, 1990: 95). The impact of these inappropriate policies, as well as the inept administration of them, was felt nowhere more strongly than in the area of rice marketing. In Java a different, more complicated (therefore difficult to regulate) system operated under very different conditions to rice marketing in Japan.

For ideological as well as practical reasons, the Occupation certainly promoted different women's roles in Indonesia. In the Japanese plans for mass mobilisation of human resources for their war effort, women had vital roles to play, although how this was to be implemented is not clear. Women were not coopted, in large numbers at any rate, into mass organisations such as Putera and Jawa Hokokai, which only had small women's sections in their central offices in Jakarta, and Fujinkai, the main women's organisation during the Occupation, never became a movement like its counterpart in Japan. Para-military groups (Seinendan and Keibodan) did not have women's sections, or women members. In some areas the Japanese coopted women into local groups with alternative activities for women. In Kendal regency immediately to the west of Central Java's provincial capital Semarang, the local information service had a women's corps with ceremonial and economic functions.

The only paramilitary organisation which did have a platoon of Karo Batak women was the KTT, the East Sumatran commando corps, an organisation aimed at Indonesian independence, set up in March 1945 by the charismatic maverick figure Inoue Tetsuro. The training for 400 KTT officers included lectures on strategy for guerrilla warfare, peasant spirit, handy fertiliser methods, ethics, applied psychology, and Indonesian history and politics. Exercises included basic combat training, guerrilla warfare, and agriculture routines. Mumi (a pseudonym for the wife of a leading East Sumatran nationalist, who was Inoue Tetsuro's lover, and by whom he had a child in 1943) taught (only to the girls presumably) first aid drill and cooking.[1] Although Tetsuro recalls in his memoirs, almost as an afterthought, that the Karo girls joined the training, they probably had to do the cooking for the men as well, as he says that they prepared warm bean gruel for the men after their morning exercises. Whether any actually graduated as leaders of the 30,000 strong KTT guerilla force is not known (Reid and Oki, 1986: 203–05).

Fujinkai: The Women's Association

The official Japanese women's association in Indonesia, Fujinkai, was of course modelled on its namesake in Japan where Fujinkai was created by combining a number of pre-war groups, all of which had mobilised women for different reasons:

> In pre-war Japan there were various women's groups and social movements serving feminist, patriotic and socialist causes. In the totalitarian mood the feminist and socialist movements were suppressed and the patriotic movements gathered strength. In February 1940, the (Japanese wartime) cabinet decided to create Dai Nippon Fujinkai (Greater Japan

---

1   Captain Inoue Tetsuro was a key behind-the-scenes figure in the Japanese wartime administration in East Sumatra. Fluent in Indonesian, his relationship with Chadidjah, the wife of nationalist leader Jacub Siregar helped him eventually understand the Indonesian Republican position. It was in response to a request from her that Inoue Tetsuro wrote his memoirs in a jungle hideout, probably in 1949 or 1950, shortly before he returned to Japan (Reid and Oki 1986, 80–81).

Women's Association) by merging existing women's associations and making membership compulsory for all women above the age of twenty. In close connection with the local administrative subunits, Fujinkai carried out activities that were considered to be suitable for it, such as preparation of comfort kits to be sent to soldiers, the collection of recyclable articles, encouragement of saving, crusades against luxuries such as permanent waves and colourful kimono, and care of those households whose men were on the battlefields. As the war situation deteriorated for Japan, Fujinkai assumed more and more militaristic features, and preparing for the landing of the Allied Forces which was considered imminent, women's combat forces armed with bamboo spears were created nation-wide in June 1945 out of the network of Fujinkai (Sato, 1990: 26–27).

In Java the Japanese did not have administrative or social networks to make Fujinkai real or relevant to poorer lower class women in rural and urban areas. In rural areas it became an organisation of the wives of Dutch trained Javanese officials (the *pangreh praja*), at least this was the perception of several informants in this study.[2] Thus the Japanese administration used *the pangreh praja* to build a system of Fujinkai branches throughout Java, 'using the influence of the wives of *bupatis, wedanas, camats* and lurahs' (Gandasubrata, 1952: 23), in other words the Javanese bureaucratic elite (regents, district and subdistrict heads and village headmen).

This association of the word Fujinkai with the wives of officials had negative connotations for lower class people during the Occupation. In Surabaya *kampungs* the word was used derisively 'as voguish slang for a high-class prostitute'. (Frederick, 1989: 176n61). As well as hatred for the Japanese, this mistaken syntax 'reflected dislike of the *priyayi* elite, since only upper class women were thought to belong to the Organisation' (Frederick, 1989: 176n61).

---

2   This study was based on field work carried out in Indonesia in July 1993, and January 1995, as well as drawing on a previous study of the Japanese occupation. The women interviewed had all experienced the Japanese occupation as teenagers or newly married women who were starting family life.

The relationship in people's minds between Fujinkai and wives of officials explains why, in a village near the temple of Borobodur in Central Java, Fujinkai was associated with *romusha* (forced labour), and the role wives of elite people (*orang tinggi* as officials were called), played in their recruitment. One of the tasks of local officials was to ensure that weekly *romusha* quotas were filled, and Fujinkai women assisted in taking those who were leaving to the transport provided for them (Ibu Raminem, interview, 7.7.93).

The other side of the coin was that Fujinkai forced the officials' wives to come into contact with non-elite women for the first time, promoting literacy classes, and cooperative kitchens (Vreede-de Stuers, 1960: 115). As famine conditions emerged in some areas of rural Java, partly because of a drought in 1944 which reduced rice production by 20%, all kinds of strange ingredients for recipes in a time of scarcity were promoted. In Pekalongan residency the local Fujinkai was known for making a virtue of necessity by promoting cooking demonstrations of snails, together with such recipes as 'Asia Bread' and 'Struggle Porridge' (*boeboer perjoeangan*) (Lucas, 1991: 37). The recipe for Struggle Porridge, rice mixed with cassava and vegetables, described as 'containing essential elements need by the human body', was first promoted by the Pekalongan Residency branch of Huzinhokokai (often abbreviated to Huzinkai), the women's section of Jawa Hokokai, the Java Service Association (*Djawa Baroe* 9, 1 May, 1945: 29). One writer tried to popularise eating Struggle Porridge, using it for the title of a short story about a young couple whose romance works out happily after the uncooperative hero relents and supports the New Life movement, eating the supernaturally powerful porridge (*boeboer sakti*) given out by a local Islamic leader (*Djawa Baroe 9,* 1 May 1945: 27). However for most people in Pekalongan residency it tasted like chicken feed and made them want to vomit.

The description Sato gives of the role of Fujinkai in wartime Japan shows us how much less significant a role it had in rural Java. For a start membership was not compulsory, or if it was, it was never effectively implemented. People were apathetic towards it, so it failed to 'get off the ground' (*nggak jalan*) (Ali Warsitohardjo, interview, 27 July 1993). While the Japanese tried to promote savings through village banks, people had nothing to save, and there were no luxuries to crusade against. Women were never drafted into para-military combat forces, although some studied women's martial arts (*ilmoe keprajoeritan poeteri*). But they were expected to play certain wartime roles, which we will examine shortly. If in rural areas, Fujinkai was too closely associated with the Dutch trained *pangreh praja*, in Jakarta, which was the headquarters of Fujinkai, perhaps the organisation had a more interesting role to play. Women joined because they wanted to show the Japanese 'that we women were not being confined or inactive' (*dibatasi atau diam*) (Arsip Nasional, 1988: 48). In the Jakarta Fujinkai branches, elite women recall a variety of functions 40 years later; promoting health care and distributing medicines, running public kitchens, helping flood relief work, distributing food rations, teaching people to plant cotton and spin yarn, showing women how to cook healthy food, and conducting literacy classes. Only amongst a handful of women, there was the issue (as recalled in 1988), that to work in the Fujinkai was 'to collaborate with the Japanese'. (Arsip Nasional, 1988: 48–53).

The background of a key figure in women's affairs during the Occupation reflects the kind of organisation Fujinkai was, or was meant to be, and the importance the Japanese placed on the support of Islamic groups. Nyonya (Mrs) S. Mangoenpoespito—her full name was Raden Nganten Siti Soekaptinah Soenarjo Mangoenpoespito—was the national chairperson of Huzinhokokai, and was previously head of the women's section of Putera, an earlier mass organisation under the Japanese. In her mid-30s with a good Dutch education, she had teaching, administrative and urban social work experience in pre-war Java. Ny. Soenarjo's Islamic credentials were also good. Her husband was a member of the national Islamic Council (MIAI) and she had been head of the women's section (*dames afdeling*) of the prewar Muslim youth group Jong Islamieten Bond. Ny. Soenarjo was also from a high priyayi background as her title Raden Nganten indicates. Priyayi women with a Dutch education and good Islamic connections were probably few and far between, which is probably why the Japanese, who always wanted to coopt Islamic leaders as well as the bureaucratic elite into their administration, appointed her to lead these women's organisations (Gunseikanbu, 1986: 475).[3] The image of Ibu Soenarjo Mangoenpoespito promoted by *Djawa Baroe,* as part of their campaign to popularise the New Life Movement, is of a highly organised woman, using every minute of the day, with no time for chatting or afternoon naps. She plants cassava in her house garden (though using old methods), she makes her own clothes (although colour and motif isn't all that can be desired), supervises the children's play, and goes to the market to do her own shopping, rather than sending a servant (*Djawa Baroe 9,* 1 May 1945: 5–6). She finds time to write an article on 'Women in Wartime', where she spells out, in the language of the New Age, what women should be doing: getting rid of all Western influences in minds and bodies, participating in air raid defence training, taking over men's jobs if they are doing wartime tasks. Well-to-do people (*orang yang mampoe*) should economise on food and clothing, look for rice substitutes, and 'educate ourselves to live simply' (*mendidik diri sendiri dalam kesederhanaan*). Women should learn handicrafts to avoid being unemployed, and do what their gender (*kodrat toeboeh,* lit. 'nature of their bodies') has set for them, to be mothers who manage their families *(Djawa Baroe* 8, 15 April 1944: 5)

These official Japanese ideologies which created new roles for women as part of the 'Greater East Asia Co-Prosperity Sphere'

---

3   Ibu Soenarjo was born in Yogyakarta, Central Java on 28 December 1907, and was educated in HIS, MULO and Taman Siswa. After teaching in the Taman Siswa School in Yogya, she became a social worker in the Semarang municipal government, providing accommodation for very poor people *(orang ropoh).* In 1938 she became a member of the Semarang Municipal Council. A member of the organising committee of both the first and fourth pre-war Indonesian Women's Congress (Kongres Perempoean Indonesia), after the revolution Ibu Soenarjo Mangoenpoespito was the only woman representative of Masyumi in the Indonesian Provisional Parliament, and one of three women members from that party in the elected parliament of Indonesia (Vreede-de Stuers 1960,117,118.).

can be seen in the agendas of a national Fujinkai congress (*permusyawaratan*) held in Jakarta from 28–30 May 1944. Over 200 women delegates from all *kabupaten* (*ken*) and municipalities (*si*) in Java attended the Fujinkai congress. They listened to Ny. Soenarjo taking a 'woman's oath' (of loyalty to the Japanese?), and discussed mobilising the population as labour for war (*tenaga perang*) for Japan's 'final victory' (*kemenangan terakhir*), and how to strengthen the people's economy in wartime. They heard speeches about nutrition in wartime, community health care in wartime, and spinning one's own yarn to make clothes in wartime. There was a demonstration by Barisan Srikandi on air raid warning procedures, a demonstration of air raid emergency first aid by the Jakarta Municipality Fujinkai Girls' Brigade (Barisan Poeteri Djakarta Tokubetsu Si Fujinkai) (*Djawa Baroe* 12, 15 June 1944: 9).

While the Fujinkai was an organisation for older married women, in Kendal kabupaten to the west of Semarang, young unmarried girls joined a local women's youth corps the Joshi Sendenbu, or young women of the information service. They wore simple uniforms which they made themselves from coarsely woven cloth, and spent a lot of time on marching drill. If there was an important Japanese visitor in the region, the Joshi Sendenbu had to line up along the road to greet the dignitaries with a deep bow from the waist (*seikere*). Joshi Sendenbu members had economic and well as ceremonial functions to perform: 'we had to plant castor oil plants, and look for *alas,* edible leaves which the Japanese took away. We also had to make long 'socks' without heels out of coarse cotton thread (lawe), which Japanese soldiers could use to store food in.' (Ibu Tejorusmi, interview, 11 July 1993)

'Indonesian Women are Slim and Beautiful'
(*Poeteri Indonesia yang tjantik molek'*) (*Djawa Baroe,* 15 January, 1943: 14–15)
As the occupying power, the Japanese authorities educated women to play social and community roles outside formal mass

organisations which would assist their war effort'.[4] These roles are marvellously portrayed in pictorial forrn in *Djawa Baroe* (New Java), an official fortnightly propaganda magazine issued to promote the ideology and practice behind the Japanese war effort. Many front covers feature pictures of beautiful, traditionally dressed Javanese (and Japanese) women, or Indonesian women dressed in Japanese dress, with Japanese hair styles, either engaged in promoting Japanese cultural activities or more often in activities appropriate for the war. At the beginning of the Occupation, women in traditional regional dress are likened to sweet smelling fragrant flowers; Javanese women are 'white and pure' like jasmine, Minangkabau women are like red dahlias, while Minahassan women are like white roses *(Djawa Baroe* 2, 15 January, 1943: 14–15). Although they have new roles to perform to support the war, yet somehow these women still stay fresh, perfumed and beautiful. Glamorous women singers and film stars (with un-Asian names such as Fifi Young, Sally Young, and Dahlia), unemployed after the Dutch film studios closed, had to join a new group called 'The Surabaya Stars' to entertain Japanese troops, which brought them 'extraordinary publicity' *(Djawa Baroe 5,* 1 March, 1943: 18–19).

In the pages of the magazine, there are stories and pictures of women in training schools learning new skills in agriculture, and pictures of women in the Japanese work force helping the war effort in Japan, examples which Indonesian women were supposed to follow, The new Wakaba domestic science school (*Sekolah Kepandaian Poeteri*) in Jakarta taught dress making, and domestic science (*ilmoe roemah tangga*), including washing, ironing, mending, and cooking. As well students had physical exercises to become strong women 'so in the future they can make their husbands contented' (*soepaya kelak memoeaskan soeaminja*) *(Djawa Baroe* 3, 1 February, 1943: 9–10).

---

4   Apart from the report of the Fujinkai congress mentioned above, I could find only two other references to Fujinkai in *Djawa Baroe*, a picture of women dressed in woven bamboo peasant's hats, traditional blouse and batik sarongs, weeding rice fields in Kedu residency to the sound of a beating drum (5, 1.3.44:14–15) and a short mention of Bogor Fujinkai activities (19, 1.10.43:5)

While these activities were certainly emphasising traditional women's roles, the experience of living together in dormitories or *asrama*, something the Japanese put great emphasis on, was new for many middle class women. Of course some village women did have pesantren experiences (Dobbin, 1980: 56), female plantation workers lived in barracks accommodation, while *priyayi* women attended European boarding schools (including convent schools) during the Dutch period. Under the Japanese women had new educational opportunities in schools for teachers (called *Sekolah Latihan Goeroe-Goeroe Poeteri*), and a very few were accepted into the Jakarta Medical School. There was much publicity for women who received training in special Japanese martial arts, and in air raid and fire drill. Women were supposed to be involved in increasing agricultural production and students had to learn agricultural skills through practical training, including planting vegetables in school garden plots. *Djawa Baru* covers featuring women include a smiling West Java peasant wearing a Muslim headscarf holding newly harvested rice, and a glamorously groomed lady wearing traditional blouse and necklace about to pick some large ripe sweet oranges.

The Barisan Mompe (Mompe Brigades)

While images of women in both traditional sarongs, and 'western' style dresses abound on the covers of *Djawa Baroe,* there are also other modern images, showing women in their new roles, marching in drum bands, doing Japanese acrobatics (*heikin undo*), peering through microscopes in the Jakarta Medical School, and marching with Japanese flags in celebration of New Java Development Day.

In both Japan and Java, the Japanese authorities encouraged women, particularly those in work brigades, to wear *mompe*, a kind of *kimono* pants suit. In Java this was supposed to replace the traditional Javanese blouse and sarong, for both tactical and practical reasons. Women could do exercises and marching drill practice more easily, and could run faster when they had to do air raid defence duty (*Djawa Baroe* 11, 1 June, 1944: 6, 14) Mompe were promoted as a cheaper more practical form of clothing; the trousers could be made from used textiles, such as old or even torn or patched sarongs. It was easier to work in rice fields wearing them. Later styles had detachable sleeves, and a headscarf could be quickly attached during air raid warnings. Those Javanese women who were reluctant to change their sarongs for *mompe* trousers were reminded that this struggle was 'war to the death' (*masa perang mati-matian*) (*Djawa Baroe* 11, 6 January, 1944).

In Sragen, a *kabupaten* town east of Solo in Central Java, a brigade of 36 women wore mompe clothes to work in the prison each day. Kishima and Maimura, two Japanese army officers who ran the large jail (which included political prisoners), recruited a group of women relatives of prison employees. Ibu Ilham (a pseudonym), who today calls the group the 'Women's Mompe Brigade'recalls:

> There were 36 women in the group. Our families all worked in the jail. My relative had to 'guarantee' my good behaviour. We had to spin yarn, sew trousers and shorts, for the military, and make blankets. The prisoners themselves also worked on sewing machines all day. Once a week we had to plant vegetables and go fishing, or plant cotton, and mulberry trees for silk worms. Starting in January 1945, we had political education sessions each morning starting at 5am about the Japanese holy war and the evils of the Allies. We had *taiso* (exercises) from 6–7am then prayers to the Rising Sun. At 7.30am we had breakfast, which we brought from home. We then worked fill 5pm. with a break at lunchtime for the same food as the prisoners ate. We weren't paid anything, but were scared to stay at home. It was better to be (working) inside (the prison) (Ibu Ilham, interview, 26 January, 1995)

Although their hours were long, women preferred to be working inside the prison. They felt safer there from the threat of being recruited by their local Neighbourhood Association heads supposedly to work for the Red Cross in Solo, but in fact to become prostitutes for the Japanese military (see below).

The women who worked in the Sragen main prison were given a ration of green khaki cloth to make their own *mompe* suits:

I didn't know what those clothes were called then, I only realised that's what they were called when you asked about them. The trousers were pleated around the waist, widened at the hips and then tapered off. You could run fast in them, for example if there was an air raid siren, we had to run and do guard duty at the jail, half the sleeves could be taken off. They were nice to wear, and practical to work in. I was moved to tears to see the clothes other people had to wear. One's own people were in such a terrible state (*bangsa sendiri tidak karu-karuan*) (Ibu Ilham, interview, 25 January, 1995)

In general however, this attempt by the Japanese to change dress styles in rural areas was unsuccessful. Probably because of the hotter climate in Indonesia, mompe were unsuited to the kind of agricultural work most women in rural areas had to perform. It was another attempt to apply Japanese wartime practice in Java where conditions were so different from those in Japan.

Japanese military style training focused on male youth during the Occupation, as part of the wartime policy of mass mobilisation. Images of the Seinendan (Youth Corps) and the Keibodan (Vigilance Corps) training in *Djawa Baroe* show they were indeed all male organisations. However the great emphasis of the Japanese on physical fitness of the population meant that women on 'leadership training', agricultural training, and teacher training courses had also to be physically fit as well as politically aware leaders *(Djawa Baroe,* 11, 1 June 1944).

Early in 1944 the Japanese authorities set up a special organisation for training women in the Jatinegara region of Jakarta. Called the Barisan Srikandi, again the emphasis was on training in dormitory life' (*latihan berasrama*), 'learning to manage one's life' (*mengatur tara usaha sendiri*), 'living simply like soldiers', and 'learning the arts of womanhood' (*tata krama adat kewanitaan*). As well women (particularly wives of Indonesian government officials) were encouraged to learn Japanese in all large urban centres, and had to learn how to lead women's groups in the grass roots neighbourhood associations (*tonarigumi*) set up all over Indonesia for rationing and surveillance purposes, and to instil the ideals of the Greater East Asia Co-prosperity Sphere (*Djawa Baroe* 8, 15 January, 1944).

The Sastra Family

While these new activities and opportunities under the Japanese probably touched only a minority of Indonesian women, those who read *Djawa Baroe*[5] saw the images and stories about how women could and should change their lives, and adapt to the New Age (*Zaman Baroe*). In a cartoon story entitled simply 'The Influence of the Times' (*Pengaroeh Zaman*), Mrs 'Sastramewah' (Mrs Sastra-Luxurious) is admiring herself in front of a mirror during the Dutch colonial periodn (cartoon No.1). The accompanying story reminds *Djawa Baroe* readers that women's lives under the Dutch were very different. The Dutch deliberately separated the Indonesian lower, middle and upper classes so there was no contact between them at all. This was the political secret of Dutch rule, sowing discord and division (*perpecahan*) everywhere. The lower classes (*golongan bawa*) needed leadership but middle class women like Mrs Sastramewah were deceived (*kena tipu daya*). Because they only thought about their own needs, they forgot their leadership obligations. Individualism *(semangat peseorangan)* was like a disease everywhere. Pak Sastramewah had a big salary but it only covered monthly household needs; there was never anything left over. This was because his wife spent it all on keeping up with her friends, and on trying to dazzle them with expensive entertaining, new clothes, and new furniture every year. All this was just so she would not be socially embarrassed.

But with the coming of the New Age under the Japanese, with its emphasis on Asianness (*ketimoeran aseli*), and enthusiasm for mutual self help (*semangat gotong-royong*) things begin to change. Mrs Sastramewah herself is slowly made aware of her position as a woman in the society. The gulf separating her from the lower class women begins to close. She feels that she has to

---

5   How many is not known, as circulation figures or print runs were not
     published; it was probably available in government offices and
     organisations in the main towns, if not at the offices of subdistrict and
     village heads.

come down to the level of ordinary people in order to get to know them better, to give them the right leadership (pictures 3 and 4). She leaves behind her luxurious lifestyle, doesn't worry so much about what she's wearing and is no longer embarrassed socially to wear simple clothes. Pak Sastrarnewah notices all these changes. He tells her that she's actually more attractive when she doesn't overdress, and how he prefers people who live simply (*orang yang bersahaja*). He wants to know what she's doing at these women's gatherings: 'Don't you read the paper Mas? Haven't you seen my name as a committee member of the local Fujinkai? 'I never thought you would have the enthusiasm', he replies.

Ibu Sastra tells her husband that she chairs meetings, organises literacy courses, first aid training, helps prepare gifts for Japanese soldiers at the front, and what's more now runs a thrifty household (picture 7). Her husband now gets a more simple birthday dinner, not like in the old days. 'Now I don't need the praise of others', she tells Pak Sastramewah, 'the welfare of the family is my main priority'. She is also saving money every month in a deposit account. Pak Sastra gets inspired enough about what his wife is doing to offer to become an information officer for Fujinkai. His offer is politely turned down, with the suggestion that he find some other avenue for his energies. The commentator ends the series by suggesting a name change for the family, they should now call themselves Sastrasederhana or Sastra-Thrifty (Djawa *Baroe* 6, 15 March, 1944: 33–34).

What are we to make of these changes in the life of Mrs Sastra? Clearly there are a mixture of ideologies at work here. There is the Javanese mutual self-help principle, which the nationalists later made part of the Republican state ideology. There is the Japanese call to value one's Asian-ness, rather than Western values. Those Japanese administrators with more traditional values believed that under the long Dutch regime, 'the native intellectual and upper classes have succumbed to a Western individualistic and materialistic lifestyle' (Reid & Old, 1986: 158). Showing the very bad kind of lifestyle that Mrs Sastra leads during the Dutch period was another way of attacking Western influence, which the Japanese tried to do whenever they could. Mrs Sastra's new lifestyle was also the result of a new element of class consciousness in her life, the rich elite have wrong attitudes and must get down and help the poor. Some Japanese officials when they arrived in Java did indeed see the bad social conditions in class terms. The Assistant Resident of Pekalongan residency, writing years later, recalled sensing a strong cleavage between a handful of rich high ranking Javanese officials versus the bulk of poor Indonesians (Lucas, 1991: 30). Yet ironically the Japanese could do little about this, having to rely solely on these Dutch trained officials to govern the occupied areas.

Juxtaposed against *Djawa Baroe's* images of what women should be in the New Age, there are contradictions which suggest that little had in fact changed, or what was hidden was now more in the open. Thus there are advertisements for herbal medicine, for 'well formed bodies' (*badan yang berbentoek bagoes*), and for healthy, beautiful, and sexually attractive wives (cartoon No.2). The 'Djago' herbal is advertised under the label 'the duties of wives' (*kewajiban kaoem isteri*) (cartoon No.4). We have seen that *kewajiban* had important wartime connotations, namely selfless service to Japan. In this advertisement, the idea of selfless service is extended to husbands' needs. 'It's not only important to look after the beauty of your face', the ad for Djago, herbal drinks entitled 'the duties of wives' says, 'you must also look after the most important part. A lot of women aren't fully loved by their husbands because they don't understand how to look after their health and their beauty'. (*Djawa Baroe* 13, 7 January, 1943: 36)

There were other potent drinks *(anggoer)* from the Tay An Ho Chinese medicine shop directed specifically at all kinds of ailments suffered by women. *Anggoer Branak* was effective for 12 different complaints, while *Anggoer Djin Som* helped cure infertility, by making menstruation more regular (cartoon No.6). Advertisements for soaps, powders and perfumes also used images of glamorous women. A women is testifying that *'Wahido Shoten* scented soap adds to beauty (cartoon No.6). Face powder advertisments in *Djawa Baroe* have wonderful names like 'youth powder', 'virgin powder' (using the English words), and the very enticing looking (but not sounding) 'Lotos powder' (cartoon No.7). The perfume advertisment features a woman half turned in her chair talking to her friend about Tosca and Flowers perfume made by Kian Gwan Kongsi, 'the largest perfume factory in Indonesia'. She is sitting at an antique Dutch dressing table with the oval mirror, carved table with a white marble top, on which are cosmetics, all in exotic and different shaped, enticing glass bottles.

What strikes one about the images in these advertisements is that the idea of beauty seems to be a very 'Western' one, at least the women look very Western-influenced. The woman asking herself 'Am I growing a moustache?' as the gecko lizard stops on the reflection of her face in the mirror looks more American than Japanese or Indonesian (cartoon No.9). There is nothing particularly related to the Asian or Eastern values that the Japanese were promoting in any of the advertisements. If Fujinkai in Japan was crusading against permanent waves, Hong Kong perms and Nanking perms (guaranteed to last eight months without using an electric current to set the hair) were still being advertised in the almanacs which were a feature of the Occupation *(Almanak Asia-Raya 26039:* 212) (cartoon No.3).

Djawa Baroe also had a 'cartoon page' in each issue, which occasionally depicted women in various roles, mostly being 'just like women' or 'unchanged' according to Indonesian perceptions of the times, despite their new roles. In one cartoon a police woman is trying to decide which eye to close to aim her pistol. Finally she decides it's easier just to close both eyes when she fires the gun (conclusion: women can't fire guns accurately); in another cartoon a police woman is on traffic duty 'but she is still a woman' (*tetapi tetap dasarnya perempoean*), because she puts down her baton and powders her face during a lull in the traffic (cartoon No.10).

In the first issue for June 1945, Embok Sarinem made her debut in *Djawa Baroe*. Embok Sarinem is a get-up-and-go young woman (wife? mother?) who gets stuck into things without mucking around (cartoon No.12). She reads about the New Life movement in the local paper. Maybe it means new clothes, everything new! She races off to find the hamlet head (*kumicho*) to ask about this New Life business. 'Look, plant empty yards with vegetables, grow your own cotton, do everything for yourself', Pak Kumicho tells Embok Sarinem. 'Be independent' she muses 'that will make Indonesian independence easier!' In another strip (cartoon No.13) she finds castor oil plants ready to harvest. Humming to herself the tune 'Crush the enemy, the British and the Americans' she picks the seeds, takes them to the local collection centre, gets paid and decides to donate it to 'Funds for Freedom', a full ten weeks before the Proclamation of Independence. Enthusiastic and idealistic, Embok Sarinem is well dressed so late in the Occupation in *mompe* trousers, with sandals, and a pretty figure, no doubt epitomising everything a *kampung* woman should be doing and thinking.

'Hairpieces were also Emancipated'
('sanggul ikut emansipasi')
     For some women, these changes in their lives during that period are symbolised with the metaphor of 'the emancipation of our hairpieces' (*'sanggul ikut emansipasi'*). During the later Dutch colonial period before the World War II there were really only two hairstyles for Javanese women, the *konde* or traditional hair piece, also called *sanggul,* worn with traditional dress, or plaits (single or double), worn loose. The Japanese introduced a new hairstyle called *Cioda:*

> The hair was parted from the back and plaited into two plaits and wound around each side of the head, in a double *konde.* The Cioda Style was used if we had to march. So the *sanggul* was also emancipated.[6]

There were other hairstyles which woman had not used before, which gave women more choice in how to arrange their hair. While the *siput* style (a single plait tied as a hairpiece) was common, women also wore the *ekor kuda* (pony tail) from Dutch days, while the *anggur 8* was the most difficult to arrange as 'you had to put your hair in curlers and sleep on your

---

6   Interview with Mrs Suremi (a pseudonym), Semarang, 12 July 1993.

stomach'. Introducing new hairstyles, like clothing also, had a wartime goal, to make it easier for women to work in essential factory production and in self defence training. In these jobs hair had to be done in manner that was both safe and practical for women working in factories.[7] Yet despite all the new hair styles, perms for women were still advertised in the Japanese almanacs. One would have thought the Japanese would frown on this 'Western' cultural influence especially as middle class Indonesian women were being exhorted to become 'Eastern' women (*poeteri Timoer*) and 'daughters of the Rising Sun' (*poeteri Matahari Terbit*) 'with ideals and actions based on 'Easternness' (*segala tjita-tjita dan langkahnja berdasar keTimoeran poela*') (*Almanak Sinar*, 1942: 179).

Juxtaposed against the advertisements, images of beautiful, well groomed almost glamorous women, reinforced by the professional black and white photography in the pages of *Djawa Baroe*, are images of working women. These are also amazingly neat and well dressed women, sometimes in dresses, sometimes in *kain* and *kebaya* with the latest hairstyles. They are all depicted in a wide range of occupations; busily working to increase agricultural production, planting castor oil plants, harvesting and marketing castor oil seed, improving the livelihood of women who depend on the sea for food, working on air raid self defence projects, learning Japanese women's martial arts, organising public kitchens, using ingredients and recipes to improve family nutrition in wartime, participating in nursing training, working in canned food, soap making and munitions factories, participating in national sporting competitions, learning Japanese singing dances, learning Japanese language and participating in language competitions, or dressing up like Japanese women.

Nevertheless there were other harsher realities for the majority of women. So far removed were these realities from the

---

7   Short hair had been adopted for practical purposes in the late 19th century by women employed in factory work in Japan. Pictures of female factory workers in Japan during the war in *Djawa Baroe* show them with short hair, although wartime Japanese street scenes show women in mompe with long hair or perms. Women in kimono have either long hair or hair pieces.

images that the Japanese wanted to construct through the glossy pages of *Djawa Baroe*, that it is sometimes difficult to bridge the gap between the two different worlds or sets of experiences. The first was the harsh economic existence nearly all women faced. The second was the recruitment of women who were forced to become prostitutes by the Japanese.

Economic Hardship

Most women's experiences of economic and social conditions contrasted sharply with how women were portrayed in *Djawa Baroe*. Even in rural areas rice was in short supply; in towns and cities people survived on a meagre distribution ration. Queues were long and rice was very poor quality, often mixed with gravel, but most certainly mixed with corn, and referred to as maize lice (*betas jaggung*).[8] In rural areas women went searching everyday for edible leaves, and Japanese suggested various substitute foods. Women found they had to cook snails (Lucas, 1990: 37). In Sragen, the rice harvest was affected by disease. People ate dried, ground tapioca (called *gogek*), which 'gave you stomach ache if you ate it all the time'. People sliced up papaya tree trunks to boil, ate a kind of black crab found in rice fields, caught and fried termites, and ate the yellow fruit of the rubber tree. Rat plagues ate all the maize plants, and with no soap, lice thrived in unwashed clothes. Ibu Ilham's mother boiled up dried rice straw and used the starchy water to wash clothes (Ibu Ilham, interview, 25 January, 1995).

'Clothes! Good Heavens! You just Couldn't Imagine what it was Like (Aaalah, klambine, mit amit jambang bayi)[9]
(Mak Warsidi, interview, 10 July, 1993)

Inflation throughout the occupation, hoarding and subsequent speculation in textiles meant that supplies were extremely difficult to obtain by 1943. In 1944 even the textile

---

8   In Japan everyone ate rice mixed with corn during the war, as part of the controlled economy (Sato 1990, 164).

9   Another gloss of this Javanese expression *amit amit jambang bayi is* 'I don't ever want my children (or descendants or relatives) to experience (or be affected by) something as bad as this'.

blackmarket disappeared. In West Java the weaving industry closed down because it was dependent on imported yarn (Sato, 1988: 97). School attendance dropped because of the clothing shortage, and women could no longer go out visiting friends and relatives. Before the war small and landless farmers bought new clothes once a year at Lebaran. These were reduced to rags in three years and totally unwearable, as people had no new clothes since the beginning of the Occupation.

Textiles were in such short supply in the last half of the Occupation that in Surabaya even middle class *kampung* residents were in rags, while the Japanese received five metres of locally made cloth every three months, and had stockpiles which could maintain this level of distribution for them for several years (Fredrick, 1989: 127nl47). Women were hurt by cloth shortages in a number of ways:

> As a woman I was very moved *(sangat trenyuh)* to see the situation of women (in the Tanjung Priok area of Jakarta) who were forced to wear rubber sarongs to cover their bodies. If they were menstruating and had to walk somewhere, the blood trickled down to their ankles, because they had no (menstrual) cloths. This was terribly sad *(benarbenar sangat menyedihkan)* (Arsip Nasional, 1988: 42)

Rubber sarungs were hot, sticky, and tore easily. What cloth was available for sarungs was hard to keep clean, as soap was in very short supply, and lice *(kutu or tuma)* was a constant problem. Some tried soaking sarungs in hot water to get rid of lice temporarily but they were soon back again (Raminern, interview, 7 July 1993). Putting sarungs out in the sun was no use either.

Concubinage and Prostitution

The Javanese *nyai* (concubine or mistress) has an established place in the history of colonial Indonesia. The practice of taking 'native' concubines was long established under the Dutch, as the large Eurasian population was created from the practice of European men entering into relationships with local women.

During the Japanese occupation these relationships produced a large number of children born of Japanese fathers and Indonesian mothers, about which little is known. A tiny number of Japanese stayed on after the war with their new families, adopted Indonesian lifestyles and became Indonesian citizens, but the majority returned to Japan. Occasionally this issue surfaces in the Indonesian press, when a Japanese ex-soldier or civilian returns to Indonesia to meet his wartime child for the first time. The commander of the Japanese Naval Base in Surabaya wrote in his memoirs that

> I felt that we were obliged to give money to the mothers for the upbringing of these children, so I issued orders to my subordinates both to make an appeal to the (Japanese military) government (in Java) and to advertise in the newspaper for this purpose. Ayukawa and Miss Yabe, who was herself born in Java, took responsibility for issuing of money. It was an extremely humanitarian action' (Reid & Oki, 1986: 348).

It is not known how many women came forward as a result of the newspaper advertisements, or of the fate of women with these children in other cities or in rural areas who didn't read the Surabaya newspapers. These women also had to survive somehow with their children after the war without support from the fathers of their children.

Because of the large number of Japanese military and civilians in Indonesia (in Java alone 60,000 were repatriated after the War), prostitution was a major issue. Japanese prostitutes had worked in the Netherlands Indies since the late 19th century (Shimizu, 1992). Although efforts were made by reform minded Protestant officials to make prostitution illegal, the Dutch regarded Asian (but not Caucasian) women's activities as a kind of 'necessary evil' (Shimizu, 1992: 36). Japanese military also brought geishas to some areas to work in restaurants, but the majority of prostitutes in the Occupation were Indonesian, Chinese, Eurasian or Dutch.

The War Rape Victims

'We had been enslaved into forced prostitution. My whole body trembled with fear. My whole life was destroyed at that moment and collapsing under my feet. Not this, surely not this!' (Ruff-O'Herne, 1994: 77)[10]

As in other areas occupied by the Japanese during World War II, in Indonesia both Indonesian and European (Dutch and Eurasian) women were forced into giving sexual services to the Japanese military during the occupation. These women, known in Japanese as *jugun ianfu*, literally 'comfort girls or women who follow the Japanese army', were recruited to work in so-called 'comfort stations'. This comfort system consisted of the legalised military rape of subject women on a scale—and over a period of time—previously unknown in history (Hicks, 1995: xv). After the invasion of Manchuria in 1931, and the occupation of Nangking in 1937, the Japanese had set up military brothels staffed by young girls and women who were tricked, coerced, and in some cases abducted, to provide sexual pleasure to Japanese soldiers (Dolgopol et.al., 1994: 15). It has been recently estimated that, of roughly 139,000 comfort women in China, Korea and the Occupied Territories of Southeast Asia (namely Burma, Malaysia, Thailand, the Philippines and Indonesia) there are approximately 58,000 surviving today (Hicks, 1995: xix).

In Indonesia female entertainers (or *wanita penghibur*) had similar functions both inside and outside military brothels. In his autobiography (written in jail during the Indonesian revolution), the veteran revolutionary Tan Malaka recalls that restaurants and other eating places in Lampung in South Sumatra 'were ordered to provide special "hostesses"…another order was for girls to bring flowers to "entertain" the Japanese "heroes" who were in the hospital on holidays. In fact this was against local custom, which 'did not permit girls to appear outside their houses, much less to offer "flowers" to semi-naked foreign men' (1991: 136). Tan Malaka relates how the daughter of a

---

10   Jan Ruff-O'Herne has recently made a film of her story, also called '50 Years of Silence', and has been active in the international movement to obtain compensation from the Japanese for East Asian war rape victims.

Menadonese doctor in Lampung who, when forced to present flowers to some Japanese, did so with such a sour face and her eyes fixed on the ground, that the Japanese made her do it again with a smile. 'I heard that this unfortunate girl ran away, probably to Jakarta.' (Tan Malaka, 1991: 136).

The comfort system of military brothels functioned on a large scale in the former Netherlands East Indies. According to Hicks, in Java the system of recruitment ran parallel to the forced labour system, i.e. via local village or kampung officials (1995, 100). In Bandung, Jakarta, Surabaya and Malang military brothels were run by 'private operators'. In Surabaya an officers' restaurant-club was staffed with professional Japanese women, while other comfort stations (for lower military ranks presumably) 'were housed in baracks-style buildings and staffed by some Korean women (Hicks, 1995: 102). In Solo, two military brothels (the Fuji Inn and the Chiyoda Inn) between them employed a hundred girls aged between 15 and 17, 'including Indonesians' (Hicks, 1995: 102).

In Central Sumatra during the Occupation, according to a later account, Muslim women set up an organisation to oppose comfort women, and to demand that the military authorities close all brothels, called yellow houses, in the region. According to the biographer of Rahma El Junusiyah, a pioneer of the Muslim women's movement in Indonesia, the Japanese then imported their comfort women from Singapore and Korea (Rasyad, 1978: 235).

While no such organisation appears to have been formed in Java, this did not mean that people were not aware of the *Ianfu*. Most people heard how women were being recruited often by false promises, accepting a job away from their home region, only to find that they ended up in entertainment centres (*tempat penghiburan*), and were forced to become comfort women 'entertainers'. Usually they were recruited by being offered jobs in restaurants, as domestic servants, nurses or promised further study (Tan Malaka, 1991: 141). Families with relatives in subdistrict or regency towns sent their teenage daughters there because it was safer than cities where the Japanese were living in larger numbers, or places of strategic economic importance, such as mines and oil refineries.

Here is an account, recently told for the first time, of an ex-comfort women, who lived near Yogyakarta in Central Java (whom the Japanese called Momoye):

> At the start I didn't know I would become an *ianfu*. I was still living in a kampung in Yogya with my parents and three brothers and sisters, who've all died. In order to lighten my parents' burden, I decided to look for work. I heard from friends that there was a Japanese Dr Sunginga offering jobs to people. I went and registered hoping I would get work in a restaurant or as an actor on the stage in Kalimantan. After getting agreement from my parents, finally I left by train for Surabaya. At the station I found lots of others who had the same destination as I did. From Yogya 40 women left for Kalimantan, but most were older women (sudah dewasa). There were only four of us 13 years or under, including me. In Surabaya we were given two sets of clothes and Rp.8 pocket money and went by boat to Banjarmasin. Now, it wasn't until we got to Banjarmasin that we found out what our real work was, when we got put in a hostel with a 3 metre high fence around it in the Telawan district near the Rambai market. I was allotted room number 11. A Japanese gave me a health check up. And that was when, for the first time, I was forced to serve the lust (*melayani nafsu*) of the health worker. After that I just suffered more and more. Especially as I had to serve up to twenty Japanese every day. Just imagine, I had to work from 12.00pm until the next morning. From 12.00pm until, 5pm we were raped (*dipaksa melayani*) by Japanese soldiers, then from 5.00pm until morning by Japanese civilians. So you could say that we were raped once an hour by the Japanese who lusted like devils (*nafsu setan*). So we could only rest in the morning. Not to mention the punishment we got for mistakes, such as keeping a customer waiting.
>
> After I was five months pregnant, I was forced to have an abortion. I was in a state of real shock over this, especially as they made me see my unborn child after the curette. I fainted, and I will never ever forget their treatment of me (*Jawa Pos,* 29 April, 1993).

While accurate numbers of the victims will never be known, in areas formerly occupied by the Japanese during World War II women in recent years have been forming solidarity groups and going public about their treatment as 'comfort women', asking for representations to be made to the Japanese government for compensation (*Jakarta Post*, 7 August, 1993).

In Indonesia the culture of *malu* or shame has in the past prevented many Javanese women from coming forward. Some victims have begun registering with private legal aid groups, hoping to be paid some form of financial compensation. For some women who were told they were going to be sent to school in Japan, but found themselves as prostitutes for the Japanese military in areas outside Java, it was too shameful to ever return to their homes in Java after the end of the war. As these women were less well off village or kampung people, probably their class background stopped them speaking out as well.

In Jakarta in April 1993, 17 former *ianfu* women met with a team of five Japanese lawyers who were in Indonesia to collect data on the *ianfu* issue in preparation for a conference to be held in Japan later in that year. After the meeting Jakarta's foremost human rights lawyer T. Mulya Lubis, called on former *jugun ianfu* and *romusha* to report to legal aid groups throughout the country. After registering 17,245 former *romusha* and 371 *ianfu*, the Yogyakarta Legal Aid Bureau closed its books, although thousands more wanted to register. LBH Yogya estimated there were 'about 4 million former *romusha* and *ianfu* in Central Java and the Yogyakarta special region (*Republika*, 16 September, 1993). A woman professor of psychology called on the women members of the Indonesian National Assembly (the DPR), to speak out on the issue. One woman member of the Muslim Development Unity Party (P3), also a member of the DPR Commission responsible for women's issues, health and social affairs, said publicly that it was more important for the Japanese to apologise than offer 'material compensation'.

Asking for financial compensation would be 'very embarrassing' said Dra Hajjah Madiniyah Koeswendar, because paying money to these women would only lower their self respect, which could not be measured in financial terms (*Suara*

Merdeka, 23 April, 1993). There were consistent reports in the press of people paying money to self appointed experts (*calo romusha*) in order to be registered for Japanese compensation payments, which the Japanese consul in Medan said they would not be able to pay because under the terms of a 1958 agreement, all war reparation claims had been settled (*Republika,* 24 August, 1993).

While the matter was raised at the UN's Human Rights conference in Vienna in June 1993, it is unlikely that the Indonesian government will take up the issue formally with the Japanese. As Japan is by far the largest aid donor to Indonesia, Japanese aid is crucial for Indonesia to continue its development programmes and to meet its foreign debt interest payments. Japan as head of the CGGI, the new intergovernmental aid group, is the most influential country in this aid consortium. In December 1994 the Japanese government finally announced that it was not paying individual compensation to any war rape victims.[11]

Conclusion

The Japanese rulers in Java, at least through the pages of the fortnightly bilingual magazine *Djawa Baroe,* seemed to be trying to uphold traditional images of women as wife, mother, family manager, also as provider of paid and unpaid agricultural labour. Women traditionally worked in various non-agricultural jobs, such as handloom textiles and batik making cottage industries since the 19th century. The Japanese extended many of these roles into factories, while allowing advertisements (in what was essentially a propaganda magazine for Japan's war effort) which promoted contradictory images of glamour and Asian beauty, which seemed little different from Western images. Promoting 'Eastern values' and 'Asianness' in terms of work + beauty (even if the beauty seemed to be based on western/international images) suggests a contradiction in their policy of eradicating

---

11   The Japanese government did announce instead that, under a 'Peace, Friendship and Exchange Initiative', they would spend $US 1 billion over ten years on programmes for women in Southeast Asia, such as youth exchanges and vocational training.

Western influence, just as promoting Ny Soenarjo's household as a model for women was a contradiction, as she was Dutch educated and worked for the Dutch government before the war. The Japanese were more successful of course in the field of education, where all Dutch schools were closed, in promoting the idea that all science and technology originated in Japan, and in replacing the Dutch language with Indonesian (Aziz, 1955: 176–77, 180).

The Occupation was a break with the past for many women. Their traditional gender and occupational roles were all affected by Japanese wartime economic policies. Women bore the brunt of the breakdown in the rice marketing system in Java, and extreme shortages of foodstuffs, daily household necessities, and clothing. They were forced to work as sex slaves for the Japanese military, a horrendous experience as the testimony of a Javanese women the Japanese called Momoye shows. Against these daily realities, the images of women (the advertisements for cosmetics using glamorous women) in *Djawa Baroe* must have seemed totally bizarre. As the Occupation continued the bulk of non-elite women (who may or may not have read *Djawa Baroe*) had no time or money for such things. Other women's activities, in civil defence groups, helping war-time agricultural production, and teaching were new roles supposedly based on Asian or Eastern values.

The worst experience of occupation for Indonesian women was as *ianfu* or 'comfort women', which from mid-1993 has become a political issue in Indonesia, although not as important as in South Korea and Taiwan. Recently the Japanese government announced that they would not pay compensation to these war rape victims, but this is unlikely to be the end of the issue.

References
Almanak Sinar, 1942, Yogyakarta.
Almanak Asia-Raya 2603, 1943, Jakarta.

Arsip Nasional Republik Indonesia, 1988, *Dibawah Pendudukan Jepang: kenangan empat puluh dua orang yang mengalaminya,* Arsip Nasional R.I., Jakarta.

Aziz, M.A., 1955, *Japan's Colonialism and Indonesia,* Martinus Nijhoff, s'-Gravenhage,

Dolgopol, Ustinia and Paranjape, Snehal, 1994, *Comfort Women an Unfinished Ordeal: Report of a Mission,* International Commission of Jurists, Geneva.

Djawa Baroe, 1942–1945, Jakarta.

Dobbin, Christine, 1980, 'The Search for Women in Indonesian History', in Ailsa Zainu'ddin et. al. (eds), *Kartini Centenary: Indonesian Women Then and Now,* Monash University Centre of Southeast Asian Studies, Clayton.

Frederick, William H., 1989, *Visions and Heat: the Making of the Indonesian Revolution,* Ohio University Press, Athens.

Gandasubrata R.A.A., 1952, *Kenang-Kenangan 1933–1950,* Bagian 11 dan III, Serayu printers, Purwokerto.

Gluck, Sherna Berger and Patai, Daphne (eds) 1991, *Women's Words: the Feminist Practice of Oral History,* Routledge, London.

Gunseikanbu, 1986, *Orang Indonesia yang Terkemuka di Jawa,* Gadjah Mada University Press, Yogyakarta.

Hicks, George, 1995, *The Comfort Women: Sex Slaves of the Japanese Imperial Army,* Allen and Unwin, Sydney.

Ilham, lbu, 1994, 'Catatan singkat berdirinya "Barisan Wanita Mompe" penjara besar Sragen pada waktu pendudukan Jepang tahun 1942–1945 di Sragen Jawa Tengah Indonesia', typscript.

Jawa Pos, 1993, 'Asian Lawyers Unite to Help "Comfort Women",' 7 August.

Kompas, 1994, '"Jugun lanfu": Utang Dibawa Mati', by Marianne Katoppo, 24 August.

Lucas, Anton, 1991, *One Soul One Struggle: Region and Revolution in Indonesia,* Allen and Unwin, Sydney.

Mori, Charlotte Manassen, 1994, *Sayonara My Friend Love Annie,* Hill of Content, Melbourne.

Rasyad, Aminuddin, 1978, 'Rahmah El Yunussiyah: Kartini Perguruan Islam', in Abdullah, Taufiq, Aswab Mahasin and

Daniel Dhakidae (eds), *Manusia dalam Kemelut Sejaarah*, LP3ES, Jakarta.

Republika, 24 August 1993, 'Jepang menolak ganti-rugi korban perang asal Indonesia'.

—— 16 September 1993, 'Romusha-ianfu Jateng/DIY 4 juta orang: LBH Yogya minta dukungan Pak Harto'.

Reid, Anthony and Oki Akira (eds) 1986, *The Japanese Experience in Indonesia: Selected Memoirs of 1942–1945*, Ohio University Monographs in International Studies SEA series no 72. Athens, Ohio.

Ruff-O'Herne, Jan, 1994, *50 Years of Silence*, Tom Thompson, Sydney.

Sato, Shigeru, 1990, 'War and Peasants: The Japanese Military Administration and its Impact on the Peasantry of Java 1942–1945', unpublished PhD thesis, Griffith University.

Schenkhuizen, Marguerite, 1993, *Memoirs of an Indo Women: Twentieth-century Life in the East Indies and Abroad*, Lizelot Stout van Balgooy (ed & trans.), Ohio University Center for International Studies, Southeast Asia series no 92.

Shimizu, Hiroshi, 1992, 'Rise and Fall of the *Karayuki-san* in the Netherlands Indies from the Late Nineteenth Century to the 1930s', *RIMA* (Review of Indonesian and Malaysian Affairs) Special Issue: Sexual exploitation and the Japanese in Southeast Asia, 26, Summer.

Suara Merdeka, 1993, 'Memalukan, minta ganti rugi para 'Jugun lanfu', 23 April.

Tan Malaka, 1991, *From Jail to Jail*, Helen Jarvis (trans. & ed.), volume two, Ohio University, Monographs in International Studies, SEA series no 83.

Vreede-de Stuers, Cora, 1960, *The Indonesian Woman: Struggles and Achievements*, Mouton & Co., s'-Gravenhage.

No.1: 'Influence of the Age' (*Pengaroeh Zaman*)

Djawa Baroe 15 March 1944

No.2: A Well Formed Body

BADAN JANG BERBENTOEK BAGOES

Adalah mendjadi perhiasan bagi seseorang perempoean serta menambah ketjantikan jang agoeng.

DJAMOE DADA
Tjap Potret
NJONJA MENIR
SEMARANG

Mendjadikan dada LEBIH KOEAT DAN SEHAT mengembalikan pada bentoek asalnja bermoela.

Harga satoe kotak (doos) . . f 3.50.

Pesenan dengan pos melainkan bisa dapat pada Poesat-pendjoealan:

NJONJA OEI HONG AN
(anaknja NJONJA MENIR)
Pasar Baroe No. 130 — Telepon Dkt. 829.
DJAKARTA

Djawa Baroe, 13, 7 January 1943

No.3: 'Hongkong' and 'Nanking' perms for women in wartime Java

Kriting Ramboet Perempoean
„Hongkong"
Krekot 49, Djakarta
Tel. 372 Djk.
Tjabang
Pekodjan No. 16
Semarang
Moelai tanggal
1 Oct. 2602
Kita mendapat
perkakas jang paling baroe *tidak pakai stroom* bisa djadi kriting, tidak bisa berbahaja apa-apa. Dikerdjakan oleh perempoean[2]. Harga : f 5,— f 7,50, f 10,—. *Pakai stroom* f 3.—. Ramboet ditanggoeng tinggal bagoes 8 boelan lamanja.

Kriting Ramboet Perempoean
„Nanking"
Pantjoran 35
Djakarta
Tel. 1162 Djk.
Adre sjang paling toea.
Dikerdjakan oleh perempoean[2] jang berdiploma dan berpengalaman. Pekerdjaan roepa[2] model, paling baroe paling menarik. Ramboet ditanggoeng tinggal bagoes 8 boelan lamanja. Harga : f 3,— f 5,—. Pakai minjak f 6,— f 7,50 f 10,—
7

Almanak Asia Raya, 1943

No.4: The Duties of Wives

Djawa Baroe, 13, 7 January 1943

No.5: Medicinal Drinks

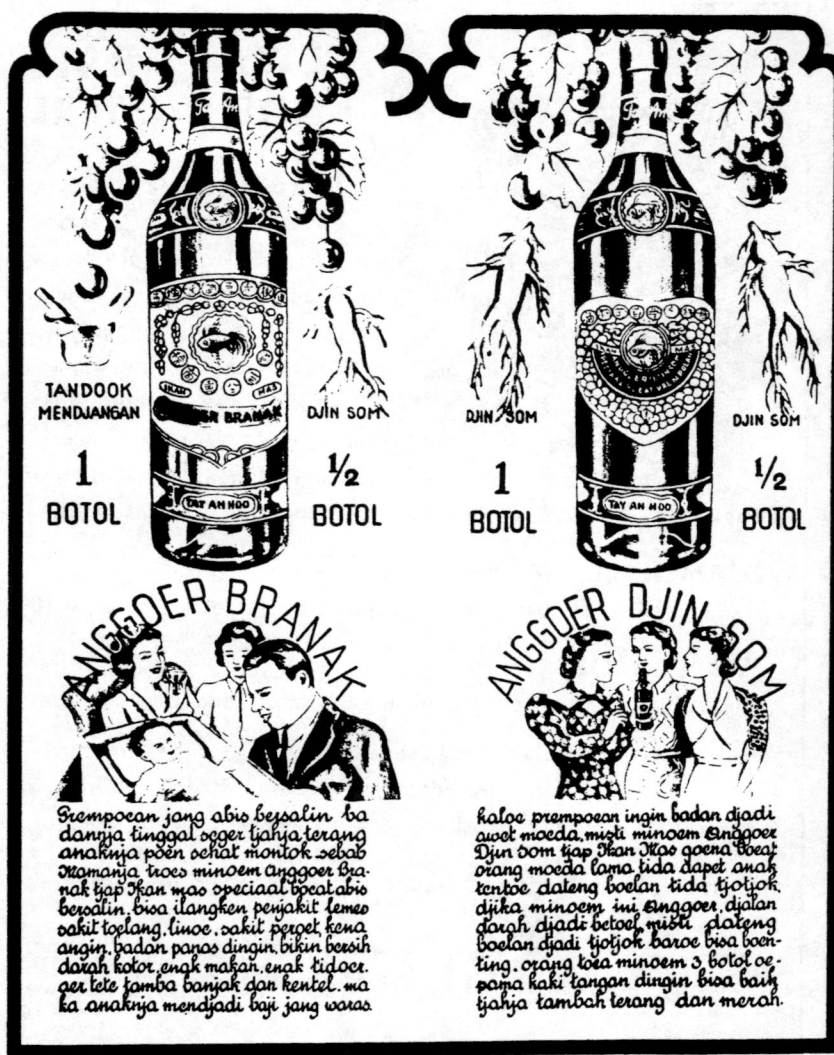

Djawa Baroe 19, 1 October 1943

No.6: Special soaps for women

Djawa Baroe 23, 1 December 1943

No.7: More special soaps for women

Djawa Baroe 1, 1 January, 1945

No.8: 'Tosca and Flowers' perfume

Djawa Baroe 14, 15 July 1944

No.9: 'Am I growing a moustache?'

Djawa Baroe 16, 16 August 1943

No.10: 'Women police, but they're still basically women!'
(Polisi wanita, tedapi tetap danar perempoean)

Djawa Baroe 13, 1 July 1943

No.11: Trying to fire a pistol

Djawa Baroe 10, 15 May 1943

No.12

Djawa Baroe 11, 1 June 1945

No.13

Embok SARINEM
(4)

Gambar SEDIADI

Djawa Baroe, 15, 1 August 1945

Official Photography, Costume and the Indonesian Revolution

Jean Gelman Taylor

This paper examines the place assigned women in the official historiography of the Indonesian revolution or struggle for national independence of 1945 to 1949. It does so by detailed consideration of photographs recording the declaration of independence and raising of the Indonesian flag.[1] They were taken on 17 August, 1945, shortly after 10.00am in front of Sukarno's private residence in Jakarta. In the first, Sukarno proclaims the independence of the Indonesian people. He stands in the centre of the photograph, flanked by Mohammad Hatta and Colonel Latief Hendraningrat. In a semi-circle behind him are a score of men and one woman. All the men wear western suits, or jackets and trousers; the woman is dressed in Javanese costume, her hair covered by a head scarf that leaves her face exposed. In the second photograph, the flag of the newly proclaimed republic is being raised. Two women are at the centre of the photograph. They are shot from behind so that we do not see their faces, but we see what they are observing, the raising of the flag. Both women are in 'traditional' costume; one woman wears a head scarf. The men to be observed in this second photograph are in western costume.

These famous photographs convey messages. If we focus on costume and posture, a specific statement seems to be made about the roles of men and women in the republic right at the moment of its birth. Through western costume Indonesian men

---

1   The photographs are reproduced in many texts. See, for example, A.H. Nasution, *Sekitar Perang Kemerdekaan Indonesia*, I, 2nd ed., 1977, p.209; *30 Tahun Indonesia Merdeka*, I, p.21; volume VI of *Sejarah Nasional Indonesia*, pp.573–74; and *Sukarno, An Autobiography*, photos between pp.156–57.

make a statement about possession of political power in the new Indonesian state. The women are assigned a different role. Through 'traditional' or 'national' dress, the women demonstrate their relationship to the men seizing power and express an association of women with the past.

Written texts on the struggle for national independence, composed long after the actual events, convey the same message. In a later section I will review some official histories and personal recollections from the time. Women make no appearance in these texts, not in the memories of former *pemuda* (youth fighters), nor in histories produced by government departments. If we turn to a text devoted exclusively to the history of Indonesian women in the struggle for national independence, we find the very topics discussed to be entirely different.

The visual record, which is the basis for my study, links costume and photography. I will examine costume on Java to explain the history behind men's adoption of western dress, and the presentation of national dress as the costume of women. Costume itself is never static. Change in costume is linked to broader social history. In the Javanese context, it carries the history of relationships between race, class, religion and gender.

Our knowledge of costume on Java does not stretch back more than three centuries. The defining characteristics of the past 300 years are twofold: this is the era of the Islamisation of Java and the creation of the state of Indonesia. Both processes developed side by side. Conversion began as Java was drawn into a Malay-Muslim zone stretching in the west to Malacca and extending north and east to Mindanao and Ternate. The creation of Indonesia involved the fusion of many states within that zone into one political entity, the Netherlands East Indies, and the transformation of that colonial state into the Republic of Indonesia. Changes to costume take place within this context of Islamisation and state formation.

Knowledge is shaped by the materials available for study. This discussion of costume is based on texts, paintings and photographs that are the work of European travellers, artists and colonial officials. Our knowledge comes, therefore, from the

Dutch part of the defining context. From the first, the United East Indies Trading Company (VOC) commissioned artists to record life in the niches the Dutch established within the Malay-Muslim zone in the 17th and 18th centuries. The first photographic studio was opened in Batavia in 1857, that is, right as the creation of the colonial state was about to get underway. We have, then, a visual record over a period of 300 years.

Photography and Costume

Before proceeding further, it is useful to remind ourselves of the limitations of photography as historical document. The official record is commissioned by the chief actors. It is not the private record of an historic moment. The official photograph is, rather, a choreographed or staged event. It reveals contemporary views of the appropriate; it records a judgement by the actors of who and what were important. It is therefore instructive, for purposes of writing women into history, to note if both sexes appear in photographs of historic occasions.

The official photograph also records posture. If women are included in official photographs, we may ask if they are placed at the centre of the photograph or at the side. Are the sexes divided equally in numbers? Posture is conditioned, to an extent, by style of dress, which itself is dictated by gender, age, class, and social status. We need to examine what body parts are actually shown. Do we see hands and feet, are heads covered, is the face exposed? What differences do we see between men and women?

We must also make some preliminary observations about the costume selected for an official photograph. Costume in photographs may not represent everyday wear, but what the commissioning actors thought suited the historical moment. The costume of those few photographed may therefore tell us about the aspirations of a society's leaders. Costume establishes the identity of the persons photographed socially and historically. Costume links the wearer to a specific community, or segment of a community. Costume makes a statement about how a society views gender differences, and it makes a statement about the wearer's moral, religious and political standpoints. In considering choice of dress for actors in a Southeast Asian setting, adoption of western costume is highly significant. Costume in the official photograph is, therefore, an important element of visual communication.

Women in Histories of the Revolution

In the construction of Indonesia's history, the national struggle for independence from the Netherlands culminating in the revolution of 1945–49 is given centre stage. It is presented as the defining moment; all events lead to it and flow from it. Periods or ages follow each other: The Pre-Historic Age, the Hindu-Buddhist Kingdoms, the Coming of Islam, the Arrival of the Europeans, the Expansion of Dutch Colonial Power, the Emergence of the Movement for Independence, crowned by the Revolution and subsequent history of the Republic of Indonesia. William O'Malley (1980) explains this linear interpretation by reference to the particular group which captured the national political leadership. Their defining characteristics were a Dutch-language education, commitment to a secular republic, and opposition to 'feudalism'. Because they were the 'winners' in 1950, scholars, Indonesian and foreigner alike, have tended to assign especial significance to their political activities in the decades preceding the revolution. As a result, little attention has been given to groups which formed in the same period to promote different objectives, such as restoration of Indonesia's monarchies, creation of a theocratic state, or reform of marriage laws.

A dominant theme of histories of the struggle for independence is nationalist fervour. Looking back at the Indonesian revolution of 1945–49, when nation and actors were young, aging participants recall a sense of fervour sweeping the country. The men interviewed by western scholars remembered their conviction that the world was in motion, being shaken up, behaviour bursting out of accustomed channels. The men who recalled this shining moment so vividly for Benedict Anderson (1972), William Frederick (1988) and Anton Lucas (1991, 1977) did not particularise. But women colleagues of western scholars may ask if Indonesian women shared this sense of a world order being upturned. Did they experience profoundly a society bursting out of its channels? Or were they too busy in the kitchen? Did women leave off performance of chores at home, abandon young children and aging parents, and believe that the new world beckoning included them?

A nationalist discourse in the Netherlands East Indies grew out of the rallies, strikes and speeches of the 1920s and 1930s (Shiraishi, 1990). It is in this period that concepts of personal freedom, self-determination, and social uplift gained currency. That new discourse was in part created by young women. The preamble to the famous Youth Oath of 1928 reads: 'We the young men and young women of Indonesia' (Vreede-de Stuers, 1960: App. 5). Women helped formulate those commitments to one country, one nation and one language. Women's ears heard the message. All the same, the nationalist discourse created in the 20s and 30s was one that placed the new Indonesian man at centre stage and directed women to subordinate positions. The leaders of the many parties formed under banners of nationalism, communism, socialism, Islam, and regional identity conceived of their membership as male. When they thought of women it was as auxiliaries. Women who wanted to work for the new nation were sent to the women's branches of the political parties. They were not invited to join as Indonesians.

The names of political parties and associations from these formative years are instructive. The parties whose membership was male chose names that indicated ideological conviction. The Islamic Union's name proclaimed religious profession as the basis of affiliation. The Nationalist Party of Indonesia, the Socialist Party of Indonesia and the Communist Party of Indonesia asserted the political goal of independence and ideological solution for self-government. None of these parties identified gender as a defining quality for membership. Consider, now, the names of a set of parties formed at the same time: Independent Daughters, Active Wives, Mothers' Group. These organisations proclaimed gender and relationship to men as key to membership. Their names did not state commitment to ending colonial rule or to philosophy of government. When 'Indonesia' was included in the name of an all-female organisation, its character as a federation of existing parties compelled a change from 'wife', 'mother' and 'daughter' to the more inclusive 'women'. This was the Perikatan Perempuan Indonesia, the Indonesian Women's Association, which was formed in December 1928. Now the organisation's name proclaimed its political objective of self-government, but it still identified gender, not ideology, as the key to membership.

Looking back on this time, male politicians do not recall women's participation in the nationalist movement at all. Abu Hanifah, for instance, devotes a whole chapter of his *Tales of a Revolution* to the 1928 Youth Congress which he attended and where the famous Youth Pledge was formulated. Hanifah's English translator entitles this chapter 'The Angry Young Men of 1928' (rather than 'angry youth'). Yusmar Basri, editor of volume V of *Sejarah Nasional Indonesia*, the official National History of Indonesia, does not include any of the women's associations in the chapter on the Nationalist Movement. Women's associations are listed, instead, in chapter four in a subsection entitled 'Women's Education'.

Cora Vreede-de Stuers examined women's nationalist associations in a pioneering work that first appeared in English in 1960. Her study focussed on the institutional history of women's parties, on their goals, resolutions and memberships. This text presented a women's history of the movement for national independence that was quite separate from the mainstream, or male-centred history. Her study revealed a cluster of concerns that had little to do with opposition to the Dutch colonial rulers. Instead, issues debated in women's congresses and in party publications concentrated on the relationship of Indonesian women to Indonesian men. It was polygamy, child marriage, and education for girls that commanded women's attention. The photographic record accompanying Vreede-de Stuers's text also suggests a separate history. It shows prominent women leaders, all-female classrooms and workplaces.

The Vreede-de Stuers text for long remained unique. If we confined our examination of the Indonesian revolution to the text and photographs in the standard histories, we would be obliged to conclude that there existed few, if any, women in

Indonesia at all. The photographic record does not show women in the streets, they are not participants in public rallies, they do not frame Sukarno in his speeches. Prominent women such as the labour union activist and cabinet minister (1947–48), S.K. Trimurti, or the lawyer Maria Ulfah, who served in Sjahrir's third cabinet (1946–47), do not command their own paragraphs.[2]

More often than not, the women mentioned in official history and autobiography alike are identified only as wives of leaders. For example, the text of *Sejarah Nasional Indonesia* identifies by name only one of the women present at the proclamation of independence, and that is Sukarno's (third) wife, Fatmawati. She was the mother of his son, Guntur, and 23 years his junior. Fatmawati is not known for any independent activity in the nationalist movement. Her contribution to the occasion was to sew the flag raised on the 17th.

The *Sejarah Nasional Indonesia* does not identify the woman standing with senior leaders as Sukarno proclaimed independence, although a footnote to its narration of events on that historic day proves that S.K. Trimurti was used as an informant.[3] The official history does, however, identify Trimurti's husband, Sajuti Melik, as one of the men standing with Sukarno. And yet, Surastri Karma Trimurti did not owe her right to witness the proclamation to her status as wife of Sukarno's private secretary. She had been active in pre-war nationalist politics since joining Partindo in 1933. Her work brought her a brief period of imprisonment by the Dutch, and a ban on teaching. The Japanese made Trimurti a leader of their propaganda

---

2   Benedict Anderson includes entries for S.K. Trimurti and Maria Ulfah in the biographical appendix to his *Java in a Time of Revolution*. Maria Ulfah is included in the Biographical Notices following the text of C. Vreede-de Stuers's *The Indonesian Woman*. In 1982 a biography of Maria Ulfah was published, written by the journalist Gadis Rasid, *Maria Ullfah Subadio, Pembela Kaumnya*, Jakarta, Bulan Bintang. A brief biographical outline of S.K. Trimurti is appended to her *Hubungan pergerakan buruh Indonesia dengan pergerakan kemerdekaan Indonesia*, Jakarta, Yayasan Idayu, 1975.

3   S.K. Trimurti is cited as the informant in footnote 245 to page 91 of volume VI.

parties, Putera and Jawa Hokokai Honbu, before imprisoning her for alleged anti-imperial actions. Even though her career in public life continued through the 1970s, culminating in membership of the Supreme Consultative Assembly, the official history is silent on her participation at the birth of Indonesia.

If we consult the commemorative *30 Tahun Indonesia Merdeka*, we find the following statement on women and the struggle for independence: 'The services of Indonesian women were so great they are indescribable' (Notosusanto, 1981: vol. I, 37). Women's participation in the revolution remains just that in the official histories, without description.

The electoral law of 1946 gave Indonesian women the vote, which right they were to exercise for the first time, along with men, in nation-wide elections in 1955. In colonial times, Dutch male tax-payers and some Indonesian men were electors for the municipal councils and Volksraad. In other words, some Indonesian men enjoyed civic and political rights which were denied Dutch and Indonesian women.[4] Supremacy of gender over race in the public arena of civic rights was the principle in late colonial times.

The enfranchisement of Indonesian women seems to be a direct result of the Youth Oath in which the young women of Indonesia had had a part. Still there is no real discussion of this accession of women to public space in the histories of the *pemuda* or of the nation written by Indonesian men. Abu Hanifah (1972: 347) attributes enfranchisement of women to their 'great sacrifices' during the revolution, surrendering husbands and sons to the cause. The implication is that women had to earn their right to vote and their equality of status with men.

Published women writers are no different in this respect. B.R.A. Partini Djajadiningrat (1986), for example, does not discuss debates about women's rights in her passage on chairing

---

4   Elsbeth Locher-Scholten discusses the debates that took place in the all-male Volksraad (People's Council) over the issue of female suffrage in her paper, 'Late Colonial Perceptions of Indonesian Women: Voting Rights, Labour, the Nyai', presented to the conference 'Gender in Indonesia', University of Washington, Seattle, June 1991.

Istri Indonesia (Indonesian Wives), the women's auxiliary of the Nationalist Party of Indonesia. Sukanti Suryochondro (1984) argues that women are part of society, and therefore, in the years leading up to independence, their main goal was simply ridding Indonesia of the Dutch.

However, if we return to the photographic record we already have, we can begin to see that the standard versions do not quite tell the whole story. Consider the photograph of the flag-raising ceremony. This photograph, as I described it above, is the version commonly reproduced in histories of Indonesia. But the uncropped version of this photograph (Sukarno, 1965) includes two other women. They are also shot from behind. Both are in short-sleeved western frocks, their hair worn up and uncovered. In *30 Tahun Indonesia Merdeka*, we find two other photographs of women from the years of the independence war. The first (1981: I, 37) is of three young women preparing food for soldiers. They wear Red Cross uniforms that expose their arms; their hair is uncovered and cut short. Neither time nor place is identified. In the second (I, 27), women in military uniform, consisting of long-sleeved shirts, trousers and boots are training (location not identified) with long sticks. The caption reads: 'The struggle to defend independence was not the work of men only. Shoulder to shoulder with the men, women formed fighting units and organisations, such as the Girls' Unit of Solo shown here'.

There is no other information in the text of *30 Tahun Indonesia Merdeka* on women's military activities. The Englishman, John Coast, was in Indonesia during the revolution. He includes in his memoir one photograph showing women soldiers in shirts and trousers, this time apparently on the battlefield (1952: opp.344). Again, they are not identified by unit or area of deployment. Nor does Coast discuss women as members of the regular armed forces or guerrilla squads. His description of revolutionary youth (pp.132–33), their emotions and sense of a new world, is written in purely male terms.

Abu Hanifah (1972: 246) does introduce the subject of all-female guerrilla units in the war for independence. Their activities at the front were not strictly military. According to

Hanifah, women guerrilla squads helped care for the wounded and cooked the soldiers' meals. In a discussion on the difficulty coordinating all the armed groups in West Java, he identifies female guerrilla squads as refusing to recognise the authority of the Republican administration (led by Hanifah) in Sukabumi. Women soldiers, he says, were 'stirred up' by 'fanatical' women guerrillas from Central Java. Furthermore, the presence of women soldiers at the front line was a distraction to the serious business of fighting the Dutch. Because of the pregnancies and general indiscipline wherever there were female squads, the (male) leaders of the various armed units operating in the Sukabumi region voted unanimously to prohibit women soldiers from their territory.

Hanifah's statement and the silent record of photography offer a tantalising glimpse of a different kind of revolution from the standard (male-dominated) versions. New research by scholars such as Marina Paath, Anton Lucas and Susan Blackburn, and personal testimonies such as the unpublished memoirs of Jo Kurnianingrat[5] suggest that there is a history of the revolution to be written that has a place in it for women. It is a history requiring a different historiographical perspective than the works we have to date. However, using the existing data, the record of photography, we can safely make one observation: women who involved themselves in the struggle for independence as Red Cross nurses and as soldiers wore western dress and left hair uncovered and face exposed. They present an image quite at odds with that of the sanctified moment of Indonesia's birth. It is now time to explore the history of costume on Java in order to understand how western clothing could become national dress for men and how an ensemble of clothing from Java could become national dress for women.

---

5   Marina Paath, 'Progress or Regress? Changing Perceptions of Women in the Indonesian Print Media', paper presented to ASAA Fourth Conference on Women in Asia, Melbourne University, October 1993; Jo Kurnianingrat Ali Sastroamijoyo, 'The Role of the Indonesian Woman', unpublished memoir written for Ailsa T. Zainu'ddin; chapters by Anton Lucas and Susan Blackburn in this volume.

'Traditional' Javanese Costume and the Record of History

It is necessary, at the outset, to establish that there is no 'traditional' costume to be described for the men and women of Java. This is because our earliest records date from the period of the Islamisation of Java, and are from coastal towns whose polyglot populations included Javanese, Madurese, Arabs, Chinese, Indians, Bugis, and Europeans. VOC employees did business amongst people whose costume was being modified by the prescriptions of Islam, by the availability of imported fabrics and articles of clothing, and by daily contact with people from all of Asia. VOC visitors to the ports along Java's north coast, therefore, recorded costumes in a context of change.

Later in the 17th century, representatives of the VOC journeyed inland to the Mataram courts. The costume they saw reflected, not some archetypal 'Javanese' costume, but an ensemble of elements testifying to the long history of international contacts of the courts. The influence of Hindu India was apparent in the uncut rectangle of cloth draped at the hips of men and women, and again Hindu notions of purity were reflected in the uncut hair of men and women. Chinese influence was visible in tailored tunics of silk, and had established gold cloth as the symbol of royalty. Long-sleeved jackets and trousers reflected Muslim influence.[6]

The many VOC etchings and paintings of port life consistently identify as Muslim those whose bodies were covered from shoulder to ankle, and whose feet were encased in sandals

---

6   Discussion and photographs of Javanese costume may be found in Mattiebelle Gittinger 1979; Alit Veldhuisen-Djajasoebrata 1984, 1988; B.R.A. Partini Djajadiningrat 1986; and Judi Achjadi 1978. Gittinger and Veldhuisen-Djajasoebrata concentrate on untailored garments, especially on batik and textile designs on the cloth rectangle. They do not analyse the adoption of tailored items such as the batik trousers or knee breeches, or of jackets and blouses. Achjadi discusses many styles of bodice. She places the origin of tailored items such as the blouse in China and Muslim India. Aart van Beek (1990) reproduces photographs of upper class male and female costume from Solo and Yogya, and of palace male and female servants. Robyn Maxwell (1990) discusses influences on clothing in terms of colour, designs and motifs.

or slippers. 'Natives' were identified as those men whose chest and feet were bare and women wearing a cloth skirt to the knees and a breast wrapper, whilst head, shoulders, arms and feet were bare.[7]

Costume cannot be considered apart from availability of materials. Cotton is native to parts of Indonesia. Western observers claimed that every village hut contained a loom.[8] Spinning and weaving cotton were described as women's work, and the consensus is that women made clothing for household needs. The Javanese also purchased imported cloth. Households substituted imported cloth for that of local manufacture when other forms of income-producing activities were available. Cloth functioned as both currency and savings. Households stored savings in the form of cloths, and exchanged cloths in the rituals of birth, marriage, circumcision, curing and death. Most commoner folk were described as wearing coarse homespun cottons dyed a solid indigo, or striped. Islamic influence was observable in the adoption of cotton and silk blends in plaids stitched to form a tube-shaped garment, the *sarung*. This garment was associated with the world of working men; it was never adopted in the inland courts. Java's aristocracy, male and female, and their retainers, wore the *kain*, a rectangle of draped cloth.

In sum, VOC employees were recorders of costume on Java in stages of transition and transformation. At the same time, the VOC made its own contribution to change in costume. It did so in its role as importer of mainly Indian cloths. In this way the VOC provided a vast array of fabrics, colours and qualities of cloths. It provided cheap wear for commoner Javanese, sumptuous cloths for the wealthy, and, for weavers and decorators of cloth, the VOC provided new models, styles, fabrics, waxes and dyes. The multiplication of batik patterns and the adoption of batikked cloth for personal wear by Java's

---

7   An example is a sketch from the 1590s reproduced by Alit Veldhuisen-Djajasoebrata (1984: 25).

8   On the history of local textile production and textile imports see Ruurdje Laarhoven (1994) and Peter Boomgaard (1981, 1991).

aristocracy were developments of the VOC centuries.[9] To the 17th and 18th centuries belong the batik 'factories' of aristocratic households. Female labour was drawn from the countryside to do the heavy work of washing, dyeing and scraping cloth. Fine cottons imported from India to Java permitted the drawing of more elaborate batik designs. This was the preserve of aristocratic women, who were also the employers and supervisors of labour in the production of batik.

The VOC was, therefore, a catalyst to costume change as importer of fabrics, tailored clothes, waxes and dyes. The VOC had a further role in the history of costume on Java, and that is in the style of garments worn. Christian values and the cool climate of northern Europe had produced a costume for men and women that covered the body from head to foot. The VOC promoted costume change in the direction of covering the whole body in several ways. First, its officers introduced variants of European clothing as the public wear of men in power. Second, the Company promoted covering the upper body of the Asian men and women in its employ. Male slaves were issued with shirts and trousers or shirts and *sarungs*; female slaves were issued with blouses and *sarungs* or *kains*. Third, the public and domestic costume of women with European status in VOC households combined a long-sleeved over-blouse with *kain* or *sarung*.[10]

In concluding these remarks on 'traditional' costume, attention must be drawn to the predominance of textiles and tailored clothes in the trading goods offered the Javanese by traders from India, Europe and China. We must also note that Muslim, Christian and Chinese representatives in Java promoted covering the body. Rulers of ports and kingdoms, whether Asian

---

9   Cotton has been cultivated on Java since the first century CE (Common Era), and weaving has a very ancient history. Gittinger (1979, introduction) dates the process of batikking to the 16th century, although she notes that other scholars argue for a much earlier origin. Hardjonagoro (1980), drawing on Javanese and Dutch sources, places the innovation of wearing batik, as distinct from using it as wallhanging and for ritual purposes, in the 17th century royal capitals of Java.

10   See Taylor (1983) for a discussion of clothing and sumptuary laws in VOC Asia.

or European, enforced sumptuary laws that dictated style and quality of clothing according to each individual's ethnic and religious affiliation, legal standing, class and gender. By the end of the 18th century, scant clothing indicated the status of the slave, the 'heathen', and the poor.

Costume Exchange between the Dutch and Javanese in the VOC Centuries

We have now established a Javanese costume that varied according to region, class and rank, and was cosmopolitan in its influences. It is now time to focus our search for the elements constituting the national dress at the moment of Indonesia's independence. That search will take us into the households of Dutch men.

In all the years of association between peoples of the Netherlands and Indonesia costume has been peculiarly linked to race and religion and powerholding. In their public wear, VOC officers always wore clothing in the styles current in Europe for their rank and class. They associated European costume also with profession of Christianity. It appears Javanese officials associated European costume primarily with power. On occasion, Javanese princes wore western costume. For example, the *Babad Kraton* states that Amangkurat II dressed in Dutch clothes when he rode with VOC forces against his brother and rival, Pangeran Puger, in 1680 (Ricklefs, 1993: 64).

Men from the 'outer offices' of the VOC, that is, the dependencies on Batavia that stretched from Bengal to Malacca and Japan, were permitted to wear local costume when appearing in their official capacity before Asian rulers. Only when they presented themselves before the governor-general in Batavia were they required to wear Dutch costume, and then in accordance with VOC sumptuary laws that dictated quality of apparel, and the style of their shoe buckles and buttons.

Most VOC employees were men from Europe. Locally born boys were not officially permitted to rise above the ranks of soldier and clerk. Immigrant men who established households in Dutch outposts in Asia lived with Asian women (Taylor, 1983). The emigration of women from Europe was banned in 1652.

Dutch men, therefore, lived with and married Asian women, as did all travelling peddlars and merchants who established themselves in Southeast Asia's ports. VOC regulations stipulated that brides of European men must be free women, baptised with European names, and take the nationality of the husband. Again, in this, VOC regulations followed the practice of Southeast Asian ports: women became part of the husband's ethnic group and subordinate to the rules regulating that group's conduct.

I have already noted that the household personnel of VOC employees were issued with blouses and *sarungs* or *kains*. It is the testimony of travellers that the wives in VOC households wore a *kain* and a long overblouse that reached the knees or ankles and had long sleeves. They wore slippers on bare feet. Their long hair was bound in a bun decorated with jewelled combs and pins, their faces exposed. The quality and kind of jewellery they wore were regulated by VOC sumptuary laws, as was the style of their carriages, wedding and funeral announcements, and the like. But the testimony of the VOC's staff artists is that wives of senior VOC men put on European female costume when their portraits were painted. So that status of the female with European standing was demonstrated by western costume.[11] By the early years of the 19th century, however, Asian costume had supplanted European as public wear for European women. The English who accompanied Raffles during the British Interregnum testified that ladies with European status always wore the long-sleeved overblouse (uniformly labelled a petticoat by the English), a long skirt, slippers on bare feet, left the head uncovered, and displayed quantities of jewellery (Taylor, 1983: 98–102).

In sum, in the VOC years, European men stationed in Batavia wore European costume at work and when representing the Company at Java's courts. European men in the outer posts wore variants of local costume. On occasion, Java's royalty wore European costume. For private wear European men removed their western suits and shoes. Women in VOC households were

---

11   See paintings of VOC era women with European status by Johannes Rach and his contemporaries in the collection of de Loos-Haaxman (1928).

usually Asian or Eurasian. They mostly wore a variant of local clothing, but sometimes wore European costume for official occasions, such as portraiture. It is in the second half of the 19th century that we see important changes leading directly to the public presentation of costume as displayed in the photographs of the independence ceremony. These changes include adoption of the western suit and of colonial whites as working costume for European men, and the adoption of batikked cloth with a short-waisted, long-sleeved blouse by women with European status for both public and domestic wear.

History of the Suit in Java

Dutch men have been migrating to Batavia since 1618. In the record of portrait they appear in the varieties of dress customary for their contemporaries in Europe. The earliest portraits, therefore, show them in somber colours, their bodies heavily draped in woollens and velvets with white collars or ruffs. By the middle of the 18th century, the governor-general was painted in thigh-length jacket, tight hose, buckled shoes, lace at neck and wrists, and long curled wig.[12]

By the middle of the 19th century, Dutch men's costume reflected two related trends in Europe. One was the rise of the middle class. Everywhere in Europe monarchies were being set aside; kings and their courtiers no longer dictated standards of dress and fashion for men. The second trend was the rise of mass manufacturing. Men's garments, accordingly, became simplified. The aristocrat's handmade costumes of richly embroidered materials, bright colours and flowing capes gave way to machine-made clothing in sturdy, dark coloured materials for the middle classes.

The basic three-piece suit makes its appearance as men's apparel in Europe in the 1850s. Now status differences were indicated by quality of materials and of tailoring. The complete costume comprised shirt and neck tie, jacket, trousers, socks and flat-heeled shoes, hat and gloves. Accessories included a walking

---

12   See, for example, *Platenalbum*, K22 and L4, and paintings in F.W. Stapel, *De Gouverneurs-Generaal van Nederlandsch-Indie in beeld en woord*, The Hague, Stockum & Zoon, 1941.

stick, watch and chain, display handkerchief and spats. Middle class men wore their hair short, and they trimmed beard and moustache or had a plain shaven face. The male body was completely covered from shoulder to foot in a costume that concealed its contours, but did not inhibit or restrict its movement. The somber-coloured suit became associated with political power after the revolutions of Europe had removed or vastly reduced the powers of monarchs. Male costume retained bright colours only in the dress uniforms of army officers. In Java, western male costume followed fashion as established in Europe, but it also responded to the demands of climate. In the mid-19th century, Dutch men adopted colonial whites, that is, trousers and jacket of light-weight materials with open neck or closed collar without a neck tie. This costume was worn for everyday official use with sun hat, shoes and socks. On ceremonial occasions it was replaced by suits of dark material, stiff collared shirts and neckties. At home, the Dutch man wore a light jacket without a neck tie, a *sarung* or batik trousers, and sandals.[13] This domestic costume remained European male attire until the last years of Dutch rule in Indonesia. It was worn by immigrant and locally born European man alike and reflected, not only the influence of climate, but also of male Javanese costume. In this context it should be remembered that the majority of Dutch men in the colony were Indonesian-born and raised in households staffed by Indonesian servants. Fully 70% of all Dutch people in Java in 1930 had been born there (Nieuwenhuys, 1940–41: 782).

In discussing the costume worn by Dutch men outside the home, it is important to stress that its wearers were those with power and authority. After the Diponegoro War (1825–30), the Dutch were in control of most of Java, and from the 1860s Dutch troops, government officials and private businessmen spread all over the archipelago. At work, that is in public space,

---

13   Nieuwenhuys has many photographs of Dutch men in batik trousers, or *kain* and shirt, relaxing at home. See, for example, *Baren en oudgasten*, pp.50, 84, 169 and 180. Photographs on pp.134, 136, 169 and 181 give examples of men in light-weight white collarless jackets and trousers. Pages 73 and 77 show official male dress uniform.

all Dutch men from the 1850s wore variants of the suit. Civilians, government staff, private businessmen, schoolteachers, policemen and soldiers wore a costume consisting of shirt, trousers, a buttoned jacket, socks, shoes and hat. Men wearing that costume were in charge. They had real force to back up their demands. Their costume was evidence of their power, their right to issue orders and to exact compliance.

Dutch numbers in the archipelago grew, particularly after 1870, when barriers to immigration from Holland were removed by government decree. The numbers of Indonesians were also growing, and at a much faster rate. But Indonesians came into a direct contact with Dutch officials in the second half of the 19th century as they never had before. The expansion of the cultivation system on Java and of government agencies brought Dutch men into regular, daily contact with Javanese men in positions of authority as district ruler, civil servant and village head.

Daily contact, arising from an expansion of business, commercial agriculture, proliferation of duties and agencies of government, increased the employment of all classes of Javanese men and necessitated the creation of a Javanese elite literate in Dutch. From the last quarter of the 19th century, the colonial government created a school system for upper class Javanese boys using Dutch as the medium of instruction. They also admitted into schools for European children the sons and daughters of the Javanese aristocracy.

At the same time, some among the Javanese started taking a particular interest in the Dutch, in their language, culture and science. Various of the *bupatis* (senior government administrators) began hiring Dutch tutors and governesses for the private instruction of their children, or demanded access to public education. Even the Central Java courts responded. It is standard in histories of the late colonial period to date this interest in things western from the appointment of C.E. van Kesteren as tutor to the children of the *bupati* of Demak in the 1850s. M.C. Ricklefs (1993), however, has established that leaders of the Javanese had always studied the Dutch and borrowed from them. During the long wars of succession that tore Mataram apart, the Javanese adopted Dutch weapons, including manufacture of matchlock muskets, within ten years of their introduction to Central Java by VOC soldiers. They adopted Dutch military techniques for training troops and instilling discipline. Mataram's rulers wanted horses from their allies in Batavia. They bought European coaches and hired European men to drive them. They also hired European men as bodyguards and trumpeters. At least by 1813, Java's royalty were drinking wines when entertaining Europeans, and male and female were dancing at balls with European dignitaries (Taylor, 1983: 107ff).

For long it appeared as if VOC men recognised the Javanese courts as arbiters of fashion and status. For Dutch men adopted such Javanese insignia of rank as parasols, betel boxes and slave retinues. They required their servants to kneel before them in the Javanese style. In the 19th century they even adopted Javanese titles. However, the balance of power had definitely shifted to the Dutch side. When it did, Dutch men began to regard the Javanese aristocracy as feudal and anachronistic.

Javanese men of the aristocracy were sensitive to this changed attitude in the Dutch. They saw their powers reduced by the regularisation of government administration, by the increased numbers of Dutch officials, especially the controleur and his assistant who now moved freely about the village. In 1867 the *bupatis* lost their perquisites to become salaried employees of the Dutch. Some began to perceive that the only way to revive their former power and expand it was to become like the Dutch in education and taste.

One of the earliest signs of accommodation to the Dutch as trend-setters is the modification of the costume of the upper class Javanese male. A bare torso, seat on the floor, and eating with fingers came to be viewed by some Javanese aristocrats through Dutch eyes and judged uncivilised. Photographs from the second half of the 19th century tell us that elite Javanese men had adopted the tailored jacket to cover the upper part of their bodies. Sometimes this jacket took the form of a tightly fitting, long-sleeved cotton garment, buttoned high under the neck. This jacket of *lurik* (striped cotton) became standard costume for the

Javanese male worn with *kain*, head wrapper and sandals.[14] *Bupatis* and princes of the courts added to the *kain* a shirt, neck tie and open jacket. Many photographs show the *bupati* in Javanese head wrapper, shirt, bow tie, dark jacket, watch and chain, batikked *kain* and slippers.[15] The next step was to wear western trousers with shoes and socks, add a walking cane and gloves, and a western hat, or to wear a western-style military uniform.[16]

The man who changed his appearance in this manner was now treated as a westerner by Dutch men. He shook hands, sat on a chair, ate with western utensils, conversed in Dutch. Manners practised between Javanese men changed of necessity, too. Javanese men in suits did not approach other Javanese men on their knees or take a seat on the floor. They walked erect into the presence of superiors, had eye contact, practised the western handshake, and spoke Dutch to avoid status differences. P.A.A. Djajadiningrat (1936) tells stories of the refusal of old-style *bupatis* to receive visits from their subordinates or junior relatives unless they wore Javanese costume and were prepared to follow Javanese etiquette.

In the 1890s Mangkunagara VI (r.1896–1916) formalised these changes in his domain. He required Javanese men in his service to cut their hair short in western style (as he did himself), and to eat with spoon and fork. He reduced to three the number of mandatory obeisances made him during an audience, permitted his subordinates to stand in his presence whilst making their reports, and he introduced chairs into the audience halls (Djajadiningrat, 1986). Upper class men came to feel belittled by wearing Javanese costume. Javanese male costume became the costume of inferiors and servants.

---

14   Examples are on page 133 of *Baren en oudgasten*, pp.32, 63 and 98 of Margono Djojohadikusumo's *Reminiscences*, 1973, and plates 18 and 20 of Aart van Beek's *Life in the Javanese Kraton*, 1990.

15   See, for example, pp. 164 of *Baren en oudgasten*, and pp.20, 53 and 55 of *Met vreemde ogen*, and the photograph of Kartini's husband between pp.380–81 of *Letters from Kartini*, 1992.

16   Examples are in the Nieuwenhuys collections *Baren en oudgasten*, p.164; and *Met vreemde ogen*, p.35.

By the early years of the 20th century, the costume of Javanese men who worked for the Dutch as colleagues and as clerks, men who represented Indonesians in the Volksraad, men in the army, in the police, on the railways, in the professions, in the household, included a shirt or collarless jacket and trousers. Shoes and socks distinguished the higher prestige positions from menial and domestic workers. Jobs in the modern sector, the Dutch world, were performed by men in variants of the suit. Men attached to the Javanese courts (and therefore divorced from real power) wore the *kain*; their feet and chests were bare.

We have now associated western costume with Dutch men in the colony holding supreme power and with Javanese men in jobs that connected them to westerners and modernity. The trends in female costume reflect a different history. The wives of the supreme (Dutch) rulers wore a variant of the costume worn by all Javanese women for most of the 19th century. It was only in the 20th century that women with European status, immigrant and locally born alike, adopted European clothing as their public wear. Now they dressed in a style that exposed their shoulders, arms and legs, and emphasised the contours of the female body. This was a style at odds with trends in women's costume in Java since the 17th century. Only a very few Javanese women took to wearing European costume before independence.

Female Costume on Java: Evolution of the Kain Kebaya

Developments in women's costume in the 19th century involved changes to the cut of the overblouse and to the fabric of the *kain*. We are considering, therefore, internal evolution within one dress style, rather than adoption of western costume as occurred for Javanese men. The changes to etiquette and deportment that followed on wearing the suit, changes that substituted egalitarian modes of greeting and freedom of bodily movement for stylised, restricted forms, were deferred for women.

The most obvious change in women's costume was the adoption of batik as a dress material. Batik had been dress material for aristocratic men and women on Java since the 17th century. It did not become a dress material for women outside the aristocracy until the second half of the 19th century. This can be explained in two ways. First, batik was a handmade item, requiring months to complete a single piece of cloth. It was produced in aristocratic households where the fine designs were drawn by the ladies, and the hard work of manufacture (the dyeing, washing and scraping) was done by their female servants. Batik was not produced for sale, but to clothe household members. This is closely related to the second reason why batik was not worn by commoners. Patterns and colours were reserved by royal decree to members of the royal families and ranks of their officials and servants.[17]

It is not surprising, therefore, that the first production of batik outside aristocratic households was the work of non-Javanese: the Chinese and the Eurasians. They introduced new modes of production, they designed batiks new in terms of motifs, patterns and colours, and they created a new clientele for batik as a dress material made up of Sino-Indonesians, Europeans and commoner Javanese.

The influence of Chinese entrepreneurs on patterns and colours, as well as on the organisation of cloth production is well documented.[18] The Chinese ran batik enterprises in two ways. One was a putting-out system or cottage industry, that engaged the part-time labour of Javanese women. The other was a workshop or factory system where male labourers applied designs to the cloth by means of a metal stamp. Now there existed batik which was hand-made, expensive, with 'forbidden' designs reserved for Java's aristocracy, and there were the mass-produced, cheap cottons produced for the commoner Javanese.

---

17   Alit Veldhuisen-Djajasoebrata lists sumptuary laws of the central Javanese courts in *Weavings of Power*. Gittinger, 1979, (Introduction) argues that proprietary rights to certain kinds of cloth and designs were already well established by the 14th century.

18   See, for example, text and photographs in Elliot 1984; Maxwell 1990; and Veldhuisen-Djajasoebrata 1984, 1988. Kitley, 1992, describes technical innovations in batik production, without however, introducing Eurasians and Chinese into his discussion. Elliot includes short biographies of leading Sino-Indonesian batik designers, along with photographs of their work. Boomgaard, 1981, describes production of batik through the putting out or cottage industry system.

Chinese capital and Chinese innovations in technical and industrial production made possible the batikked *kain* as daily wear for Javanese women. The particular combination of *kain kebaya* that became the national dress for Indonesia's women derives from the Eurasian contribution to the batik industry.

The Eurasian share of the batik industry was minuscule, compared to the Chinese.[19] This is because it was the work of women. Their supply of capital confined their enterprises to backyard workshops. By this mode, Eurasian women continued a Javanese production pattern in which the female head of household was the employer and supervisor of labour. Dating from around 1840, we find in Java the emergence of batik workshops run by Eurasian women. Such women had European legal status, though not the highest social standing. They used their capital to accumulate supplies of cloth, dyes and waxes, and to employ Javanese women to wash, dye and scrape cloths. Eurasian women drew on their twin cultural heritages of Europe and Java for the designs to be batikked.

Eurasian women had to create their own motifs and designs for two reasons. First, they could not, as outsiders, use the designs reserved by Java's princes for royalty and the aristocracy. Second, they had to appeal to a clientele made up of European immigrants and locally born women who might be Eurasian or Javanese or Chinese-Indonesian. Freed from the rules governing colour and design, Eurasian women could choose their own colours, patterns and images. They borrowed from Chinese decorative textiles, from European folklore, and from European pattern books and manuals. An innovation was to cover the whole length of material with the design framed within elaborate borders. Eurasian women batiksters must have had a sense of themselves as creative designers, for they signed their cloths. Their contribution to the 'national' costume of modern Indonesia was the wresting of batik from its realm of exclusive

---

19   For information and photographs of batik designed by Eurasian women, see again Elliot 1984; Maxwell 1990; and Veldhuisen- Djajasoebrata 1984, 1988. Kahlenberg, 1979, discusses the influence of European pattern books of printed fabrics, pattern books of floor tiles, and of embroidery manuals on the designs of batik by Eurasian women.

privilege and sacred associations to transform it into the public and domestic costume of women attached to men who had political power.

Production of fabrics covered in design led to changes in the overblouse. This ceased to be a long garment reaching to the knees. The photographic record for the second half of the 19th century shows that the blouse worn with batikked *kain* reached only to the hips, allowing the full design on the cloth to be seen. The blouse, or *kebaya*, was made in a variety of styles: it could be square-necked, tunic-like, or worn closed with brooches. In all cases it was long-sleeved. Eurasian dress style did not meet climate needs. Instead it met cultural values for female modesty shared by the dominant foreign cultural influences on Java: European, Middle Eastern and Chinese.

What then distinguished the Javanese woman married to a Javanese man from the Javanese or Eurasian woman married to a Dutch man? The distinction needed to be made if the wife of the Dutch man were to be accorded the privileges of the white ruling class. The wearing of slippers was one sign of the woman with European standing. The other was that the hip-length blouse was white cotton, trimmed with European lace, or black silk,[20] whilst the woman with Javanese status wore a blouse of floral material.

It was not until the 1890s that the *kain* and *kebaya* became exclusively domestic wear for women with European status and the western frock their public wear. This development is related to the rising number of women amongst the immigrants from Europe to Java after 1870. It is also related to the kind of woman who set the trends in fashion and taste in Dutch circles in Java. Until 1880, the leading ladies (defined as wives of the governor-general and senior officials) were Eurasian. After 1880 the wives of all governors-general were women born and educated in Europe. This foreign-born element at the top of

---

20   Nieuwenhuys gives many examples of wives and housekeeper-mistresses wearing the white blouse or *kebaya* in the day-time and the black silk *kebaya* for evening in his photographic collections. See, for instance, *Baren en oudgasten*, 1981, pp.50, 75, 84, 170, and 175; and *Met vreemde ogen*, p.180. See also Taylor, 1983, pp.137 and 143.

colonial society wore and sponsored European fashions in female dress.

Elite women's wear underwent profound changes in Europe during the second half of the 19th century and early 20th, and these changes were reflected in the colony. It is therefore time to consider western female costume.

The Frock in Java

Portraits of Dutch women in Holland's Asian possessions in the first half of the 17th century show them wearing wide skirts in heavy materials that conceal the female figure. Colours were dark and the dresses without ornament save a starched white lace collar or ruff. This costume covered the body from shoulders to ankles (de Haan, 1923: L4, M3).

As noted earlier, the VOC imposed a ban on female emigration from Holland that was to last until the end of the 18th century. Very few Dutch women actually went to Indonesia before 1870. The earliest photographs taken of European women in Java show them in high-necked crinolines, with loose sleeves and skirts spread wide over hooped petticoats. The body was covered from shoulder to feet, the hair worn in a bun and uncovered (Nieuwenhuys, 1981: 14, 47). The bustle replaced the crinoline in the 1870s. This costume emphasised the distortion of the female body due to corseting. Hair remained uncut, covered by a hat in public. Sleeves were long, also hemlines (Nieuwenhuys, 1981: 95, 96).

By the time numbers of Dutch women were moving to Java in the first decades of the 20th century, western female costume had undergone several revolutions. Tight lacing and the wearing of many layers of petticoats over hoops had been discarded, in part due to the influence of reform movements in Europe for women's health and suffrage. Women's costume at the turn of the century required a high-necked, long-sleeved dress or blouse, with hem length at the ankles. This costume was worn over undergarments that included a brassiere, corset, petticoat, stockings and shoes. When out, women added a hat and gloves (Nieuwenhuys, 1981: 118, 122, 132, 133, 136). Women still wore their hair long and piled high in a bun from their mid-teen years.

By the inter-war years Dutch women had shortened skirts and sleeves to expose part of their legs and arms. For evening occasions they wore a costume cut low to bare the shoulders (Nieuwenhuys, 1981: 118, 140; Buitenweg, 1977: 75). Their hair was worn either long or cut short. This female costume differed from its male counterpart in volume of material and brightness of colours, and in the amount of body exposed or left uncovered. The shortening of skirts and abandonment of hoops and bustles were related to well-to-do women entering college and the professions. A less restrictive form of costume was a key demand of those women active in the movement to give women the vote and the right to stand for public office. That is, simplified costume and exercise of citizenship went together. At the same time, high fashion still promoted a view of women as related to holders of power through bright colours, the corset and exposure of the body.

In the Javanese context, 20th century western female costume was associated with a female elite born and bred in Europe. This elite accepted and took seriously the role assigned European women by senior Dutch officials who promoted the Ethical Policy: that of promoter of (western) civilisation. As wives of senior men in the colony, they expected to mix socially with the men and women of Java's aristocracy. European social functions crossed gender lines, as well as race, making the social class of individuals the basis on which society's divisions were drawn.

Eurasian women adopted western women's clothing from the last years of the 19th century (Nieuwenhuys, 1981: 81, 96). This change of costume was accompanied by other changes. Eurasian women in Java now sat on chairs, ate with spoon and fork, went to school, and became literate in Dutch. They shook hands, and came into close physical contact with men through the ballroom dancing that replaced Javanese entertainments such as the *wayang*.

Upper class Javanese women were affected by these changes too. They learnt Dutch, western-style embroidery, cookery and piano from their Dutch governesses in the last quarter of the 19th century, and some of them started attending European elementary schools. All the photographs we possess of Kartini show her in Javanese *kain* with varieties of long-sleeved bodices in silk, velvet and cotton. Kartini died in 1904. Girls attending European elementary school of the next generation started to wear western frocks.

We see photographs recording this change in collections from Nieuwenhuys (1961, 1988). Photographs of upper class Javanese families show the married and marriage-age women of the family in long-sleeved bodice, *kain* and slippers, their hair in the bun ornamented with hair pins. Husbands and sons wear costumes ranging from shirt, jacket and bowtie teamed with *kain* and slippers to full suit, shoes and socks. School-age boys appear in western clothing; little school girls wear frocks, stockings and shoes. Photographs of Partini (1986), eldest daughter of Mangkunagara VII (r.1916–44), show her in a variety of western costumes that included frocks, skirts, blouses and jackets. Her hair is decorated with bows, arranged in plaits, or covered with a hat. In all photographs of her in western costume she wears shoes and stockings. In her father's residence, by contrast, she wore the Javanese costume of long-sleeved bodice, *kain* and slippers over bare feet, her hair in a bun. When married, she added a fan to this costume.

This pattern of western frocking for Javanese school girls and *kain* with blouse for married women is repeated in photographs from autobiographies of Sukarno (1965), Ali Sastroamijoyo (1979) and of Margono Djojohadikusumo (1970). By the 1930s some Javanese women continued to wear western clothing after their school days were over. They used their educational qualifications to pursue careers in the public domain, and wore western costume as workers in modern occupations. Their numbers were limited and restricted to a few cities. The adoption of western costume as everyday work dress awaited the development of a middle class of western educated women and large-scale recruiting of poor women into factories. These were developments of the decades following independence.

In considering adoption of western costume by elite Javanese women before World War II, we have to note again essentials of that costume. In Europe in the inter-war years female costume had evolved in the direction of comfort and reduction of restriction to body movement. The Javanese upper class woman who adopted western adult costume could now walk with a larger stride than the tightly wrapped *kain* allowed. The western frock of the 20th century required her to expose her legs from mid-calf or the knee, and also to expose her arms and neck. Western frocks emphasised contours of the female body, especially the waist and bust, in ways that the breast wrapper and loose bodice did not. To wear western clothing as an adult thus made the Javanese woman more like Dutch women in terms of manners, personal liberties, and standards of decency, and distanced her from the body language, decorum and learned behaviours of the great majority of Javanese women.

Campaigners in Europe for women's rights linked freer clothing to the vote. In Indonesia campaigners for national independence linked costume to self-governance. The subject of costume entered the political discourse during the teens and twenties. Western dress versus 'native' was a subject of debate in nationalist circles. It is now time to turn to Sukarno and the views of his group, expressed ultimately in the independence day photographs.

Sukarno and the Invention of National Dress

From his founding of a study club in Bandung, Sukarno always wore western male costume. He rejected the halfway costume of his Surabaya Dutch high school days, that is, Javanese head cloth with western shirt and bowtie, jacket and batikked *kain* (Sukarno, 1965, opposite p.156). Not as leader of the pre-war Nationalist Party, not as negotiator for statehood, not as president of independent Indonesia, nor yet in international forums did Sukarno wear any variant of Javanese costume. Even when he performed before the press the quintessential Javanese ceremony of kneeling in respect to his mother (Sukarno, 1965, photograph between pp.156–57), he wore a western-style suit. The one photograph Sukarno staged in loose trousers, bare torso and feet (Sukarno, 1965) was on his pilgrimage to Mecca.

When not dressed in civilian clothes, Sukarno wore western-style military uniform with braid, ribbons and swagger stick. The armed forces over which he presided as commander-in-chief was also outfitted in western-style uniforms. No rhetoric of nationalism caused Sukarno to recreate the image of the Republic's army. Mangkunagara soldiers in the 1880s wore batikked *kain*, with torso and feet bare (Veldhuisen-Djajasoebrata, 1988). Sukarno's soldiers wore shirts, trousers, socks and boots, and head gear that included helmets, berets and peaked caps. Officers' insignia were not ear rings, finger rings, or batik motifs, but stars, braid, ribbons and medals.

Two reasons explain Sukarno's opting for western costume. First, he aspired to lead all peoples of the archipelago. To wear a Javanese (or Balinese) costume would have particularised his claim to leadership, and identified his authority with one ethnic group only. Second, costume symbolised power. Those issuing orders in colonial Indonesia wore suits; those taking orders wore *sarung* or *kain*.

In his 1965 *Autobiography as Told to Cindy Adams*, Sukarno recreated a discussion he had with fellow nationalists in 1928:

> I further suggest that we condemn the sarong even in private practice. This old-fashioned native dress has a demeaning effect. The minute an Indonesian dons trousers he walks erect like any white man. Immediately he wraps that feudal symbol around his middle, he stoops over in a perpetual bow, his shoulders sag. He doesn't stride manfully, he shuffles apologetically. He instantaneously becomes hesitant and servile and subservient.

In response to the objection that the *sarung* was part of Indonesia's tradition he continued:

> Indonesian tradition of the past—yes. Not with the new Indonesia of the future. We must be divested of that influence which chains us to the cringing past as nameless, faceless servants and houseboys and peasants. Let us

demonstrate that we are as progressive as our former masters.
We must take our place as upstanding equals. We must put
on modern clothing (Sukarno, 1965: 80–81).

We may now note that Sukarno conceived of political power
as male power. In the same memoir he expressed his dislike of
short skirts, fitted blouses and lipstick on women (Sukarno,
1965: 142–43), the costume, in other words, habitually worn by
lawyer and cabinet minister, Maria Ulfah. It was also the
costume selected by some women witnessing the raising of the
flag on 17 August, and who are usually cut out of that historic
photograph. Western costume was associated in 1945, not just
with the privileged, unmarried school graduate, but with women's
participation in the public arena of politics, in the world of
modern education and jobs. It was a costume associated with the
personal freedoms of citizenship.

Western costume held another meaning for pre-independence
generations of Javanese women. This is made clear by a passage
in a letter from Kartini to Rosa Abendanon-Mandri in 1903.

> Now I suddenly remember that the daughters of the
> Regent of Ciamis, when they were still going to school in
> Batavia, had not always worn European clothes. However it
> had become so difficult for them that they put aside their
> national costume and wore European dress (Kartini, 1987:
> 431, 14/7/03).

In other words, western women's costume could be a shield or
armour against Javanese men. Dressed in *kain* and *kebaya*,
Javanese upper class girls could not prolong their studies past
puberty, or walk in the street unattended without criticism from
Javanese men. In European attire they appeared to the observer
to be Eurasian, that is, women with European status and rights.
Young Javanese women had to be able to pass for Eurasians if
they wanted personal freedom. They appeared to have what
Achmad Djajadiningrat sought when he enrolled in Batavia's
European high school under the alias Willem van Banten:
European legal status. These considerations were not in the
president's mind when he promoted *kain kebaya* as 'national

dress' for Indonesian women. Not personal freedom or escape from convention for them, but a statement about the past, about the home, about dependency.

Let us now consider all the components of the female national dress in Sukarno's invention of tradition. The long-sleeved *kebaya* in Java's history combines Christian and Muslim ideals of personal modesty in the covering of shoulders and arms. The hip-length style of the *kebaya* owes its origins to Eurasian female costume, without its tight association with European status, for the white lace was rejected in favour of the floral and coloured *kebayas*. The batikked *kain* stems from Java, but a Java divorced from the royal courts and their world of hierarchy and exclusiveness. The *slendang* or display scarf owes its origin to the carrying cloth of commoner women. Slippers are associated in Java's history with status and distance from servitude. The uncovered head represents a rejection of Islamic ideals as expressed in Arab female costume.

The national costume Sukarno promoted for Indonesian men was the western suit, worn with shoes and socks, and the *pici*. This headcovering is a modified variant of the Muslim fez. It therefore bore a link to Islam as the religion of most Indonesians. Sukarno, however, promoted the *pici* as the headgear of the working man, again rejecting models from royalty and articles specifically tied to any one ethnic group. It was in this costume of western suit and *pici* that he proclaimed Indonesia's independence.

During his presidency, Sukarno promoted batik as the symbol of Indonesia. In 1955 he commissioned Go Tik Swan to design a style of batik that could be worn by Indonesians of all ethnic groups, that is, a style that would release batik from its tight association with Java and the courts.[21] Sukarno's successor, President Suharto, continues to make the same public statements through costume. One of batik's old functions, as the uniform of retainers, has been revived in the 'dress batik' for Golkar, the

---

21   Go Tik Swan (b.1931) came from a Sino-Indonesian family that had long been in the batik business. In 1972 he was elevated to the nobility by the susuhunan of Solo as Kanjeng Raden Tumenggung Hardjonagoro and made court advisor for cultural affairs.

party of the New Order government. The official costume of civil servants is batik shirt and trousers for men, batik blouse and short skirt for women. Daily use of Indonesian costume remains associated with poverty and low status. Courtly Javanese wear is to be seen now only on ceremonial occasions, such as the wedding. The *sarung* is now almost exclusively identified with mosque and domestic wear.[22]

Conclusion: Symbols in the Independence Day Photographs

Let us conclude by returning to the two photographs documenting the declaration of Indonesia's independence. We note that all men wear variants of western costume. There is no man in any kind of regional costume visible in either of the photographs. No image connects Indonesian men to the status of inferior, either to an indigenous ruler or to a colonial one. The two women at centre stage observing the raising of the flag wear the costume of long-sleeved bodice and batikked *kain*, which we now know to have been a product of the last half of the 19th century. In the uncropped photographs of the flag-raising ceremony two other women may be seen to the right, wearing western short-sleeved dresses. Their costume links them to the world of modern men, to careers and to personal liberties.

Taken together, both images represent the history of Indonesia's women. The central image makes a statement about connection to the past, to men, to status and the family. It is a staged presentation of official views on women. It represents a partial truth about women's lives. Looking around that central image we learn, too, about women's entrance into the modern world of mass education, the paid workforce, and the commitments of citizenship.

22　The *sarung* and the *kain kebaya* figure in nostalgic pieces by Indonesian and Eurasian alike. See, for example, Goenawan, 1994; Nieuwenhuys, 1963; and Schenkhuizen 1993.

References

Achjadi, Judi 1978, *Pakaian Daerah Wanita Indonesia*, Djambatan, Jakarta.

Anderson, Benedict R.O'G. 1972, *Java in a Time of Revolution, Occupation and Resistance, 1944–1946*, Cornell University Press, Ithaca.

Barnes, Ruth and Joanne B. Eicher 1991, *Dress and Gender: Making and Meaning*, St. Martin's Press, New York.

Beek, Aart van 1990, *Life in the Javanese Kraton*, Oxford University Press, Singapore.

Boomgaard, Peter 1991, 'The Non-Agricultural Side of an Agricultural Economy, Java 1500–1900', in Paul Alexander et al. (eds.), *In the Shadow of Agriculture*, Royal Tropical Institute, Amsterdam.

—— 1981, 'Female Labour and Population Growth on Nineteenth Century Java', *Review of Indonesian and Malaysian Affairs*, XV(2).

Coast, John 1952, *Recruit to Revolution*, Christophers, London.

Djajadiningrat, B.R.A. Partini 1986, *Partini, Tulisan Kehidupan Seorang Putri Mangkunagaran*, as told to Roswitha Pamoentjak Singgih, Jakarta, Djambatan.

Djajadiningrat, P.A.A. 1936, *Kenang-Kenangan*, Kolff-Buning/Balai Poestaka, Batavia.

Djojohadikusumo, Margono 1973, *Reminiscences from Three Historical Periods*, P.T. Indira, Jakarta.

Elliot, Inger McCabe 1984, *Batik, Fabled Cloth of Java*, Clarkson N. Potter, New York.

Frederick, William H. 1989, *Visions and Heat: The Making of the Indonesian Revolution*, Ohio University Press, Athens.

Gittinger, Mattiebelle 1979, *Splendid Symbols: Textiles and Tradition in Indonesia*, Textile Museum, Washington, D.C.

Goenawan, Mohamad 1994, 'On Sarongs and Other Such Things', *Sidelines: Writings from Tempo*, translated by Jennifer Lindsay, Monash Asia Institute, Hyland House.

Haan, F. de 1923, *Oud Batavia gedenkboek: Platenalbum*, C. Kolff, Batavia.

Hakim, Abdul 1988, *Jakarta Tempo Doeloe*, P.T. Metro Pos, Jakarta.

Hanifah, Abu 1972, *Tales of a Revolution*, introduction by Chr. L.M. Penders, Angus and Robertson, Sydney.

Hardjonagoro, K.R.T. 1979, 'The Place of Batik in the History and Philosophy of Javanese Textiles: A Personal View', *Batik and Related Textiles*, Irene Emery Roundtable on Museum Textiles, 1979 Proceedings, Textile Museum, Washington, D.C.

Hobsbawm, Eric 1983, 'Introduction: Inventing Traditions', in Eric Hobsbawm and Terence Ranger (eds.), *The Invention of Tradition*, Cambridge University Press, Cambridge.

Kahin, George McTurnan 1969, *Nationalism and Revolution in Indonesia*, Cornell University Press, Ithaca, 7th printing.

Kahlenberg, Mary Hunt 1979, 'The Influence of the European Herbal on Indonesian Batik', *Batik and Related Textiles*, Textile Museum, Washington, D.C.

Kartini, R.A. 1987, *Brieven aan mevrouw Abendanon-Mandri en haar echtgenoot*, F.G.P. Jaquet (ed), KITLV Press, Leiden.

—— 1992, *Letters from Kartini, An Indonesian Feminist, 1900–1904*, translated by Joost Coté, Monash Asia Institute, Hyland House.

Kemper, Rachel H. 1977, *Costume*, Newsweek Books, New York.

Kitley, Philip 1992, 'Ornamentation and Originality: Involution in Javanese Batik', *Indonesia*, 53, April.

Laarhoven, Ruurdje 1994, 'The Power of Cloth: The Textile Trade of the Dutch East India Company (VOC) 1600–1780', unpublished dissertation, Australian National University.

Legge, John D. 1972, *Sukarno, A Political Biography*, Penguin Books, Ringwood, Victoria.

Loos-Haaxman, J. de 1928, *Johannes Rach en zijn werk*, Kolff, Batavia.

Lucas, Anton 1977, 'Social Revolution in Pemalang, Central Java, 1945', *Indonesia*, 24, October.

—— 1991, *One Soul, One Struggle*, Allen and Unwin, Sydney.

Maxwell, Robyn 1990, *Textiles of Southeast Asia. Tradition, Trade and Transformation*, Oxford University Press, Australian National Gallery.

Nasution, A.H. 1977, *Sekitar Perang Kemerdekaan Indonesia*, I, Angkasa, Bandung, 2nd edition.

Nieuwenhuys, Rob 1940/1941, 'Over de Europese samenleving van "tempo doeloe" 1870–1900', *de Fakkel*, I.

—— 1961, *Tempo doeloe: Fotografische documenten uit het oude Indië, 1870–1914*, Querido, Amsterdam.

——1963, *Vergeelde portretten uit een Indisch familiealbum*, 5th ed., Salamandar, Amsterdam.

—— 1981, *Baren en oudgasten*, Querido, Amsterdam.

—— 1988, *Met vreemde ogen: Tempo doeloe-een verzonken wereld*, Querido, Amsterdam.

Notosusanto, Nugroho (ed.) 1981, *30 Tahun Indonesia Merdeka, I, 1945–1949*, P.T. Tira Pustaka, Jakarta, 5th printing.

O'Malley, W.J. 1980, 'Second Thoughts on Indonesian Nationalism', in James J. Fox (ed.), *Indonesia: Australian Perspectives*, vol. III, Australian National University Press, Canberra.

Poesponegoro, Marwati Djoened and Nugroho Notosusanto (eds.) 1960, *Sejarah Nasional Indonesia*, volumes V and VI, Balai Pustaka, Jakarta.

Reid, Anthony 1974, *The Indonesian National Revolution 1945–1950*, Longman, Hawthorn, Vic.

Roach, Mary Ellen and Kathleen Ehle Musa 1980, *New Perspectives on the History of Western Dress*, Metropolitan Museum of Art, New York.

Sagimun, M.D. 1988, *Jakarta dari Tepian Air ke Kota Proklamasi*, Pemerintah Daerah Khusus Ibukota Jakarta, Dinas Museum dan Sejarah, Jakarta.

Sastroamidjojo, Ali 1979, *Milestones on My Journey*, edited by Chr. L.M. Penders, University of Queensland Press, St. Lucia.

Schenkhuizen, Marguerite 1993, *Memoirs of an Indo Woman: Twentieth Century Life in the East Indies and Abroad*, Lizelot Stout van Balgooy (ed. & trans.), Ohio University Southeast Asian Series No. 92, Athens.

Shiraishi, Takashi 1990, *An Age in Motion: Popular Radicalism in Java, 1912–1926*, Cornell University Press, Ithaca.

Sukarno 1965, *Sukarno, An Autobiography as told to Cindy Adams*, Bobbs-Merrill, New York.

Suryochondro, Sukanti 1984, *Potret Pergerakan Wanita di Indonesia*, C.V. Rajawali, Jakarta.

Taylor, Jean Gelman 1983, *The Social World of Batavia: European and Eurasian in Dutch Asia*, University of Wisconsin Press, Madison.

Veldhuisen-Djajasoebrata, Alit 1984, *Bloemen van het heelal: De kleurrijke wereld van de textiel op Java*, Sijthoff, Rotterdam Museum of Ethnography, Amsterdam.

—— 1988, *Weavings of Power and Might: The Glory of Java*, Museum voor Volkenkunde, Rotterdam.

Vreede-de Stuers, Cora 1960, *The Indonesian Woman: Struggles and Achievements*, Mouton, 's-Gravenhage.

Wilson, Elizabeth 1985, *Adorned in Dreams: Fashion and Modernity*, Virago Press, London.

Equality?
The Influence of Legislation and Notions of Gender on the Position of Women Wage Workers in the Economy: Indonesia 1950–58[*]

Janet Elliot

Introduction

Considering that the viability of the Republic was in real doubt with the determination of the returning Dutch to secure their former colonial possession, the introduction of labour legislation by the fledgling Republic of Indonesia in 1947–48 was remarkable. The desire to protect and nourish the workers of an independent Indonesia, in ways which had been sadly lacking during the colonial era, was in a real sense a reward for the years of struggle and impoverishment workers had suffered during the revolution and the Japanese occupation. It follows that one should commend those who nourished this early idealism. Therefore, in writing this paper, I do not suggest all those in power, either in government or the bureaucracy, were entirely unconcerned with working-class conditions. Where women workers were concerned, reference was often made to the State's commitment to equality for the sexes enshrined in the constitution. But a review of legislation, and of the position of women wage workers in the economy until 1958 (the year Indonesia ratified ILO Convention 100 on the principle of equal

[*] An earlier version of this paper was presented at the Fourth Women in Asia Conference, Melbourne University, 1–3 October 1993. A summary appeared in *Asian Studies Review*, 17(3), April 1994. This paper has been substantially revised and has benefited from the helpful comments of Dr Jean Taylor. I owe her a special word of thanks. Naturally, any errors remain my own.

pay for equal work),[1] raises serious doubts about the strength of that commitment. Ideas of 'equality' for workers were accepted, in the main, for a workforce gendered as male. Women workers may have been wage earners in a 'new' Indonesia but old notions about gender continued. It is to history that we must turn to find the reasons why.

The new nation-state of Indonesia succeeded the old colonial entity as determined by its boundaries: in the terminology of political theory it was a successor state.   However, just as the entity itself was influenced by European ideas so too were the intellectuals who led the nationalist struggle. Those upwardly mobile men (and a few women) 'laid the foundations for the structure of attitudes and beliefs that would constrain and channel future behavior' (Hindley, 1966: 4). The political culture of post-independence Indonesia, both with regard to the state-qua-state and the relationships within civil society, was deeply embedded in the colonial era. And dominant ideologies in the colonial and wider European discourse about the rights of workers, the protection of workers, and the 'duties' of workers, were reflected in the labour legislation announced by the fledgling Republic in 1947–48.

European derived ideas, however, were not the only influence on the political culture. The political leadership was also the product of cultures where notions of gender had been historically and culturally constructed.[2] Along with European derived ideas about the state-qua-state went ideas about civil society. European derived in the shape of legal and political institutions, they were also rooted in pre-colonial traditional cultural thinking about society in general, and on the differences of men and women and their different roles in the community (Woodcroft-Lee, 1983: 190). For colonial Indonesia, Locher and Niehof comment (that) 'inevitably, [the] sources reflect a white male perception of Indonesian society' (Locher-Scholten & Niehof, 1987: 3). Yet, even the post-colonial indigenous sources are not immune from class-based and gendered perceptions. In thinking about the

---

1   *UU* No.80/1957.
2   See Joan Wallach Scott, (1988), and William H. Sewell, (1990: 71–82) for a discussion on this point.

nature of the extant material on labour (for example from the Ministries of Labour, Information, and Manpower, or personal histories of Prime Ministers, or various Ministers of Labour)[3] one is reminded of the elite nature of the discourse concerning the relationship of workers with the state. A discourse which included the formulation of legislation, policy implementation, and writings on the working-class.

The legislation drawn up in 1947–48 was enacted in early 1951 after the unitary state of Indonesia became a reality. Still, Government commitment to the principles of the legislation was too often long on rhetoric and short on action. Even before the legislation was enacted there was some wavering from the idea of 'equality' for workers, but unions, workers, and labour supporters rallied to ensure the legislation was passed (Iskandar Tedjasukmana, 1958: 118).

However, in the new Indonesia women remained disadvantaged in the workplace. If we keep in mind Catherine MacKinnon's (1989) dictum (that) 'social power shapes the way we know and the way we know shapes social power', the ideas about gender and class that underlay and reinforced that disadvantage can be brought to the surface. In support of this I want first to show the historical grounding of the low wage levels of women workers; and second to focus on the ideologies of gender which underlay the 'protective' and the 'negative proscriptive'[4] articles (and the exceptions granted to these) in the legislation promulgated by the new nation-state.

---

3   See for example Iskandar Tedjasukmana, (1958), and (1961). Tedjasukmana served as Minister of Labour in three different cabinets: the Sukiman Cabinet (27 April 1951–2 April 1952); the Wilopo Cabinet (3 April 1952–31 July, 1953); and the Burhanudin Harahap Cabinet (12 August 1955–27 March, 1956). He was Chairman of the Political Bureau of the Labour Party from 1951–56 and a member of the Indonesian Parliament (except while serving in a Cabinet) from 1946–56. (Tedjasukmana, 1958: iii).

4   See Virginia A. Leary, (1982). Article 7 (1) of the Labour Act, 1948, is an example of a negative proscriptive article. It begins... 'woman may not work in the evening...'.

The Colonial Period

For Java and Madura, figures published in the 'Declining Welfare Survey' (1905) show an 'already quite high level of proletarianisation in non-farm activities as well as in agriculture' (White, 1991: 46). 40% of the agricultural labour force, and 36% of those engaged in non-farm activities were wage workers (White, 1991: 46). In the 1930 occupational census, out of a total Indonesian population of 60,731,025, 34.4% (48.5% of all the males and 20.6% of all the females) 'were gainfully employed', with the majority engaged in agriculture (Thompson, 1947: 117); approximately 10% employed in industry, the majority of these in small and home-based industries (*Bank Indonesia Report*, 1952–53: 176). The survey numbers do not of course include the large numbers of women engaged in unpaid labour, either in the home, on the family's plot of land, or in family cottage or small-scale industries. This under-enumeration of working women 'has been relatively consistent over the years in Indonesian census records.[5] The figures, however, do illustrate the extent of women's participation in wage labour, or at least, in 'gainful employment'. Women's increasing participation in wage labour had its impetus in the 'dramatic changes in all sectors of the economy' during the 19th century. which 'took place against the background of an expanding colonial state…and the ongoing expansion of Western enterprise' (Boomgaard, 1991: 29).

In the decade before the war the colonial government actively pursued an industrialisation program. Between 1930-1940 the number of factories, excluding small or home industries and those connected with agricultural industries, increased by approximately 71.7% (*Monthly Labour Review*, 1944: 980); and in the years between 1935 and 1939 the number of workers engaged in factory production tripled (Thompson, 1947: 120).

---

5   White, (1991: 52 and fn.5). see also Hazel Moir's (1987) analysis of the 1971 Indonesian census in which she identifies the rate of female access to non-primary occupations, stresses the importance of recognising the contribution of both female and male unpaid labour; particularly as non-recognition 'perpetuates a tradition of undervaluing the contribution of women's work'. (Hazel Moir, 1987: 178).

The largest number of workers were employed in the food, metal and textile (weaving) industries (*Monthly Labour Review*, 1944: 971). The onset of World War II accelerated this expansion and in 1940 alone 500 new factories providing employment for some 25,000 workers were established (Thompson, 1947: 138). In 1938 unskilled factory labour earned around ƒ0.35 to ƒ0.40 per day and an eight hour working day was common for industry. There was no general system of paid vacations, family allowances or social insurance (except workers' compensation) which provided an assured supplement to wages, although some employers did make voluntary grants to their workers. Wages and salaries varied according to racial groups, skills, location of the enterprise (*Monthly Labour Review*, 1944: 971–84) and gender.

The better paid European workers, for example, were found in printing establishments, electric power stations and various machinery plants. Conversely, the lowest paid workers were found in the textile plants using a high proportion of female labour. In the *batik* industries males received ƒ0.18–0.42 for a working day ranging between 7.5–11 hours. Females received ƒ0.15–0.18 for a slightly shorter working day of 8–9.5 hours. On this calculation women had to work a longer day than male workers to receive the lowest wage paid to males. Bakeries, rice mills, candy, tile and pottery factories reported similar wage differentials for equal length working days. Only in the cigar factories were wage ranges similar for males and females, although the unskilled category, into which large numbers of women fell, were paid lower wages. There were no uniform overtime rates, but in workplaces where overtime was paid women usually received less. On the rubber estates, for example, overtime was usually paid at ƒ0.6 for men and ƒ0.5 for women. In manufacturing industries the temporary worker rates were at the following level: daily wages for unskilled adult males—ƒ15-25; for women and children—ƒ05-15. Similarly in the tea plantations in the Buitenzorg Residency, in the harvesting and preparation of cinchona bark in West Java, and in the manufacture of palm oil and other products on Sumatra's east coast minimum, as well as other rates, tended to be higher for males than for females for the same hard work (*Monthly Labour Review*, 1944: 985–86). In secondary industry women numbered about 600,000: approximately one quarter of all the workers engaged in factory production. In tobacco factories they were 39% of all the workers, and in the textile industries 34%. Overall, where a comparison could be made between male and female wage rates women invariably received less (Thompson, 1947: 149).

In addition to the low wage rates little legal protection was provided for the industrial worker, and through the first half of the 1920s there was strong union and worker agitation over wages and working conditions. This so concerned the Indies Government that it removed from the country those it believed to be the root cause of the discontent (Trimurti, 1980: 13). It was not until the last years of its rule that the Indies Government, worried both by the international situation and the political atmosphere in Indonesia, moved to put some regulation into the settlement of labour disputes. The 'Agency for the Settlement of Disputes between Employers and Workers' was formed on 24 November, 1937. On 20 July, 1939 a 'Commission of Civil Servants' was established to oversee serious disputes in private businesses other than the railroad companies, and on December 16, 1940 a Law concerning the 'Resolution of Labour Differences in Vital Businesses' which had more than 20 workers was promulgated (Trimurti, 1980: 14). Provisions of the 'Coolie Ordinance of 1931' required employers to pay 'sufficient' wages for the normal necessities of life, and limited the workday to nine hours in surface employment, and eight and a half when work was carried on partly or wholly underground. Even so there were no general minimum-wage standards fixed by law. Amendments involving overtime pay provisions were made in 1936, but the repeal of the ordinance in 1941 removed any compulsion to comply with the standards (*Monthly Labour Review*, 1944: 987).

There was, however, legislation restricting the employment of women and children, and an important duty of the Labour Inspectorate in Java and Madura was to oversee the regulations concerning these two groups of workers. The 1926 regulations prohibited the employment of children in any enterprise between 8pm and 5am. Nor could they be employed in some specified pursuits, including work in factories. Women were prohibited from working between the hours of 10pm and 5am, except for certain industries and enterprises which had special industrial needs as provided for by a decree of the Governor General (*Monthly Labour Review*, 1944: 987). This meant that women as a general rule were prohibited from night work, but could be employed to suit industry needs. In 1939, 69% of the sugar factories employed women on the seasonal night shifts.[6]

Locher-Scholten writes of the non-interest in the actual condition of Indonesian women by those debating the legislation concerning night work, whether they represented the 'Western or the orientalist view'. The result was a compromise bill 'between Western opinions about a woman's place and the economic demands of employers' (Locher-Scholten, 1987: 80). The compromise allowed four hours more of night-work than was permissible in Europe at that time. The later 1948 legislation fell into line with the European 'standard'. In the 1925 Volksraad debate on the abolition of female night labour in industry all the discussants were male and Locher-Scholten concludes (that) 'it is to the higher social classes that we should look for any influences of colonial ideology concerning women. During the colonial period it went over the heads of the Indonesian working class' (Locher-Scholten, 1987: 93).

The Japanese Occupation

During the Japanese occupation unions were banned and all labour organisations were put under the umbrella of the *Kenpeitai*. Negative labour legislation concerning regimentation of labour and the prohibition of strikes was passed, and the regimentation of the population along communal, occupational,

---

6   Thompson, 1947: 149. With the declaration of martial law in 1940 emergency measures giving the Government special powers for the mobilisation of human and material resources were promulgated. The Industrial Cooperation Act of 1940 authorised the government to make stipulations on pay scales, and in 1941 new rules were established for the employment of native or foreign Asiatic labour. Hours of work were limited to 9 in any 24 but no wage standards were prescribed. 'Labor Conditions', *Monthly Labor Review*, p.987.

religious, sex and age groups lines was undertaken. Recent work by Shigeru Sato (1994) on labour mobilisation during the occupation gives new information on the poor working conditions which affected both rural and urban people. A worker was anyone mobilised to work for the Japanese war effort and labourers were viewed as working soldiers (*perajurit pekerja*). Labour mobilisation was coercive and the conditions extremely harsh, but where labour was in short supply or, where skilled labour was necessary, better wages were paid. For unskilled labour the level of wages depended on the type of work, but rapid inflation meant that wages did not keep pace with the rising cost of living (Sato, 1994: 167). Although there is little comparative information on wage differentials available Sato points out that when the Malang Residency set a minimum wage level of *f*0.40 for urban areas in 1944 the rate for women was 80% of this amount. The minimum level was calculated on the cost-of-living per day for a family of five—the total calculated expenditure equalling that of the minimum level (Sato, 1994: 167–68). Since large numbers of male workers were coercively mobilised for overseas work,[7] there can be an assumption of many households headed by a female worker, where 80% of male wage rates would be inadequate for daily living. Desperation and privation was the lot of Indonesians, generally, during the occupation.

Independent Indonesia

As has been noted in the introduction, given the difficulties under which the Republic operated during the revolutionary period it is remarkable that any legislation was produced. And unremarkable that the fight for better working conditions was subsumed under the struggle for the Republic's survival. A worker's group, the *Barisan Buruh Indonesia,* was formed in September 1945, and a women's section of this group (*Barisan Buruh Wanita*) at the end of the year. In 1946, the BBW became an autonomous section of the BBI with a brief to act as an educational and 'go-between' body. The worries of female workers were to be directed to the major union or the BBI in each region (*Tindjauan Masalah Perburuhan* 4 August 1950;

---

7   The workers were known as *romusha*.

Ichtisar Isi Pers 4, 21–27 February 1946). Nonetheless, political partnership[8] during the revolution did not translate into full working equality on independence. A 'defining and confining of roles' (Manderson, 1980: 86) which was both gender and class-based began. Clearly, women were not excluded from wage labour. An analysis of statistical and pictorial representation shows that their wage-force participation continued after independence. The question becomes to what extent did legislative changes after independence reflect a change in labour relations for women wage earners?

The waged formal sector, at least in theory, was the sector protected by legislation. (The formal/informal sectors were not mutually exclusive since many wage earners might, whilst working, draw income from the informal sector to supplement their income.) (Boomgaard, 1991: 15) The largest proportion of women wage earners was found in the primary sector. For instance, as tea pickers on the plantations, or in the rice mills, or sugar and rubber factories. Apart from the primary sector, women were engaged in labouring work across a wide spectrum of occupations. They were to be found in the transportation industry, and in factories associated with the manufacturing industry. In the latter they were concentrated in certain industries, often within certain tasks.[9]

Any assessment of the number of women wage earners is difficult in countries with a large number of cottage industries. The producing unit can range from the proprietor and family members, to others with a few paid workers, to others where a hundred or more workers may be employed—many of them working from home for piece rates and paid by merchants or middlemen. The wage rates themselves are generally hard to assess and workers, large numbers of whom are women working in exploitative conditions, often lie outside any legislative

8   An informative account of the attitudes of the late President Sukarno on the role of Indonesian women in political life is given by Colin Brown, 1981: 68–92.

9   *International Labour Review Reports and Inquiries* (1953: 310). In industry in Asian countries generally, women were largely employed in the unskilled occupations in the old established industries such as textiles.

provisions (*International Labour Office Studies and Report*, 1956).

By 1953, the number of employed persons had risen to 30 million (from the approximate 21 million shown in the 1930 census). Around 8 million of this number worked for a definite wage or salary (Hawkins, 1963: 85). Of the wage and salary earners the largest number was still engaged in agricultural production on the large estates many of which processed rubber, sugar, palm oil, or sisal (Hawkins, 1963: 85). Workers were divided between large firms with over 500 employees, those employing between 100 to 500 workers and small industrial firms with less than 20 workers (Hawkins, 1963: 86). There was a shortage of skilled workers and a great disparity between the skilled and unskilled wage rates existed.

Women's historic limited access to education and to vocational skill training meant they were concentrated in this unskilled section, with very little opportunity to advance their position. This was particularly true when women sought work in the towns and cities where more skills were generally demanded. It also partially explains why so many women entered the informal sector in urban areas. But rural and urban women wage earners were similarly affected. Not only did the wage rates of women workers illustrate their position at the lowest end of the wage labour force, they also illustrated their comparable position to unskilled and skilled male labour. In the West Java tea factories unskilled female labour received Rp.4.75 per day: male labour received Rp.5.75. Skilled machinists were paid about Rp.20, over four times the amount paid to unskilled women workers (Hawkins, 1963: 109). Often the pay differential had little to do with a 'skilled' classification, and more to do with the sexual division of labour. The tobacco, *batik*, and food processing industries employing a high percentage of women were at the lowest end of the industrial wage scale, with the low daily minimum wage of these industries reflecting a large pay differential of around 25% between men and women workers (US Department of Labour, 1963: 38).

Examination of newspaper and journal photographs of factory production in the early 1950s, both in cities and rural areas, shows women on the production line in workplaces as diverse as cigarette, margarine, soap, and toothpaste factories, and rubber mills and printing establishments. At many of the workplaces where there was a production line, such as in the rubber mills and cigarette factories, women appeared to be in the majority, were mostly in 'traditional' dress with few visible safety/health measures. At the printing establishments, on the other hand, where more skilled work was being undertaken women were not in the majority and were employed stacking the loose-leafed or finished product. The range of women's tasks in factory work can be seen in a gelatin (*agar-agar*) factory in Surabaya employing around 140 labourers and a few laboratory assistants. Women were pictured doing both inside and outside work. That is, sorting the washed seaweed and drying it in the sun; purifying the seaweed (washing it in large tubs); putting it into baskets after the washing process and trundling the gelatin bricks outside to dry. Men and women worked side by side in some of these tasks. In many other factories, usually where there was a production line of sorts, women alone worked.[10]

From the statistical and pictorial overview a number of points can be made about the structure of labour relations in the workplaces where women were employed. First: women often worked alongside men performing the same work; second: in occupations that required vocational/technical training, as in the printing establishments women, because of their limited access to training and education, were relegated to the unskilled section;

10 Pictorial sources are: *TMP* 3, July 1950: 27 (working machines in a tin can factory in Bali); *TMP* 4, August 1950: 30 (cigarette factory—cigar section); *TMP* 9, January 1951: 23 (tea factory); *TMP* 3/4/5 July/August/September 1952: 19 (factory production); *TMP* 6, October 1954, front page (women tea pickers); *TMP* 7, November 1954: 17 (factory production); *TMP* 1, May 1955: 1 (conveyor belt factory production); *Indonesia*, 1958: 22–2 (toothpaste factory); *Indonesia* 1958: 13–16 (*agar-agar* factory); *Indonesia* 1958, (as part of the process of sugarbag making:washing fibre and tying it into bundles). By 'traditional' dress is meant the *kebaya, sarong* and the *selendang*: some workers are pictured wearing the *kerudung* headress. In other factories there appears to be a mixture of traditional and western dress. In some workplaces, such as the modern toothpaste factory in Jakarta, women wore safety caps for hair covering.

and third: many of the tasks within an occupation category, such as the sheet feeders on the rubber production line or the brick sorters at the gelatin factory, had clearly become tasks which only women performed. Gender both influenced the wage differentials between male and female for the same work and defined occupations, or tasks within an occupation, as women's work for which less remuneration could be offered.

As has been noted this sexual division of labour affected the stratification of skilled and unskilled work. Yet more job opportunities in these industries, already large employers of women, would not have affected women's subordinate position in the wage scale because the work itself had become a 'bearer of gender' (Elson & Pearson, 1981: 26). Even when occupations are not so categorised the rigid stratification of workers as skilled or unskilled means that some forever remain second-class labour. While this is true for both men and women, recruitment for men is into both categories, recruitment for women usually into the unskilled (Boserup, 1986: 141).

Elson and Pearson argue that investigation should centre on the relations by which women are integrated into wage labour, rather than on their being 'left out' of wage labour (Elson & Pearson, 1981: 19). In looking at the position of women workers in the early 1950s the way in which they were integrated into wage employment was indeed part of the problem; grounded as it was in the historical capitalist labour process of the colony, and dominant ideologies concerning gender.[11] The dominant ideologies were reflected in the mixture of protective (maternity leave) and proscriptive (prohibition on night work) legislation which, while giving support to women worker's 'duties' as mothers and wives, paid 'lip-service' only to their rights as workers.

---

11   Boomgaard in his work on 19th century Java warns against seeing the sexual division of labour as 'timeless', and of generalising across the archipelago. He argues changes in labour roles occurred with different influences, and often at different times for ethnic groups. (Boomgaard, 1981: 13). Cf. Douglas, (1980), on both these points. Women's increasing participation in wage labour in the capitalist economy, and the legislation were a continuum of those 'influences of change'.

The Legislation

The Amir Sjarifuddin Cabinet established the Labour Ministry in July 1947, but political conditions within Indonesia meant that the Labour Act and the Labour Inspection Act, although prepared, were not ratified until 1951 when, along with the provisions of the Accident Act (the first piece of social legislation introduced by the Republican Government) all of the regulations became law for the whole of Indonesia (Trimurti, 1980: 13). Between 1947 and 1951 legislation to provide some protection for workers; to 'define' a worker; to lay down policy on workplace conditions such as hours of work, periods of rest, etc., and to outline an arbitration scheme which placed limitations on the right to organise and bargain collectively, and on the right to strike was introduced.[12] These were the Accident Act, the Labour Act, the Labour Inspection Act, the Central Military Authority Regulation and the Emergency Law, which changed the provisions of the Military Authority Regulation, and the Emergency Law, which changed the provisions of the Military Regulation, and the Act on Collective Labour Agreements between Trade Unions and Employers.[13] Together with these acts there were decrees and recommendations from various Ministers of Labour concerning official holidays for workers; the registration of labour unions; the problem of mass workplace dismissals; Lebaran[14] payments; permission of absence

---

12 The International Commission of Jurists commented in 1979 that the Indonesian Labour Law is rather ambiguous, and in the case of the limitation on the right to strike has a real weakness in that governments resort to prohibition as a means to control worker unrest. Further, the ILO Committee of Experts in reference to Act No.21/1954 states the protection offered under the Act is extremely limited and does not satisfy the requirements of ILO Convention No.98 on the right to organise and to bargain collectively. (Thoolen, 1987: 125)

13 *UU Kecelakaan* (1947); *UU Kerja* (1948). Article 1 defined adults (male or female 18 years of age or older); youth (male or female over 14 years but under 18 years of age); children (male or female under 14 years). As well the daytime was defined as between 6am and 6pm, and night time the period between 6pm and 6 am. *UU Pengawasan Perburuhan* (1948); *Peraturan Kekuasaan Militer Pusat* (1951); *UU Darurat* (1951); *UU* (1954).

14 The *Lebaran* festival celebrates the end of the fasting month.

for elections; contracting out of work; overtime pay; and legislation on the execution of binding P4P (Central Disputes Committee - *Penjelesaian Perselisihan Perburuhan Pusat,* hereafter *P4P)* decisions.

The Accident Act provided employer liability compensation for injury, disablement, or death, for workers in undertakings defined as dangerous: amongst others this included a large range of industrial, farming, plantation, mining and forestry enterprises. Employees working in their own home, but not using a specified range of chemicals and gases known to be dangerous or injurious to health, were excluded from its provisions.[15] It is thus possible to see how many women (and men) small-scale, piece-work and contract wage earners could fall outside the compensation provisions. This is not to detract from the intention of the Republican Government to provide, under extremely difficult political and economic circumstances, the beginnings of a program for some form of social security. Quite clearly, in 1951 when the Act became law for the whole of Indonesia, similar economic difficulties were present. Nonetheless, workers needed and deserved protection against the contingencies of work-injury, and limitations such as the exceptions to payment mentioned above impacted unfairly, particularly on women. The ability of the employer to pay (as in the case of bankruptcy) is an inherent limitation in individual employer liability schemes and thus a cause of anxiety for employees (*International Labor Office Review,* 1960: 164). In the legislation the Government indicated its intention to establish a pooled fund to overcome such difficulties. As late as 1960, however, the International Labor Office reported that 'no information was available on the creation of the fund and payment by the Government had been reported in relatively few instances' (*International Labor Office Review,* 1960: 164).

The Articles in the Labour Act specifically concerned with women were as follows: **Article 7** (1) states women may not work in the evening except where work, because of its nature, place and condition, should be performed by women (for

15   Article 3, paragraph 2 did allow for other undertakings to be dedicated dangerous by law.

example, hospital work); (2) allows for exceptions to (1) in instances where the employment of women cannot be avoided in connection with the public interest or welfare; (3) exceptions allowed for in (2) to be determined by Government Regulation together with the conditions to guard the health and morality of women workers so excepted. **Article 8** (1) women may not work in mines, underground or other places where minerals and other materials are extracted from the earth: (2) provided for exceptions where women had to descend underground but do not perform manual work. **Article 9** (1) women may not perform work which is dangerous for their health and safety, or work which because of its nature, place, and condition presents a danger to their morality. The accompanying explanation (*Penjelasan*) stated that articles 7, 8, and 9 placed limits on the type of work which women could undertake because in the judgement of the Government women (were) physically weaker and (needed) to have their health and morality guarded. **Article 13** (1) women are not obliged to work on the first and second day of menstruation; (2) a rest of one and a half months before giving birth and one and a half months after confinement or miscarriage; (3) the rest time before giving birth can be extended to three months if a medical certificate states it is necessary in order to guard the woman's health; (4) during work-time women workers still breastfeeding to be given time to suckle their child. And a regulation (*Peraturan Pemerintah* 1951: Article 1, 4) determined that full pay should be given to the worker for the period of leave provided for in the Act.[16]

An analysis of the implications of legislation designed specifically for women workers, either to give benefits to women within their work, or prohibit them from performing certain tasks, or entering certain occupations, can be approached from two different perspectives. In the first it can be argued that women are 'better off' not performing night work, particularly under exploitative labour conditions. Since exclusion from night work allows women time for their domestic duties exclusion appears as an obvious benefit for women. A 'benefit' further

---

16   See *Peraturan Perburuhan dan Peraturan Administrasi Perburuhan* (1953), and *Labour Legislation Republic of Indonesia 1945–72* (1972).

validating the domestic role as belonging to women. The second way is to ask who does it benefit to prohibit women working at night particularly when exception clauses allow women to work in occupations, or at tasks, usually performed by women? The exclusionary clauses, in fact, followed a similar course to that taken in the colonial legislation and contained in International Labour Conventions and were, by their nature, 'negative proscriptive'[17] in that they were an institutional stricture which prevented women making an act of free choice about their own work.[18] Studies have shown that they are also a 'serious impediment to the employment of women in large-scale industries' (Boserup, 1986: 113) particularly where multiple shift work has been introduced.

Moreover, negative proscription with exceptions, that is, the permitting of night work for tasks which women would 'normally' undertake, such as nursing, suits established gender ideology about the sexual division of labour. Additionally, the exclusion of women in need from certain occupations in the waged formal sector forces them to seek alternative means of obtaining money, most generally in the informal sector: but also in prostitution where they are certainly in situations 'dangerous to their health and morality'. Since exception clauses also define times when women may be brought into the night workforce for other, specific, purposes, often in relation to seasonal work loads, women wage earners become a large reserve labour force for the state: limited through gender ideology to time and place of work but able, at the state's behest, to be used and expelled when necessary.

Apart from the danger to their morality, the legislation was concerned with the danger to women's health and safety. Rather than placing restrictions on the employment of women in particular occupations a better method would have been to 'lay

---

17   ILO Convention Nos.41 and 89 Night Work (Women) (Revised), 1934 and 1948. Leary, *International Labour*, pp.8,183.

18   The focus of this paper is on how and why certain limitations were placed on women's entry to work and their position within occupations. The question of whether women could, in reality, make a 'free choice' given the general dire national economic conditions is beyond the scope of this paper.

down conditions that would have rendered these occupations innocuous to them without limiting their opportunities of employment' (*International Labour Review*, 1954: 548). Often work not inherently dangerous was carried out under unhealthy conditions: this was particularly true where unskilled manual work was undertaken. Although this was a general problem for all workers it affected women specifically when certain factory work, which had become part of the sexual division of labour, was assigned to them (*International Labour Review*, 1954: 548). This limiting of women's employment opportunities for paid employment because of the 'dangerous nature' of work was compounded when other, possible areas of work had themselves been limited owing to the lack of educational and vocational training open to women.[19]

---

19   The lack of opportunity in these areas was in itself connected to gender ideology. Certainly it appears that the literacy campaign established by the Government in 1950 was successful in raising the literacy rate for all Indonesians. The 1930 census had shown a literacy rate of 7.4%—13.2% of males and 2.3% of females. (Widjojo Nitisastro, 1970: 85). By the 1961 census the overall rate was 47%—24% of females aged ten and over having had at least some formal schooling. (See Yulfita Raharjo and Valerie Hull, 1984: 101). By the end of the decade educational facilities at all levels had been increased. Vocational training centres catered for a wide range of occupations: metal, automotive, radio-electrical, building and also for a special category of 'home economics for women'. (See *United States Department of Labor Report* 246: 28). Note: Jean Taylor has directed my attention to a paper by H.M.J. Maier, 1993, 'From Heteroglossia to Polyglossia: The Creation of Malay and Dutch in the Indies', *Indonesia*, 56, October, pp.37–65. With regard to the 1930 Dutch census Maier sounds a strong note of caution 'that figures and numbers are dangerous and poly-interpretable...(and) a more careful exploration of terms like literacy and illiteracy...' and the numbers of those able to read Arabic and Javanese scripts, or receiving schooling in religious institutions needed to be included. 'The number of people who knew the Koran and were able to read it...or the number who can read Javanese or Batak or Bugis script for that matter...can not be found in the report...'. *ibid.*, pp.38–39. As contrast see a Ministry of Labour family living survey for Jakarta. In a sub-sample of family heads 72.29% were literate, that is; could read and write a language. *International Labor Office Report to the Government of Indonesia on Social Security*, 1958: 13).

The maternity benefit measures contained in the Labour Act were protective rather than negative proscriptive in nature. The intent for further protection was given in a 1952 Government Regulation which provided for support to bodies prepared to make arrangements for women workers' hostels/dormitories, workers' clinics, pregnancy clinics (either for workers or the wives of workers), child care, and kindergartens for workers' children.[20] In 1979, the International Commission of Jurists assessed the Indonesian maternity legislation as 'reasonably strong' (Thoolen, 1987: 133). Nonetheless, even in this area women experienced discrimination and validation of these benefits was not widespread.[21] Overall, their concentration at the lowest paid, unskilled, seasonal, industrial homework end of the labour market, where there was abundant labour oversupply, meant that women could be easily dismissed. Single and widowed female labour (still at the lowest wage scales) could replace them. Moreover, since a women worker had to pay a cost for confinement the full pay provision of the legislation somewhat lost its meaning. Despite knowing that cost was an extra impost on working women the Government wanted a three-sided arrangement of payment: government, employers and a contribution of as much as 1% from a woman's pay to establish the public clinics. This was in addition to the state wage tax. Overall, the financial cost imposed on the employer was carried by women workers (International Labour Review, 1954: 545).

Although negative proscriptive and protective legislation was enacted during the period, 'promotional' legislation,[22] such as

---

20   See *Peraturan Perburuhan dan Peraturan Administrasi Perburuhan.* This regulation also provided for support for the arrangement of holiday, sporting and other welfare measures designed to help workers generally.

21   *Pikiran Rakyat*, January 1953. In 1955 the *P4P* handed down a decision in favour of nine women kretek factory employees. Sometimes, as in this case, women were able to force employer compliance with the law but the process was long and difficult. (*TMP* 6, 1955: 17–18). As late as 1982 a Government handbook stated that: 'maternity leave provisions may be used as an excuse for not assigning important and responsible tasks to female employees'. (Department of Information, Republic of Indonesia, 1987:40).

22   Promotional legislation sets 'objectives of a more general character, such as equal remuneration for men and women workers, equality of

equal pay for equal work and minimum wage legislation was not. Whilst minimum-wage legislation helps all workers women, because of their position at the lowest paid end of the labour market, have more to gain: equal pay recognises their value as workers. A 1958 study of the *batik* industry in Central Java[23] typifies all of the difficulties under discussion for women wage earners.

Between 1950–55 the industry experienced a period of rapid growth and the number of enterprises increased by at least 100%. Enterprise size varied between those employing 21 or more printers and hand drawing (*tulis*) workers, to those employing 11–20, to those employing less than 11. The industry employed 43,000 full-time workers, half of them women; and 1 million part-time workers all of them women. In the full-time jobs men did the printing, blue-dyeing, brown-dyeing and finishing. The scraping, rewaxing and hand drawing of the cloth was done by women. The work was no easier than printing but because it was performed by women, and classified 'trained', not 'skilled', the wage rates were lower.

Cloth printers received between Rp.2.50 to Rp.4, with average daily earners of Rp.15. Blue dyeing, brown dyeing and finishing rates were slightly lower with average daily earnings of Rp.7.50 and Rp.10 respectively. The full-time workers received cash for meals and drinks, and medical services at the *batik* cooperative clinics. Not all of the scraping, rewaxing and hand drawing was undertaken at home. Under what was known as the

---

opportunity and treatment in employment and occupation and active employment policy' (Leary, 1982: 8).

23   The information in this section is drawn from Kertanegara (1958: 107–08). The report states that *batik* began as a handicraft when wives of the serving men of the king needed to earn money to supplement their husbands' meagre incomes. Although in other sources there is general agreement that batik was practised as a form of meditation in Java they differ as to those involved and the commercial genesis of the craft. Perhaps the last word should be left to the authorative voice of KRT Hardjonagoro who says... 'because in former times *batik* was a vehicle for meditation...truly realised beings in the social fabric of the Javanese community all made batik-from queens to commoners. And it is almost *inconceivable* (my emphasis) that in those days batik had any significant commercial objectives' (KRT Hardjonagoro, 1980: 229).

pengobeng system a group of workers 'practically lived within the plants', working day and night: they were all female and the managers were not obliged to feed them. For their work they received between Rp.0.75 and Rp.1.50 with an average daily wage of Rp.5. Conditions industry-wide were unsanitary, while the simple social allowances available were applicable only to full-time workers. In handicraft industries generally (which were large employers of women), industrial relations were underdeveloped. Collective agreements were, 'for all practical purposes, non-existent' (*International Labour Office Report*, 1958: 34). Where workers were united in a labour union for the most part it was outside the plant, and comprised the better educated, skilled male workers.

All of the factors connected with the general poor conditions of women wage earners were present in the study of the *batik* industry (Saptari, 1991: 127–50). For both full-time and part-time women workers the sexual division of labour ensured their concentration at the 'less skilled' end of the workforce. The lower rate paid for scraping and rewaxing-which was time consuming and skilled work-was compounded by the piece-rate payment system because, at the most, workers could only finish two pieces of cloth a day. The part-time nature of the work of the greater majority of the women left them outside legislative benefits (such as maternity benefits and accident insurance), and all were affected by the lack of such promotional measures as minimum wage legislation. The absence of minimum wage legislation affected both male and female workers, but female workers were already subject to a wage differential because of gender.

Further, while all workers were affected by the unsanitary plant conditions, the women under the *pengobeng* system suffered particularly. The proscription on women's night work was clearly not applicable under the *pengobeng* system because the work had been categorised as women's work, and their 'morality' was safeguarded by living in. But what of their health? This issue slipped by. In the *batik* industry women were pushed into the less protected, unorganised part of the labour force (Boomgaard, 1981: 16). In other industries where night work was undertaken, such as the sugar factories (permission was given at milling times because women were considered more 'patient and thorough' than men), and fibre factories (where selecting fibre required the same 'womanly expertise' of patience and thoroughness) (*TMP*, 1954: 13–14), exceptions to the proscription on night work simply confirmed these occupations as belonging to women. Work certainly, but work both defined and confined by ideas about gender.

Despite the many individual calls for better conditions and equal rights for women workers (Surjotjondro, 1948: 12–13), there was a failure on the part of the national leadership of organised labour and women's groups to push for the recognition of women as workers in their own right, in need of, and deserving, promotional help for economic independence. Only very rarely did a union put equal pay for equal work amongst its demands, and then, only at the branch level.[24] To the extent that issues such as creches, kindergartens and *asramas* (worker dormitories) were raised women workers were not forgotten. That these were critical issues for working women is indisputable, but they nevertheless reflected gender and class perceptions of the needs of Indonesian working women. Leadership was content to concentrate on protective measures that confirmed the centrality of the ibu/istri role for women workers.[25] The early calls for equality for women workers showed that the idea of the secondary role of work for women was not uniformly held. Indeed, some writers were certain that the new Indonesia meant a new role for women:

> the time is different to Kartini's…a radical change… women are now free to demand the direction of their lives… to achieve their own economic freedom. (The times) allow

---

24   In 1953 this demand was put forward, with others, by the Bandung branch of the *Serikat Buruh Tekstil* (*TMP* 9/10, 1953: 59). *Serikat Buruh Tekstil* Versus N.V. Wevery Yoeng Ngi di Djakarta. The P4P decision was in favour of the women.

25   Of 40 listed changes taken at union conferences, meetings and congresses in the first half of 1951 to do with pay rises, rest times, right to demonstrate etc., not one concerned women's wages (*TMP*, 1951: 50–51).

the possibility that women are now able to earn their livelihood the same as men (*TMP*, 1950: 29–30).

These views were themselves class-coloured perceptions. Work had never been secondary to the lives of Indonesian working-class women. Equality for them should have concerned fair wages and opportunity, not a denial of one and a limiting of the other.

Even when the union movement and some women's groups began to focus specifically on the poor conditions of women workers, and on principles such as equal pay the politics of gender and class were ever present. Unions were overtly political. In the early years of the union movement leaders were male, often from the intellectual class and usually unconnected with the industry they were representing. Most of the unions were connected with a federation of trade unions which was in turn affiliated to a political party. A spectrum between the communist party at one end and Islamic organisations at the other called forth different political and religious loyalties from workers. Similar class and ideological problems were present in national women's groups. At its 1952 conference, the women's federation, *Kowani*,[26] as part of its 'urgency program' resolved to investigate the wages of women civil servants and women workers. It also urged the arrangement of child care for women workers. At its eighth congress in Surabaya in 1955 there was a resolution for every field of work to be opened to women, and a call for vocational training so that the principle of equal pay could be implemented (Soewondo, 1967: 142–54). *Kowani's* role as an umbrella group, with its need to accommodate diverse views, limited its effectiveness. It was difficult to achieve consensus of support for measures, or consensus of opposition.[27]

---

26 *Kowani* was an umbrella organisation of many women's groups with different political and ideological loyalties. The name *Kowani* came from the merging of organisations in February 1946.

27 See the opposing views amongst members concerning Government Regulation No.19 (*Peraturan Pemerintah* 19) on the capacity of a civil servant to nominate more than one wife for his pension (Sukanti Suryochondoro, 1948:100).

The social origins of the leaders of *Gerwis*, the left-wing women's organisation were almost entirely middle class. In its early years of formation the organisation was more concerned with political action rather than any real attempt to organise women at the mass level. Still, between the first national congress in 1951 and the second in 1954, when the conference was urged to concentrate on discussing the concerns of women workers because the issues had been neglected in the past (*Harian Rakyat*, 1954), *Gerwis* achieved remarkable membership growth. Membership expanded because *Gerwis* began to change its character and start organisational work at the mass level: running kindergartens, anti-illiteracy campaigns, mutual assistance programs, and cadre courses. At the second conference the organisation changed its name to *Gerwani* 'to indicate the end of its sectarian character' (Hindley, 1966: 203–04).

The male-dominated leadership of the communist party and the party's labour federation, SOBSI (*Sentral Organisasi Buruh Seluruh Indonesia:* the Communist Party labour organisation), was much slower in turning its attention to the concerns and conditions of women workers. Not until 1956 did left-wing organised labour indicate through resolution its desire to support the principle of equal pay; to oppose discrimination in government offices, services etc.; to fight for the implementation of maternity provisions, and also its willingness to have women share in the work of the organisation. Before 1956 SOBSI had one lone woman member, this was increased to five. By 1957, there were 49 women cadres in the central and regional leadership committees of member unions (Hindley, 1966: 208–09).

Nonetheless, even where workplace organisation of women had been successful the numbers in leadership positions remained small. There were four women out of the 39 central membership council of the estate worker's union where the membership was 45% female; 9 out of 29 in the cigarette worker's union with a membership 65% female, and 3 out of 21 in the textile worker's union with a membership also 65% female (Hindley, 1966: 208–09). The greater determination on the part of the political left to place issues concerning women workers on to the political agenda did achieve some results with the ratification of the convention on equal pay. Ratification, however, is not sufficient without a belief in the fundamental principle of the convention (Ward, 1965: 13–99). By the early 1960s, the PKI *(Partai Kommunis Indonesia:* the Communist Party), SOBSI and *Gerwani* congresses were still pressing for real government commitment to the implementation of the protective legislative measures for women wage earners, and to the principle of equal pay (Njoto, 1959).

Conclusion

Notwithstanding a political atmosphere of an almost universal rejection of capitalism and espousal of the socialist ideal (Castles, 1965: 34), the 1950s were difficult times indeed for Indonesian labour.[28] That this was so '…can be understood largely in the light of the Indonesian class structure and its evolution' (Castles, 1965: 34). Women wage earners' double disadvantage was located within this structure of class relations, and within the gender ideologies that underlay that class structure. It is clear that legislation which, on the one hand, accepted the reality of women in the workforce, but on the other, sought to shape sexual difference to fit with historically and culturally constructed ideas of gender was a critical influence on women's position in the workforce.[29] Herein lies the conundrum. Even in more contemporary times industries which

---

28   An ad-hoc sampling of selected industry sub-groups in Java in 1956 (63 cotton textile undertakings with 4,377 male workers and 3,048 female workers) revealed 77.1% of the males and 94.4% of the females earning under RP.225 per month including allowances in kind, but not overtime or special bonuses. RP.275 per month was the 'just above starvation line' for Jakarta; Rp.220 to Rp.260 for other Java towns; RP.275 to Rp.330 for large towns in Sumatra. Wages were frequently higher in Sumatra and some of the Outer Islands, which were more sparsely populated, but were offset in many places by the higher cost-of-living. *ILO Report on Social Security*, p.21 and *ILO Report on Wage Policy and Industrial Relations*, p.16.

29   The Ministry of Labour journal is replete with examples of the tension between acknowledgment of the reality of women workers, and the 'ideal' of Indonesian womanhood. see for example the photo and caption in *TMP*, 1953: 3.

are large employers of women, such as the handicraft industries of *batik* or weaving; or factory tasks which women perform, such as selecting fibre, are not in themselves 'bad' for women. It is only when these occupations are labelled 'women's work' that they become so.

Legislation allowing women to work at night would have widened their job opportunities, but without, as I have argued, a fundamental belief in the principle of equality, uninfluenced by gender ideologies, would not by itself have improved women's working conditions. Legislation which comes imbued with these notions cannot deliver on workplace justice for women workers. Gender was a defining influence on women's position in the workforce. Because it was used to maintain differentials in wages and workplace conditions it was also a limiting factor on their opportunities for mobility within that workforce. In any analysis of the position of Indonesian women wage earners during the decade of the 1950s it is for the above reasons that it is crucial to take account of gender.

References

Boserup, Ester, 1986, *Women's Role in Economic Development*, Gower, USA.

Brown, Colin, 1981, 'Sukarno on the Role of Women in the Nationalist Movement', *RIMA*, 15(1).

Boomgaard, Peter, 1981, 'Female Labour and Population Growth on Nineteenth-Century Java', *RIMA*, 15(2), pp.1–31.

—— 1991, 'The Non-agricultural Side of an Agricultural Economy: Java, 1500–1900', in P. Alexander, P. Boomgaard, B. White (eds), *In the Shadow of Agriculture: Non-farm Activities in the Javanese Economy, Past and Present*, Royal Tropical Institute, Amsterdam.

Castles, Lance, 1965, 'Socialism and Private Business: The Latest Phase', *BIES*, 1.

Department of Information, 1987, Republic of Indonesia, *The Women of Indonesia*, Jakarta.

Douglas, Stephen, 1980, 'Women in Indonesian Politics: The Myth of Functional Interest', S. A. Chipp, J. J. Green (eds.), *Asian Women in Transition* Pennsylvannia State University.

Elson, D. and Pearson, R., 1981, 'The Subordination of Women and the Internationalisation of Factory Production', in K. Young, C. Wolkowitz and R. McCullagh (eds), *Women's Subordination in International Perspective,* CSE Books, London.

Hardjonagoro KRT, 1980, 'The Place of Batik in the History and Philosophy of Javanese Textiles: A Personal View', in Mattiebelle Gritlinger (ed.), *Indonesian Textiles,* Textile Museum, Washington DC.

Hawkins, Everett D., 1963, 'Indonesia', in Walter Galenson (ed.), *Labor in Developing Economies,* Institute of Industrial Relations, University of California Press.

Hindley, Donald, 1954, 'Conditions of Employment of Women Workers in Asia', *International Labor Review,* 70, July-December.

⸺ 1966, *The Communist Party of Indonesia 1951–1965,* University of California Press.

Ichtisar Isi Pers, 21–27 February, 1946.

International Labor Office Report to the Government of Indonesia on Wage Policy and Industrial Relations, 1958a, 7, Geneva.

⸺ 1958b, 10, Geneva.

International Labor Office Studies and Report: New Series, 1956, 'Problems of Wage Policy in Asian Countries', 43, Geneva.

International Labor Organisation: Monthly Labor Review, 1944, 'Labor Conditions in the Netherlands Indies', 58, May.

International Labor Review Reports and Inquiries, 1953, 'Women's Employment in Asian Countries', LXV111(3), September.

Kertanegara, 1958, 'The Batik Industry in Central Java', *Economi dan Keuangan Indonesia,* July.

Labour Legislation Republic of Indonesia (1945–1972), 1972, Erlangga, Djakarta.

Leary, Virginia A. 1982, *International Labour Conventions and National Law: The Effectiveness of Automatic Incorporation into National Legal Systems*, Martinus Nijhoff, The Hague.

Locher-Scholten, Elsbeth and Niehof, Anke, (eds.), 1987, *Indonesian Women in Focus: Past and Present Notions*, Foris Publications, Dordrecht.

Locher-Scholten, Elsbeth 1987, 'Female Labour in Twentieth Century Java: European Notions—Indonesian Practice', in Locher-Scholten and A. Niehof (eds.), *Indonesian Women in Focus*, Foris Publications, Dordrecht.

MacKinnon, Catherine A., 1989, *Towards a Feminist Theory of the State*, Harvard University Press.

Maier, H.M.J., 1993, 'From Heteroglossia to Polyglossia: The Creation of Malay and Dutch in the Indies', *Indonesia*, 56 October.

Manderson, Lenore, 1980, 'Rights and Responsibilities, Power and Privilege: Women's Roles in Contemporary Indonesia', in A. Thomson Zainu'ddin (ed), *Kartini Centenary: Indonesian Women Then and Now*, Centre of Southeast Asian Studies, Monash University.

Mempertahankan dan Memperluas Hak-Hak Kaum Buruh Dilapangan Politik, Ekonomi, Sosial dan Kebudajaan, Laporan Umum sentral Biro kepada Sidang Keempat Dewan Nasional SOBSI, 1959, disampaikan oleh Njono, Sekretaris Djenderal DN SOBSI.

Moir, Hazel, 1987, 'Female Access to Non-Primary Occupations in Indonesia', in L. Manderson, G. Pearson (eds.), *Class, Ideology and Women in Asian Societies*, Asian Research Service, Hong Kong.

Nitisastro, Widjojo, 1970, *Population Trends in Indonesia*, Cornell University Press, New York.

Njoto, 1959, *Pidato Pengantar Untuk Rentjang Perubahan Program PKI: Program PKI disahkan oleh Kongres Nasional ke-VI PKI*, Depagitprop CC PKI, Djakarta.

Peraturan Perburuhan dan Peraturan Administrasi Perburuhan, 1953, Diterbitkan oleh Kementerian Perburuhan R.I.

Peranan Buruh Wanita dalam Pembangunan: Dari Seminar Nasional Buruh Wanita, 1961, diselenggarakan oleh D.N. SOBSI. tanggal 11–14 Mei 1961 di Djakarta.

Raharjo Yulfita and Hull, Valerie, 1984, 'Employment Patterns of Educated Women in Indonesian Cities', in G.W. Jones (ed), *Women in the Urban and Industrial Workforce*, Development Studies Centre Monograph 33, ANU, Canberra.

Ratna Saptari, 1991, 'The Differentiation of a Rural Industrial Labour Force: Gender Segregation in East Java's Kretek Cigarette Industry, 1920–1990', in P. Alexander, P. Boomgaard, B. White (eds), *In the Shadow, of Agriculture: Non-farm Activities in the Javanese Economy, Past and Present*, Royal Tropical Institute, Amsterdam.

Sewell, William H., 1990, 'Review Essay', *History and Theory*, 29(1).

Shigeru Sato, 1994, *Java Under the Japanese Occupation 1942-1945*, ASAA Southeast Asia Publications Series with Allen and Unwin, Sydney.

Scott, Joan Wallach, 1988, *Gender and the Politics of History*, Columbia University Press, New York.

Soewondo Nani S.H., 1967, *Kedudukan Wanita dalam Hukum dan Masjarakat*, Timun Mas, Djakarta.

Sukanti Suryochondro, 1948, 'Wanita dan Kerdja', *Mimbar Indonesia*, 18, 1 May.

—— 1984, *Potret Pergerakan Wanita di Indonesia*, C.V. Rajawali, Jakarta.

Tedjasukmana Iskandar, 1958, *The Political Character of the Indonesian Trade Union Movement*, Cornell University Modern Indonesia Project, Monograph Series, Ithaca.

—— 1961, 'The Development of Labor Policy and Legislation in the Republic of Indonesia', PhD dissertation, Cornell University.

Thoolen, Hans (ed.), 1987, *Indonesia and the Rule of Law*, Frances Pinter, London.

Thompson, Virginia, 1947, *Labor Problems in Southeast Asia*, Yale University Press, New York.

Tindjauan Masalah Perburuhan, 4 August, 1950.

Trimurti Dra. S.K., 1980, *Hubungan Pergerakan Buruh Indonesia dengan Pergerakan Kemerdekaan Nasional,* Yayasan Idayu, Jakarta.

United States Department of Labor Bureau of Labor Statistics BLS Report 246, 1963.

Ward, Barbara (ed), 1965, 'Men, Women and Change: An Essay in Understanding Social Roles in South and South-East Asia', *Women in the New Asia,* UNESCO, Paris.

White, Benjamin, 1991, 'Economic Diversification and Agrarian Change in Rural Java, 1900–1990', in P. Alexander, P. Boomgaard, B. White, (eds.), *In the Shadow of Agriculture: Non-farm Activities in the Javanese Economy, Past and Present,* Royal Tropical Institute, Amsterdam.

Woodcroft-Lee, Carlien P., 1983, 'Separate but Equal: Indonesian Muslim Perceptions of the Role of Women', in L. Manderson (ed), *Women's Work and Women's Roles: Economics and Everday Life in Indonesia, Malaysia and Singapore,* ANU, Canberra.

Building the Future: The Life and Work of Kurnianingrat Ali Sastroamijoyo

Ailsa Thomson Zainu'ddin

On 19 December 1948, when the Dutch launched their second military action against the Republic of Indonesia by bombing Yogyakarta airport at 5.30a.m., George Kahin, the author of *Nationalism and Revolution in Indonesia*, was in Yogyakarta as a participant observer in the events which he later described.[1] Of the unannounced abrogation of the Renville Truce by the Dutch and their consequent capture of President Sukarno; Vice President Hatta, the Prime Minister; and half the Cabinet of the Indonesian Republic, he later wrote:

> Of great importance to the Dutch was the fact that they were able to knock out the Jogjakarta radio station before Soekarno, Hatta and Natsir were able to deliver the speeches of exhortation and guidance to the population that they had begun to prepare...The content of these speeches was not known to Indonesians outside the vicinity of the Jogjakarta area nor to the Good Offices Committee until almost mid-January, 1949, after an American secured copies of them from the Republican underground in Dutch-occupied Jogjakarta through the help of two courageous Indonesian girls, Jo Abdurrachman (Paramita Rahayu Abdurrachman, 1960: 184–85) and Jo Kurnianingrat.[2]

The unnamed American was Kahin himself and, as he makes clear in his eyewitness account, this Dutch offensive and the

---

1   (1952: vii–viii). He spent a year in Indonesia from mid-1948 to mid-1949 as a graduate student and also had press accreditation.
2   (1960: 338). He notes (p.337, n.15) that 'The Dutch attack was witnessed by the writer who was then in Jogjakarta'. He was there from 24 August to 19 December 1948. (p.251 n. 76)

subsequent Dutch occupation of Yogyakarta initially led to a severe food shortage in the city. Kahin noted that

> at the time the writer was in Jogjakarta and for some weeks thereafter the situation remained extremely critical. Considerable credit for meeting this situation must go to Indonesian women such as Mrs Suriadarma,[3] Dr Sulianti Suleiman, Miss Budiardjo and Miss Kurnianingrat who set up clandestine 'rice kitchens'. Here Indonesian civil servants who did not wish to collaborate with the Dutch, but who had no food in reserve, could obtain the minimum to keep themselves and their families alive (Kahin, 1952: 397).

Christine Dobbin, in 'no more than a random sampling' of the writings of three academics who had studied various aspects of the Indonesian nationalist movement, looked in vain for any consideration of the role of women (Zainu'ddin, 1980: 56–66). Through the above excerpts from someone who was actually there, we catch a glimpse of five individual women actively involved in the revolution. They have in common their membership of the Indonesian élite and they are representative of many, although by no means all, of the women who actively supported the Revolution.

*****

One of the five, Miss Kurnianingrat—known to her friends as 'Jo'[4]—is the subject of the biographical sketch which follows. It is based mainly on her reminiscences, 'Other Worlds in the Past', which she began writing in 1990 as a 'last story' for her grandchildren, Rini and Ruli, 'who used to ask for a story at any time of the day when they were little'. I have also drawn on

---

3   See p.177.
4   I have used 'Jo' (pronounced 'Yo'), the name and signature she used with members of the Volunteer Graduate Association, rather than her given name, 'Kurnianingrat'. She continued to spell it 'Jo' even after the change in Indonesian spelling, perhaps because it was initially Dutch-derived. As it is her story, I refer to friends and family members as she did when writing for her grandchildren.

correspondence in my possession,[5] on her article, 'The Role of the Indonesian Woman'[6] and on two taped interviews.[7] Having entrusted to me the typescript of that last story, Jo has posthumously become co-author of this one. Initially she intended to conclude her account in 1950 when Indonesian independence was recognised by other nations and the world familiar to her grandchildren came into being. I persuaded her to take the story further and she planned additional chapters with the general title, 'Building the Future',[8] to include the introduction of English as the first foreign language of the Republic. Only one more chapter was completed before her final illness.

In her memoirs we glimpse some of the other women mentioned by Kahin, as well as several others who are not. Jo spoke for them all when she stressed to her grandchildren that 'there are still many others who have their own stories to tell. You must remember that the revolution has been won not only by the leaders but by the Indonesian people as a whole'.

*****

When, after considerable hesitation, I agreed to write about Jo, it was in celebration of the friendship begun when we first met in August 1954 and continuing until Jo's death in October 1993. In August 1954 Betty Feith and I arrived in Jakarta as new members of the Australian Volunteer Graduate Scheme for

5   From 1954 to 1956 letters from Australian Volunteer Graduates for
      Indonesia to their families, friends and each other; from 1956 to 1993 I
      also draw on letters from Jo to Tommy (the name by which many friends,
      including my husband, address me); from 1979 to 1993 both sides of the
      correspondence are in my possession. Jo and I use 'Din', an
      abbreviation of his given (and only) name, Zainu'ddin, when referring to
      my husband.
6   Mss copy in possession of author.
7   Conversation/discussion with Tommy and Din, Cipinang Muara,
      3 February 1992; interview with Herb and Betty Feith at Cipinang
      Muara 12 June 1993.
8   I have used the title 'Building the Future' here as more appropriate to
      creating Indonesia. Quotations not otherwise acknowledged come from
      this typescript.

Indonesia pioneered by Herbert Feith, who was returning to the Ministry of Information. Betty and I joined the Ministry of Education, Instruction and Culture as members of the English Language Inspectorate (*Inspeksi Pengajaran Bahasa Inggeris:* IPBI), established in 1953. By 1951 English had officially replaced Dutch as Indonesia's first foreign language and the task of this inspectorate was to plan and set in motion the practical aspects of the transition. On our first morning we met our new colleagues and I wrote enthusiastically that:

> Our immediate superior is a most charming Indonesian woman, Jo Kurnianingrat, who looks most aristocratic and is indeed a member of the Sundanese aristocracy...She seems taller than the average Indonesian woman, probably in part due to her regal carriage and she has a dignified, even noble face. It comes hard to a democratic Australian, bred on mateship and 'educating down', to admit that there is perhaps something in the notion of aristocracy after all, particularly when her graciousness had no hint of condescension in it at all. She has been very helpful and considerate.

The head of the section was Mr Fritz Wachendorff, not that we learnt his first name until much later. He was an Eurasian who had chosen the Republican side and had taken Indonesian citizenship. I recorded my opinion that, for all his German name, he seemed a typical Central Sumatran. At that stage, even though I was unofficially engaged to a Minangkabau and had met several others in Canberra and Melbourne, I was hardly qualified to generalise so confidently. Herb was most impressed when first visiting him and wrote that, as 'one of the Indo-Europeans who has been accepted by Indonesians, he seems to be much freer from the duality of Indos than any other Indo I've met'. The third member of the professional staff was Mrs Nini Rudolph, whom Jo described as imaginative and full of initiative.[9] She had

---

9   Interview 3 February, 1992. (See also Belben, 1995: 71–73). Another of her initiatives was to suggest that Jo, when losing her sight, might write her memoirs and that I might 'do the prodding' to urge her on. Nini to Tommy 5 January, 1990.

studied as a Fulbright scholar at Barnard College and Columbia University Teacher Training College as well as completing the Ministry of Education B I course for English Language Teachers. I noted that our senior colleagues 'were very sympathetic, anxious to fit us smoothly into the running of the office and to give us something really useful to do'. Later Jo admitted that

> To be frank, we were very hesitant about taking in two foreigners without knowing much about them and, after your stay in Indonesia I'm sure you understand why: there is often so much misunderstanding between Indonesians and foreign 'experts' that foreign aid, which I'm convinced is offered with the best of intentions, can become quite a burden, especially when people have the bad taste of trying to impress upon us how valuable this aid is, whether in manpower or in money. It is often forgotten that we certainly cannot have fought for our independence to be dictated to again in building up the country (*Djembatan,* 1959: 15).

In 1980, at our request,[10] Jo wrote an article on Indonesian women which began with a comparison between her own upbringing and that of Kartini and her sisters 40 years earlier.

> In the 1920s the *kabupaten*[11] no longer confined girls within its walls; it was a centre from which youngsters went forth to pursue their studies. Many cousins of mine, boys as well as girls, came to live in the *kabupaten* and we grew up together as equals. Never were the girls made to feel that the boys were superior and the younger did not have to humble themselves before the older. ...Whereas Kartini craved for the opportunity to get Western schooling, we were

---

10   From Betty Feith and me, by then long back in Australia. It was for a series to be called 'Sisters International' which, for reasons beyond our control, failed to eventuate.

11   This was the residence of the *bupati* (Regent), the aristocratic head of a Regency and the highest indigenous administrative official in the Dutch-ruled areas of Java, but responsible to the European administration represented by a Dutch Resident (Sutherland, 1979). For Priangen *bupati* see pp.96–97

encouraged to learn as much as possible about Western culture.

Jo saw the *kabupaten* as 'a haven of peace and harmony, where I could blend into my own cultural background again'.

Early Childhood and Life in the *Kabupaten*

Jo was born on 4 September 1919 in Ciamis, which she describes as 'a friendly, prosperous little town', near the border between West and Central Java. Her father, R.A.A. Sastrawinata, a member of the *bupati* family of Krawang/Purwakarta, had been appointed *bupati* of Ciamis in 1916.[12] His wife, a daughter of the *bupati* of Rangkasbitung, came there as his *Raden Ayu*.[13] As they remained childless, they adopted a niece and nephew from Purwakarta. When the *raden ayu* became ill with dysentery she was taken to Garut for treatment, but even the best Dutch doctors could not cure her. While there she met and became very fond of a 15 year old girl, a teacher at a girls' school in Garut. Before her death, she asked her husband to marry this girl, the daughter of a well-do-do landowner from Gadog, a small village on the slope of one of the mountains near Garut. They had a quite spacious brick house, the only one in the area.[14]

A few months after his wife died, her father married the girl of his wife's choice whom he came to love deeply and they went to live in the Ciamis *kabupaten*, although 'the great social gap between aristocrat and non-aristocrat still remained as unbridgeable as did the gulf between the Dutch and their Indonesian subjects'. Therefore, as this wife was not of noble birth, she could not become his *Raden Ayu* although she did give him a daughter. When Jo was born, her father, delighted to have a child of his own at last, called her '*Kurnia*' meaning 'Gift'.[15]

---

12   Sutherland, (1973) indicates that 'in 1915, Ciamis was detached from Cirebon and became part of the Priangan' and that 'The ambiguous location of Krawang between the centers of Batavia, Cirebon and Priangan was reflected in the colonial authorities' vacillation over its identity' (1973: 127).
13   His official wife, which only a woman of aristocratic birth could become.
14   Later destroyed by Darul Islam *gerombolan* (guerrilla squads).
15   And added '*ningrat*' to indicate aristocratic descent.

Ten days later, he married, as his *Raden Ayu*, a widowed daughter of the *Pangeran* of Sumedang, whom the children called Ibu Gedong, Mother of the Big House. Jo and her mother moved first to a house near the *kabupaten* and later to a simple, comfortable house near the mosque. This was Jo's home and her base, although she was taken every day to spend a few hours at the *kabupaten* and often went with her father on his tours of inspection.

The people who influenced her most in those formative years were Ibu, her birth mother, 'warm hearted, emotional, full of humour and with a great capacity for endurance' (something which Jo only came to understand at a later age)—her father 'big-hearted, trying to do what was best for those for whom he was responsible and protecting us with his position, his name and his love' and Ibu Gedong, 'proud and wise...who treated me like her own child'. It was only later in life that Jo also realised that Ibu Gedong must have been a very good administrator to be able to make both ends meet with so many people under her care. It was only later too, when reading her father's diary, 'a factual summary of what happened to him' that she realised that 'his love for me shone through every dry statement and I know I must have hurt him often, being very selfish, while thinking of myself only as being rebellious'.[16]

When Jo was about three or four she was sent to the village school,[17] close enough to the *kabupaten*, she realised later, for the teachers to be anxious 'when the spoilt brat started crying' as 'it was easily heard in the *kabupaten* and they were afraid of the consequences'. Although never forced to visit, she was always welcome at the *kabupaten* and became increasingly absorbed in the life of her extended family there, with its army of servants; its spacious grounds; its various animals—horses to draw the *bendi*; cows to provide fresh milk; a goat and a small

---

16   Jo to Tommy 26 September 1987. 'Isn't it strange, only at a later age do we learn fully to appreciate our parents. Only much later do we realise their love'.

17   Unfortunately I did not check with her whether this was, as I assume, a vernacular language school, whether it was a government or a private school, whether it was an Islamic school. See Ailsa Zainu'ddin, (1970: 17–55) for an outline of educational provisions under the Dutch.

deer—the fruit trees, which were her father's hobby; the poultry; the fish. Ibu Gedong knew each fish by name. Of those early years Jo recalled that 'My home...with Ibu was my warm nest, in which I felt safe and secure but the *kabupaten* was where I learned how to cope with the outside world'. It was an entirely Sundanese aristocratic outside world while her mother's family provided links with the village, where she enjoyed occasional holidays.

Primary Schooldays

When Jo was four, her father decided to send her to Tasikmalaya, half an hour's drive from Ciamis, to stay with an Indo-European family to learn Dutch, a necessary prelude to a good education or a good job in colonial times. Initially, when she felt herself abandoned there by her parents, she was inconsolable, refusing for a whole day to eat or drink anything. Although treated as part of the family and, in age, fitting between the two daughters of her host family, she 'lived for the times when they drove me to Ciamis for an evening or when my father came to fetch me home'.[18] Later she wrote:

> Thinking of my father, I am reminded of a film I once saw about horses: A baby horse sought the protection of its mother but the mother...forced her child to stand alone and so learn to stand on its own feet.

By the time she was five, her Dutch was sufficient to enter the Dutch medium European Primary School in Tasikmalaya. Her village school year meant that she was promoted straight to second form.[19] Then, when she was seven, she was sent even further away to Bandung, which had better schools than Tasikmalaya. There she boarded, initially with 'a simple living, friendly, Indo-European family', the Hoedts, whose house was

---

18   The family had a car, which was a rarity of which the children were all very proud.

19   Her emphasis on the work covered in the year at the village school perhaps raises doubt about my generalisation about the education 'offered in the poorly staffed, poorly equipped village schools' (1970: 55) at least for a non-villager child.

close to the Girls' Primary School which she attended. Her father arranged with the *Bupati* of Bandung, R.A.A. Wiranatakusuma, for her to spend week ends at the *kabupaten*, which she found far more luxurious than theirs in Ciamis. After the *Bupati* of Bandung returned from Mecca (Soedarpo, 1994: 11), he had installed an Arabian room with a pond and fountain in the centre, thick carpets on the floor and low cushioned divans around the walls. His daughters always made a *sembah* when handing anything to an older person, something the girls in Ciamis never did and Jo felt no desire to emulate this.

Heather Sutherland has noted that 'the Priangan *Bupati* had succeeded in renewing the old *volkshoofd* contact between Regent and people' in the mid 20s and were 'still the focus of popular reverence'. When Sarikat Islam and Sarikat Rakyat 'began to mobilise popular hostility against the status quo, the Sundanese *Bupati* reacted strongly' (Sutherland, 1979: 96–97). Jo, drawing on the account in her father's diary, describes the increasing activity of Sarikat Rakyat around Ciamis and Banten from 1923 to its culmination in the riot of 1926, while she was at school in Bandung.

A mob of people entered the *kabupaten* from the front, molesting the guard. A shot was fired 'by a man who saw his own face in the mirror of the umbrella stand and, in his nervousness, mistook it for another person's face'. Then the people went to the *alun-alun* (city square) where they murdered the head of the Chinese. Her father's diary did not record his own role but 'as he told it to us' his first idea was to end the chaos so he went to the *alun-alun*, with the police commissioner and one guard, to face the mob. 'As if by a miracle, after three shots, I don't know fired by whom, the people withdrew and dispersed'. Next day the rioters were imprisoned. During their trial they were asked why they had not entered from behind the *kabupaten*, which had no rear wall to protect it. They replied that it was strongly guarded by soldiers although in actuality nobody at all had been there. It was believed in Ciamas that *onom*, 'spirits that can materialise' had protected the family. Certainly, 'if the people had entered from the back the whole family could have been massacred, as happened in other places'.

Her father did not see the rioters—who were deported to Digul—as his personal enemies and regularly visited their families during the period of exile. 'In the same way the exiles didn't seem to consider my father their personal enemy for when they returned, they brought small gifts from Digul' including a gaily coloured bird like a parrot which lived with the family until it reached a ripe old age.

Meanwhile in Bandung the Hoedt family moved, so Jo was found other more luxurious accommodation in a place with more boarders. The children boarding there were treated quite differently from the children of the family. Her brother, Dicky,[20] five years her junior, joined her when he was four and she was unhappy that she did not know how to protect him in this loveless atmosphere. Afterwards she wondered why she had not complained to her parents, who would certainly have moved them. Instead she stuck it out for five years, completing the seventh year of primary school. Although she liked the nuns and other teachers at the girls' school, she had no friends among her classmates. She wrote:

> We were friendly enough with each other and I don't think they looked down on me. They couldn't very well because I easily equalled them in class but they lived their own lives and I mine. There was just no contact.

So, with no friends at school and none at her accommodation, she spent her Sundays at the cinema and, watching silent movies, gradually became a film fan.

Back in Ciamis, when Jo's paternal grandmother visited them, she never

> tired of letting me demonstrate how the pupils of the Roman Catholic school I attended, first crossed themselves, then folded their hands, closed their eyes and said their prayers before class began. At the end of such a demonstration she used to chuckle, shake her head and mutter something like 'Those foreign fashions!'. Never did

---

20   He was given this nickname because he was such a chubby little baby—
     'dik' (Dutch) means 'fat'.

it enter her mind that those foreign fashions might change the grandchildren. She was so convinced that they were too firmly rooted in their own customs and ways to change much. That was my father's attitude too, so he had no qualms about sending me and my brother from home to live with foreigners at a very young age.

High School and Teacher Training

After seven years of primary schooling, it was decided that Jo would enter the three year High School run by the Ursuline Sisters. She returned to Bandung after the holidays the proud owner of a bicycle, a present from her father. She enjoyed lessons, especially foreign languages. Sound films had now been introduced and German films were popular, so they learnt German the easy way. When she was among a group of girls asked to entertain guests at an international conference at the Bandung *kabupaten*, she found she could easily converse in German.

High School was less lonely too as she made friends with other students. Of three special friends one was from Sumatra, one from Ambon and one Eurasian. Ida, her Sumatran friend, introduced her to tennis. Now, in her leisure time, she played tennis, making many new friends through the game. She also announced that she did not want to stay in their former boarding house. Although their next place also proved unsatisfactory, they then moved to the family of a retired planter, Mr Andrée Wiltens, whose wife encouraged Jo's study by giving her articles and books to read. She felt very much at home with the two daughters, one about her own age and one younger, yet, while there, she began 'to realise the great gap that existed between Indonesians and people of the ruling race'. Although the family treated them as friends, Jo noted that when friends of the daughters came to visit, they

> just did not acknowledge Dicky's and my existence. You could say Dicky was too young for them but I was their age and had a similar education to them. It did not hurt because then I had my own Indonesian friends, but it registered.

Dicky, she later realised, may perhaps have found this woman-dominated household less congenial than she did. He attended 'the so-called best primary school in Bandung'. When her father went to enrol him there, Jo recalled that the headmaster kept him 'sitting on a hard wooden bench on the gallery in front of the classrooms', the first time that she had ever seen her father treated discourteously by anyone. He refused to budge, waiting there for hours 'until it pleased the head master to see him' and to admit his son to the school.

After her three years of junior high school Jo decided to undertake vocational training, as by then her father had retired. He rented a villa in Bandung for Ibu Gedong, where Jo stayed during term. The cousins who had lived at the Ciamis *kabupaten* moved back to their respective parents in Purwakarta or out into the wider world. A new house was built in Purwakarta for Ibu. There Jo's sisters—Bibib,[21] 13 years her junior, 'a chubby little child...pampered by all' and Yettie, born two years later and 'received with as much joy and love as her elder sisters and brother before her'—were brought up because

> Father was not entirely satisfied with the result of the Western-oriented education he had given his two eldest children. He decided to give his two youngest ones quite a different education. They were to stay with Ibu and have an education like every other Indonesian child.[22]

Jo registered at the Indo-European Society's Teacher Training School (*I. E. V. Kweekschool*). There she learned with pleasure from teachers who were mostly very good. The psychology teacher, Sybesma, aroused her interest in a subject

21 As Indonesian terms of address are generational and as there was such a gap between the ages of her father's four children and his even older adopted children, many nieces and nephews older than she was, called her 'Bibik' (Aunty) which became her nickname.

22 As most other Indonesian children had very limited access even to vernacular primary schools one needs to add 'of comparable background'. The two younger sisters later studied Medicine and Dentistry respectively. They may possibly have attended Taman Siswa schools, which Jo herself did during some of her vacations. ('The Role of Women'.)

she later pursued further. Both her Indonesian and Indo-
European classmates were pleasant and, through them, she was
introduced to a party-going set of friends. For her dancing was a
sport which she enjoyed as she did tennis, noting that 'at that
time the girls danced in *kain* and *kebaya*'. She was not interested
in the flirtation which usually accompanied it. She also enjoyed
living in the quiet household of Ibu Gedong[23] even though it was
quite a distance to cycle to and from lessons. Looking back, she
saw her childhood as a time when the love of their parents gave
the children 'a feeling of security which came in good stead
when, in later years, life played havoc with us'.

After passing her initial teacher training course, Jo took the
Hoofdacte, a more advanced two-year course, and also taught
part time at a girls' school. Dicky was then at the five year High
School. The difference between their ages seemed to diminish
and they became very close, which did not stop them from
debating endlessly about all kinds of problems, neither one ever
giving in to the other. Perhaps this convinced her father that
'those foreign fashions' had indeed influenced his two elder
children.

'Schoolmarm'

Once Jo was well qualified to begin her teaching career, her
father took her to the Ministry of Education in Batavia. Her
first appointment was at the Dutch-Chinese Primary School in
Glodok. There, from 7.30 to 11, she taught third grade. Her
salary of f.100, was enough to cover her monthly needs. With
great trepidation she set off by tram to Glodok that first
morning, mentally rehearsing what she was about to teach. Her
headmaster told her later that, for the first three days, she had
been so nervous and anxious to do things well that she had not
touched the blackboard. Her more experienced colleagues all
seemed to her to handle their classes with ease. Again she met
people from different parts of Indonesia. An Latuassan, who
took the first grade, Jo remembered as an Ambonese with a
lovely voice. Loes Djajadiningrat, in charge of the second grade

---

23   It became livelier when father brought Bibib with him from Purwakarta
      to visit.

in the next room to Jo, 'seemed so sure of herself'. Mrs Tjindarbumi, who taught the fourth grade and 'seemed very popular with her class', was to become a good friend. A pleasant Chinese colleague, The, took the fifth class and Mr Dahlan Abdullah, 'an elderly Sumatran',[24] the sixth, while the headmaster, Mr Geleynse, took year seven. She admired all these much more experienced colleagues and 'felt so small and insignificant compared to all of them'. As for the pupils, she later confessed that

> I was not used to Chinese faces and, in the first weeks they all seemed alike; only after some time I managed to distinguish one from the other. Those poor little pupils must have had a terrible time with me.

From her Sumatran colleague, Mr Abdullah, she first learnt about the national movement for independence, in which he was strongly involved.[25] She then discovered that:

> So far my life had been so protected that I did not notice the injustices around me. I did not know that there were certain swimming pools with the notice: 'Dogs and natives not allowed entrance'.[26] I had no idea that it was difficult for Indonesians to be accepted at the European Primary School, which paved the way for future good schooling. I did not realise that for most Indonesian children it was made difficult to get a good education and I was oblivious of the fact that the masses were kept ignorant and poor.[27]

Through Ibu Gedong's daughter, Cheuk Patih, Jo was introduced into the household of the *Patih* of Weltevreden

---

24   Jo herself was only in her late teens or early 20s then, so 'elderly' could have meant anyone from about late thirties upwards.

25   In January, 1942 when Husni Thamrin, the famous nationalist leader, died of typhoid fever while under Dutch house arrest, Mr Abdullah was among those who suspected foul play (Satyawati Suleiman, 1979: 63).

26   See Mien Soedarpo, (1994: 25) for whom it was equally a rude awakening, although some of the town's notables in Fort de Kock (Bukittinggi) were exempted from the rule.

27   See footnote 22.

(Gambir), whose eldest daughter had married Ibu Gedong's only son. Another daughter, Cheuk Ijoh, was married to Kang Sanusi, one of Jo's favourite cousins, already a police officer in Batavia. She also became a very close friend of a cousin, Toos Prawira Adiningrat and, through Toos, learned to know her brother, Jusuf Prawira Adiningrat, who was then a law student in Batavia. In Bandung, Jo had been concerned because 'left and right I saw my friends fall in love, finding a partner' and wondered why she alone could not do so. At 21, she found that she could and did. Soon she and Jus were deeply in love, taking long evening walks together, quite oblivious to how they 'inconvenienced and shocked others' by always coming home late. Finally the *Patih* told her that he did not want to take any further responsibility for her and asked her to find another boarding house. She, in turn, was shocked to feel unwanted but, fortunately, could stay with her cousin, Kang Sanusi, by then assistant *wedana*[28] in Jatinegara, and his wife, the *Patih's* daughter.

Finding one's own partner by falling in love was a very Western concept. The traditional view of marriage saw it as 'not an affair between two people (but) an alliance between two families'. Jo wrote that ' with our new-fangled ideas we did it the western way'. Jus himself, at Jo's urging, asked her father for permission to marry her but 'later everything was done in the correct way. The *Bupati* and *Raden Ayu* of Cianjur, cousins of Jus, came to propose officially' on his behalf so they were then 'properly engaged' but, because in Jakarta she could not be properly chaperoned, her father wrote to the Ministry of Education to ask for her to be transferred to Purwakarta. She then received a letter, endorsed 'Transferred on request', appointing her to the European primary school in Purwakarta. When she told Mr Lukman Djajadiningrat, secretary of the Department of Education,[29] that this was not *her* request, he was most understanding. Although he did not rescind the transfer, he kept his promise to call her to Jakarta sometimes, providing the

---

28 The *wedana* was an indigenous official in charge of a district under the *bupati*.
29 Brother of the Patih of Weltevreden (Gambir) with whom she had first stayed in Batavia. (See Satyawati Suleiman, 1979: 62)

young couple with a few rare 'oases of privacy', something they valued greatly. In Purwakarta her own people were very happy to have an Indonesian teacher appointed to the European school where Jo taught many of her young nephews and nieces as well as her sister, Bibib. Jus came each weekend to Purwakarta, where he had relatives living and, while there, the young couple were heavily chaperoned by their many younger relatives.

Meanwhile war had started in Europe. The headmaster of the European school at Purwakarta left to join the Home Guard (*Landwacht*). Jo, as the most highly qualified staff member, was then in charge of the school. Neither the other teachers, mostly older Eurasians, nor the Dutch Assistant Resident liked this but, in any case, the Dutch parents soon began leaving, especially after the Japanese bombing of Pearl Harbour on 7 December 1941, when the threat of a Japanese invasion became more real. Some Dutch people left for Australia, others unable to do so faced internment under the Japanese. Soon the school closed and her father, along with many other families, decided to evacuate with Ibu Gedong, Ibu and the children to the country.

Jo's Dutch education had equipped her for a vocation in the Netherlands Indies world in which she had reached adulthood. Her engagement foreshadowed a marriage of the kind envisaged by Kartini, in which a couple who had already met as friends chose each other as future partners (Coté, 1995: 46–47). Despite the Japanese occupation they, like many of their contemporaries (Soedarpo, 1994: 49, 51), were planning married life together once Jus completed his legal studies. They had already

> arranged that, when the Japanese came, he would join me in Purwakarta and, as he would then be in possession of an emergency diploma, he could get a job and we would ask to be married.

So when the family evacuated, Jo, with one male servant, waited in her mother's house for Jus. After some time, when he did not come, she 'decided, though with a heavy heart, to join the others in the country'. Antagonism between Chinese and Indonesians had flared up again as an added problem. In March

1942, the Japanese occupied Purwakarta and the surrounding areas but still there was no sign of Jus. After some time, Jo could no longer bear waiting. She told her father that she wanted to return to Purwakarta to make enquiries. Accompanied by the same servant, despite his mortal fear of the Japanese,[30] she walked to Purwakarta. At the *kabupaten* the *bupati* and his wife welcomed her and made enquiries about Jus.

It was soon found out that Jus had safely arrived at his brother-in-law's house in Barangdan and, from there, had set out to Purwakarta on foot. He had been intercepted by some village people who took him for a Chinese. Whatever he said or did to convince them that he was a Sundanese and a Muslim, they refused to believe him and killed him.

Recalling this terrible time she wrote that

> I shall never forget how nice people were in their efforts to console me...I felt very responsible for Jus's death to his family but they were very nice to me and, till this day, I am still considered one of the family.

Her cousin, Kang Sadeli, assistant *wedana* in Cianjur, came to fetch her, taking her on foot through the woods to avoid the Japanese. 'It was peaceful and quiet where we walked on moss covered soil and heard a solitary bird singing now and then.' They crossed a big river and arrived in Cianjur where 'Kang Sadeli and his wife, Cheuk Ida, did everything to divert me but, after some time, I went home with the same heavy heart.'

The Japanese Occupation

For many Indonesians the Japanese occupation was the fulfilment of an ancient prophecy by Joyoboyo, king of Kediri, that 'a yellow race of short people would come and reign over Java for as long as the maize plant lives'. Once they departed, said the prophecy, Indonesia would be independent (*merdeka*) and justice would then reign. A modern translation into Javanese by a late 19th century poet had drawn people's attention to it

---

30   Something which she always remembered with gratitude.

again so the arrival of the Japanese in 1942 seemed to fulfil the first stage of the prophecy.

> Now the life span of a maize plant is about three and a half months and most people took the prediction literally. A friend of mine even planted a maize plant in front of his window on the day the Japanese invaded Java. Unfortunately, a few weeks later, a goat nibbled at the young plant and that was the end of the experiment.

The Japanese stayed three and a half years, so Jo saw the phrase as a poetic expression implying a short time. It convinced many Javanese that the occupation would be temporary and would lead to independence. This gave hope to many while under Japanese rule. Jo wrote of that period:

> Three and a half years is a relatively short time but it was a devastating period. I am not thinking of the cruelty of the crash troops because crash troops, no matter what nationality, seem to be cruel everywhere, but their *Kempeitai*, a kind of Japanese Politbureau, was notorious for its cruelty. The wealth of Indonesia was scooped up and used for Japanese war purposes, leaving the people poor and hungry. The Dutch and the Indo-European men and women were put in separate camps and often the men were transported to other countries to do forced labour. This happened to a lot of Indonesians too. When they did come home they were emaciated and not capable of much.

Yet she also recognised that, in spite of these great hardships, some good things did come out of this time. For one thing the suffering strengthened both Indonesian nationalism and the desire to be free from all foreign domination; for another the Japanese-trained troops became the nucleus of the future Indonesian independence army. The Japanese also established hundreds of primary schools, extending formal education to many more people than in colonial times and using Indonesian as the medium of instruction. Also 'the aristocracy no longer had any special privileges but were poor and hungry like all the others. The feudal society ceased to exist'.

The pension her father had received as a retired *bupati* ceased, leaving him without income. Jo recalled that '(t)his was the time when we had to live from the sales of anything we had. Tablecloths and bed sheets were cut up for underwear; curtains for dresses. Yet many people came to stay with us, some for a short time, others more permanently'. Jo herself, after several months unemployed, decided to look for a job in Jakarta, staying again with Kang Sanusi and Cheuk Iyoh. She was fortunate in meeting her former colleague, Mr Dahlan Abdullah 'who had become an important person because he had always opposed the Dutch government'.[31] He offered her a job at the Municipal Office, initially weighing and doling out sugar but later she was employed to translate from Dutch into English. She suspected that, as her experience was confined to school English, her translations 'must have been rather poor' but they satisfied her superiors. Also through Dahlan Abdullah, Kang Sanusi obtained a better and bigger house. This and his small salary were both shared generously and more people came to stay there, including Dicky, by then at the first Indonesian High School under Mr Adam Bachtiar.

Jo's own salary was very small. She recalls the time when Dicky needed a new pair of shoes and they went in and out of shop after shop all along Pasar Baru without finding a single pair she could afford. When she heard that a Girls' Teacher Training School (SGP) in Yogyakarta needed a psychology teacher, she applied at the Japanese Ministry of Education. She recalls that

> The Indonesian official who received me, told me that this was *not* the time to walk about with one's chin in the air; you had to bow a lot, especially women. (What he perceived as) my haughty demeanour must have irritated him. I was really sorry, for I did not mean to be haughty and did not feel superior at all.

---

31   Abeyasekere (1987: 136) refers to an Indonesian, H. Baginda Dahlan Abdullah, who was head of the municipal administration for some months before a Japanese filled the position of mayor. (Cf. Mien Soedarpo, 1994: 45)

He may also have been reacting to her name, as *'ningrat'* indicated her family status. Then, because 'the Japanese official in charge of the applications was an elderly, fatherly man who did not stand on formality', she took it at face value when 'he told me that if there were any difficulties at school I could always report to him and count on his help'. Her new colleagues in Yogya, when she told them this, initially suspected her of being a spy for the Japanese. She had unwittingly given the wrong impression as she moved into a new world.

For her Yogyakarta was completely unknown. Her father, who had visited there, arranged for Sumarsono, his late friend's son, a boy whom Jo knew from his Jakarta schooldays, to meet her at the station, where her train was due at midnight, and take her to his younger sister, Mustinah, a student at the first Indonesian High School in Yogya. Next morning, barely recovered from her long journey, Jo was summoned to undergo scrutiny from Mustinah's mother, an aunt of Hamengku Buwono IX, Sultan of Yogyakarta and saw, sitting on the wooden couch, 'a thin, wiry woman with sharp features, cross-legged and bolt upright. She asked me all kinds of questions about my family and then she left'. Jo must have passed muster as she was soon treated like a close relative.

Her appointment was to a secondary boarding school providing post primary teacher training for girls. As she went to report there she found that

> All along the road young men were stationed at regular intervals to urge the passers-by not to speak a foreign language but to use *Bahasa Indonesia*. That was very necessary for people like me, who spoke Dutch all the time.
>
> The directress, Ibu Sri Umiyati, had the nightmarish task of being responsible for hundreds of girls in their teens, including the ultimate responsibility of seeing that they had sufficient food.
>
> Once in a while the girls had to learn cooking special dishes from material that we had never used before in our diet; for instance, they were taught to cook snails (*bekicot*) that were becoming a plague in the gardens. These cooking lessons took place in the homes of Japanese men. It was on

these occasions that the girls had to be guarded with extra care and several teachers always accompanied them.

Jo was provided with a big house next to Ibu Sri Umiyati. Sumarsono obtained furniture for it from Dutch people forced to leave Yogyakarta. Her parents sent a cousin to look after the house and, on one occasion, even undertook the long train journey to Yogya to see how she lived. Meanwhile she faced a special difficulty in her teaching. Although she knew hardly any Indonesian, it was the language of instruction in which she had to teach Psychology.

> Fortunately one of my colleagues, Ibu Nurseha, translated everything that I wanted to say into Indonesian and I learnt it by heart. I was always in mortal fear that the students would ask me questions but it seemed a good way to master Indonesian. After some time things became easier and I even learnt to answer questions unprepared.[32]

As Japanese currency declined in value, she could no longer live on her teaching salary. By bartering kain batik[33] and selling her jewellery she kept her enlarged household going. It now included several high school students—one was her fiancé's youngest brother, another the son of her step-brother; then later, 'to my great joy, Bibib was entrusted to me' and enrolled at a good junior high school.

As hardships under the cruel Japanese regime continued, rebellions occurred in West Java at Singaparna near Taskimalaya and in Indramayu in 1944. Then in mid-February 1945, at Blitar in East Java the PETA[34] forces rebelled.[35] Dicky was by then

---

32   For many of the students Indonesian would have been their second or third language so they may have been as uneasy about asking questions as she felt about answering any.

33   She could barter a batik kain (length of cloth worn as a skirt) for 100 kg of rice.

34   Pembela Tanah Air (Protectors of the Homeland) founded October 1943. (Ricklefs, 1981: 192

35   Benda, (1958) refers to the Singaparna rising in February 1944 and the rising in June 1944 at Kaplongan village near Indramayu on pp.160–63

enrolled at the Medical School set up by the Japanese in Jakarta.
He told Jo that the students had risked Japanese retribution by
refusing to have their heads shaved. Several leaders were expelled
for this.[36]

During a vacation when all the family members were in
Purwakarta, they heard about the fall of the Japanese Empire.
There too Jo also 'heard something that shook me awake. All
that time I was stunned by Jus's death. Then I heard about the
kidnapping of Bung Karno and Bung Hatta to Rangasdengklok by
a group of young people' who urged their leaders to proclaim
independence before the arrival of the Allied Forces. Back in
Yogya she witnessed the end of Japanese rule and the attempts
of young people 'armed with bamboo spears (*bambu runcing*)
with or without the help of PETA 'trying to obtain arms from
the Japanese before the Allied Forces arrived. Then, we heard
about the Proclamation of Independence by Bung Karno and
Bung Hatta on 17 August 1945.'

The Early Years of the Republic

The proclamation of Independence signed by Bung Karno and
Bung Hatta, was read to a very limited audience outside Bung
Karno's residence in Jakarta.[37] Although the broadcasting station
was still controlled by the Japanese and heavily guarded, some
young Indonesians who worked at the station broadcast the
Proclamation several times. They were beaten and imprisoned
by the Japanese but then the Japanese retreated and the young
men were freed. News of the Proclamation did not reach Yogya
for a few days. Radios were sealed during the Japanese occupation
and listening to overseas broadcasts was a capital offence. Even
so quite a few young people manipulated their radios to pick up

---

and p.268 n. 46. For the Blitar rebellion see p.182, p.270, n. 62 and
p.283 n.44–45

36   Mien Soedarpo, (1994: 48–49). Her future husband, Soedarpo, was
among those expelled. Later he was press attaché to the United Nations
delegation of which Sujatmoko, who had also been expelled, was a
member (p.85)

37   It was then known as *Gedung Merdeka* (Independence Building). was
later called *Gedung Proklamasi* (Proclamation Building) and is now
known as *Gedung Pola*.

the Australian Broadcasting Commission[38] or Voice of America and it was mostly from the former that news of the Proclamation of Independence reached many parts of Indonesia. Jo noted that

> In Yogyakarta spirits were high too. People felt the need to voice their support of the Republic, Bung Karno and Bung Hatta, and often gathered in Malioboro, Yogya's main street, to do so. We yelled 'Merdeka!' (independence, freedom) when we met, we shouted 'Merdeka!' when we parted; we called 'Merdeka!' before starting a speech. 'Merdeka!' became our national greeting.

She recalled that although 'the schools were not exactly closed' the students and teachers were 'more intent upon following the political developments than upon regular lessons'. They used their limited English to produce hundreds of brightly painted posters which they pasted on trains arriving in Yogya. These read 'Long live our Republic', 'Never more under foreign domination' or, by contrast, 'Free, free, like a bird in a tree'. Resistance to the Allied Forces, which arrived in September 1945, convinced the English that the Dutch-Republican dispute should be solved by negotiation.

Not long after that, to ensure the safety of its members, the Republican government moved to Yogyakarta.[39] 'The people in Yogyakarta were wild with enthusiasm and Sultan Hamengku Buwono IX, who was a staunch supporter of the Republic, prepared everything'. The residence of the former Dutch governor of Yogya became Bung Karno's Presidential Palace.

> We were very proud when we saw our 'Red and White' hoisted in front of the building and were elated when we

---

38 News had reached Australia via an Arabic-language broadcast from Bukittinggi Radio in West Sumatra early on 18 August. Molly Bondan, *Spanning a Revolution: the story of Mohamad Bondan and the Indonesian Nationalist Movement*, Pustaka Sinar Harapan, Jakarta 1992, p.202

39 There is an account of this journey in Ali Sastroamijoyo, 1979: 119–20.

heard the official band playing the national songs, most of which were still in the making.

Soon Yogya was full of new arrivals, including members of various government departments; the top command of the Armed Forces; State visitors; American, English and Indian journalists. Jo's household was extended to include a sister of her fiancé and her army officer husband.

> All kinds of things started happening. Japanese money was replaced by Republican money; we had a broadcasting station for overseas, the Voice of Free Indonesia; the first Indonesian University, Gaja Mada, was opened, temporarily located in a front part of the *Kraton* (the Sultan's residence). Many teachers were eager to study again and many of us enrolled at the new university. For some time we managed to attend the lectures but soon most of us had to quit, because our teaching took up too much of our time.

Jo was moved to the Senior High School to teach English.[40] Utami Suriadarma, her fellow teacher, was the wife of Indonesia's first Air Commander, 'a very beautiful woman, always elegantly dressed' and idolised by many people yet 'very earthy too' with a hearty appetite.

Not many people spoke English in Yogya at that time so 'those who did were recruited to entertain foreign guests and visitors'. Thus Jo and Tami attended many state dinners at the presidential palace together and became close friends. KOWANI[41] gave Tami the task of contacting the outside world to inform them about the situation in the Republic. She wrote the articles and Jo read them on Voice of Free Indonesia. Jo recalled that

> (w)hat I remember of this time...was the general atmosphere of real friendship. We were all equals—only

---

40   One third year student, Achmad Jayusman, became her brother-in-law.

41   *Kongres Wanita Indonesia* National Women's Congress, established in 1945 to organise first aid posts, refugee services, food and clothing supplies.

some got more important tasks to perform than others but we appreciated each other. Nobody, no matter how high in rank, felt superior.

The High School organisation, GASEMA,[42] previously a sporting, cultural and social union, grew into a combatant organisation, later officially accepted as the 17th brigade of the Indonesian National Army (TNI) and known as the Students' Army.

> At this time the Central and East Javanese youth thought the West Javanese young people very inactive. So they sent them a mirror and face powder to challenge their fighting spirit. Maybe the West Java youth was slow at the outset but, in the course of the revolution, they too showed their mettle.

Meanwhile the Allies were anxious to complete their first task, freeing the prisoners in Japanese camps. A combination of Allied troops and the International Red Cross were to escort them to certain harbours for evacuation to Holland but the Indonesian Republic did not want Allied troops in the interior. Mrs Maria Ulfah, Minister of Social Affairs, offered the Republic's assistance in bringing the ex-prisoners safely to the appointed harbours. The offer was accepted and its accomplishment demonstrated to the outside world that 'the Republic was capable of acquitting itself of its responsibilities.' Many Chinese, who did not feel safe, left Yogya with the ex-prisoners for the port of Semarang. Those Chinese shops on Malioboro which therefore closed were occupied by the young people, declaring in their enthusiasm 'that from then on Malioboro would be only for indigenous shopkeepers' but later, when the Chinese returned, they were allowed to occupy their shops again.
Still more people came to live in Yogya including Jo Abdurrachman, then a leading figure in the Indonesian Red Cross (Vreede de Stuers, 1960: 184–85; Soedarpo, 1994: 36; Suleiman,

---

42   *Gabungan Sekolah Menengah Mataram* Union of Mataram (Central Java) High Schools

1979: 61). Dicky, whose Medical School had been closed when the Japanese surrendered, enrolled at the Military Academy in Yogya. 'Bibib and I were very happy to have him in Yogya, but he did not feel very happy at the Academy.' When Dicky and Bibib visited Purwakarta in school holidays—by then she was at Senior High School—the first military attack by the Dutch, on 21 July 1947, made return to Yogya impossible.

Even more refugees arrived in Yogya after the Dutch attack. Titi Sukonto,[43] on holiday, could not return to Jakarta so stayed in Yogya. Tambu, a Singalese from Singapore who published *The Indonesian Times*, arrived after being banned from Jakarta for reporting the true situation in the Republic. He was engaged to Titi's younger sister, Cing, his assistant on the newspaper, and she arrived in Yogya shortly after he did. They all became good friends and, looking back, Jo recalled: 'at that time nobody felt poor in spite of the many deprivations. We were all in the same boat and shared whatever we had with each other'.

An Englishman, Mr Ratcliffe, whom Jo thought may have been from British Intelligence, was in Yogya when an Indian plane, carrying an International Red Cross representative and medicines from Singapore, was shot down by the Dutch. Ratcliffe wrote a plea to the outside world on behalf of the Republic which Jo read over the Voice of Free Indonesia. As a result medicine was sent from everywhere and the foreign press quoted her as 'the head of the Indonesian Red Cross' although, as she was anxious to emphasise, she 'was only a means to get the appeal across'.

State dinners continued although Jo, reduced to two *kabaya*, was obliged to keep appearing in the same clothes. She continued attending 'in the hope that I would help dispel the image of Indonesians being ignorant half savages.' On one occasion she and Cing had the opportunity of going to Jakarta by plane. There, after the lack of good detergents in Yogya, she was impressed by 'the white towels and the clean clothes of the people' and enjoyed the films. 'In Yogya we had one cinema and for months it had shown the same film, *Gone With the Wind*.'

---

43   A niece of Ali Sastroamijoyo. In 1990 she helped Jo to prepare and type her reminiscences.

When she found it difficult to return to Yogya she felt very
unhappy, although able to stay with Kang Sadeli and Cheuk Ida.
He 'had joined the Dutch Police Force and was very well-off. So
we were in opposite camps but it did not alter our sisterly and
brotherly relationship.' Purwakarta was in Dutch occupied
territory so, afraid that she would not be able to return to Yogya
at all, she did not go home.

> I heard that Father, who was then practically the head of
> the Purwakarta family and a very influential person, was
> sought out by the Dutch. He received his pension back-dated
> to 1942; so he was very well off. I could not help being glad
> for him; he had suffered enough in his old age.

Dicky and Bibib, still in Purwakarta, were convinced
supporters of the Republic so when Dicky and a friend hoisted
the Red and White there one day they were thrown into prison.
Father went to the Assistant Resident declaring 'No child of
mine shall be in prison' and the two were set free, though Jo
doubted whether Dicky liked that outcome.

She and Jo Abdurrachman finally managed to get a lift in the
jeep of an International Red Cross officer. It gave her 'an eerie
feeling to drive through deserted areas; not a single person was to
be seen in no man's land' in one of the most densely populated
parts of the globe. They arrived safely to find that many more
people were now arriving in Yogya as the Three Nations
Committee (KTN), established by the Security Council came to
arbitrate between the Republic and the Dutch,[44] Among them
was Adik Budiardjo, later Mrs Simatupang, who came from
Jakarta to join the secretariat for these discussions. Jo
remembered that

> (t)he womenfolk of Yogya could not take their eyes off
> her modern 'new look' dresses, which came right down to
> her ankles. in Yogya, where there were no fashions, we still
> wore our dresses very short, barely covering the knees.

---

44   The delegate from Australia was the choice of the Republic, the delegate
     from Belgium the Dutch choice and they jointly chose the third member,
     from the United States of America (Kahin, 1952: 217ff; Reid, 1974: 114).

The discussions were continued on the deck of the American ship 'The Renville' and Jo, 'flabbergasted but elated', was chosen as one of the secretaries for these negotiations.

Although she felt capable of helping with translation work she had never done secretarial work and could barely type. Cing was also 'one of the happy few to go to 'The Renville' as a secretary'. They were flown to Jakarta where the secretariat was housed in a pavilion of the Hotel des Indes[45] and they shared a room there. She recalled that

> (t)he waiters and servants of the hotel were very nice to the people from Yogya, though they were not dressed with the chic of the other guests at the hotel. We always got first class service from them and, when there was a pork dish during the meals, they always warned us.

Most of their translation work was done at the pavilion and they went in shifts to 'The Renville' by motorboat, which 'was very enjoyable, especially at night time'.

After the Renville agreement the Dutch began establishing puppet states to form a Federal State of Indonesia on which they would confer independence, hoping to exclude the Republic from the federation. Meanwhile Jo and Cing returned to Yogya and she recalled that

> (i)t was about this time that we learned to know George Kahin. At that time he was a young academic, doing research on nationalism and the Indonesian revolution. He needed people to translate the material he collected and so we learned to know him well.

On 19 December 1948, Jo, at whose house the previous night there had been a party ending 'late by Yogya standards', was woken at half past six by violent explosions as the Dutch launched their second military attack on the Republic by bombarding the airport. Dressing quickly she found Jo Abdurrachman and, after much persuasion, obtained a Red Cross band so that she could check on the safety of her friends. George

---

45   Perhaps one might call it the Raffles Hotel of pre-war Batavia (Jakarta).

Kahin had been taken to Jakarta by the Dutch. She discovered that his housemate, Hamid, was a political prisoner in Wirogunan prison along with many other friends. The captured Republican leaders were imprisoned either in Prapat on Lake Toba in Sumatra or on the island of Bangka and, as planned in advance, an emergency government was established in Central Sumatra under Syarifuddin Prawiranegara (Sastroamijoyo, 1979: 170–88).

In Yogya NICA money[46] replaced Republican money. Many people were unemployed and, in such confused times, looting took place nearly everywhere. Many wives and children were on their own as husbands were imprisoned or joined the Republican forces. Jo wrote:

> Schools were closed at that time; the Dutch tried to run a school but very few Indonesians wanted to make use of Dutch facilities. Most of the boys and, this time, more girls than before, had gone to the front. For those who stayed Mr Prijono and the senior high school teachers organised a regular timetable for every year of Senior High School; students had to go from one house to another, and sometimes had to cover quite a distance. But they came regularly.

Once one of her former students threatened to tell the Dutch about their clandestine school. She pointed out that, if he did, 'he stood in as much danger from his friends as they did from the Dutch and that it was better to leave everybody free to choose'. She never saw him again.

When not teaching Jo did administrative work at the Indonesian Red Cross, including the compilation of casualty lists, which were reported daily. One day George Kahin, who had been allowed to return to Yoga, visited the Red Cross office, escorted there by NICA soldiers, to obtain the latest casualty lists.[47] 'Some friends, who thought this a good opportunity to tell the

---

46 Netherlands Indies Civil Administration. See Reid, 1974: 43, 51 and for NICA money p.126

47 Although a graduate student, as he also had press accreditation he was entitled to see these lists.

outside world what was happening inside the Republic, had put some more information among the lists, unnoticed by Dutch soldiers'. It took nerves of steel to hand the lists to George without a flicker of recognition passing between them.

Jo's house was also a depot from which parcels were forwarded to the guerrilla troops. Once her house was searched by NICA soldiers but 'as if by a miracle they overlooked the cupboards where I had put the parcels.' Another time she was sorting things for the troops when an Ambonese NICA soldier entered her front room. 'He stayed for hours; fortunately only to vent his great love for Jo Abdurrachman, who had been imprisoned by the Dutch' and, fortunately too, he failed to notice the telltale goods spread all over her bedroom floor.

Meanwhile world opinion had turned against the Dutch in favour of the Republic whose leaders made a triumphant return from imprisonment (Sastroamijoyo, 1979: 197–200). Then schools were reopened and life became more normal.

Australian Experiences

In his capacity as Minister of Education for the Republic,[48] Pak Ali Sastroamijoyo had met Jo several times and knew of her capabilities. One day she was offered a scholarship[49] by the Australian Office of Education entitling her to one year's study in Sydney in subjects of her choice. To her this scholarship seemed a miracle, although she did, in discussion, accept that possibly the experience she had already had in English may have had some relevance.[50] She chose to study 'the Australian educational system in practice to see what we could learn from

---

48   When he became a member of the delegation to the Round Table Conference, Pak Ali relinquished his position as Minister of Education and Culture and was replaced by Sarmidi Mangunsarkoro on 4 August 1949 (Sastroamijoyo, 1979: 200).

49   Although she describes this as a Colombo Plan scholarship, the Colombo Plan itself was not established until 1951 and Indonesia did not become a member until 1953. Her scholarship must have been part of the 'modest amount of emergency and technical assistance to Indonesia and other Asian countries in the immediate post war era' (Varma, 1974: 195, 188)

50   Interview 3 February, 1992.

other systems in other countries' and also took a few courses in psychology, because she liked the subject. With evenhandedness the Australian government had also awarded one scholarship to Amisah Bekti from the Dutch sponsored United States of Indonesia and they were placed at the same accommodation. Jo found Amisah 'a very likeable person and in spite of the fact that we were candidates from opposite camps, we had many acquaintances in common.'

In preparation for her departure Jo went to Purwakarta to see her parents.[51] She had to choose her wardrobe carefully so that, with very few *kebaya*, *kain* and *selendang*, she could vary the combinations to give quite a different impression.[52] She was helped by Ibu Sri, aunt of Cing and Titi,[53] who 'was known for her good taste'. On 17 November 1949, farewelled by Father, Ibu and many other relatives and friends Jo eagerly left Kemayoran airport for Australia on her first journey abroad.[54]

In Sydney she was met and taken to the Office of Education to meet

> Mr Morrison and Mr Phillips, who were to look after me, and the two secretaries, Ruby Dyer and Bette Gray, who were to become close friends of mine. I had my first 'morning tea', to be followed a few hours later with 'afternoon tea' and I learned that people had an hour off for lunch.

Later she received a telegram of welcome from the Indonesian *chargé d'affaires*, Pak Usman Sastroamijoyo, younger brother of Ibu Sri and Pak Ali Sastroamijoyo. She had known Usman from tennis days in Bandung.

---

51   Ibu Gedong had died in 1947 as the aftermath of a bad fall.
52   *Kebaya* the fitted blouse worn over the *kain*, a length of *batik* cloth worn pleated at the front, with the *selendang*, a long scarf, over one shoulder
53   She added 'whom I was later to see more as Pak Ali's elder sister', the great aunt of the two young people for whom she was writing her memoir.
54   Although she often thought of visiting Australia again she was the only IPBI member not to do so. Wachendorff came in 1957 and Nini in 1987.

So far my impressions had been very pleasant; the only disappointing thing was that there were no windows in my room to let the sunshine through. I always had to switch on the electric light. I had seen so many advertisements— 'Come to Sunny Australia'—that I was very surprised to be walled in like that.

She was also surprised by the pace of life in Sydney, commenting that

I was so used to the leisurely pace of Yogyakarta that I had the impression that the people of Sydney were all running. 'Where are they running to, and why?' I thought.

Yet the underlying pressure of life in Yogya under siege had taken its toll. After meeting the head of Sydney's psychology department, Professor O'Neill, and purchasing the books she would need for the course

I eagerly opened the books and started to read but, to my horror, nothing really registered. I understood the words but nothing made sense. I understood that it was because of the tense time in Yogya, with all its emotion and stresses, that I could not think properly. I tried not to panic and kept reading a little every day. And one day it was as if something clicked in my brain and I could digest everything normally.

She first boarded with a pleasant elderly woman whose alcoholic daughter and eight year old grandson were staying with her, causing Jo to reflect that she 'had never thought much about the problem of alcoholism but I soon realised that it was a problem in Australia.' Another problem was her discovery that 'small, black insects were hopping around in the bed' and had also infested her clothes. When she told her friends at the Office of Education about these they were identified as fleas and she was moved to bed and breakfast accommodation run by 'an elderly woman with a hoard of lapdogs which followed her everywhere. When you came too near their idol, they bit you in the leg, as I was to experience one day.' She found that she 'did not care very much for the food they served in restaurants; all the restaurants smelled invariably of lamb. At that time there was no good coffee to be had in Sydney' so she resorted to drinking tea. Home cooking she found delicious, introduced to it through a good friend, Bernice Julius, who also took her to visit the Australian countryside where she met her first leech and, with trepidation, rode a horse; to an agricultural show and for a trip along the coast.

She visited many schools in Sydney as well as the country, including a rural migrant hostel where the teachers were 'young people who seemed to enjoy their work and (seemed) self-sufficient, capable and humane.' The Australian schools she did not find very different from Dutch schools in Indonesia but was struck with the number of single sex schools and noted that this 'segregation between the sexes seemed to continue in adult life. ...I wondered whether the two sexes were really so different that they had to live as if in two worlds.'

When, accompanied by Mr Morrison, she visited the Boy Scouts headquarters with a message for them from the Indonesian scout movement, she was puzzled by the response of the Scout leader who accepted her message.

> The man got red in the face; he hummed and hawed, stuttered and stammered. I thought his behaviour most peculiar. On our way back to the office I asked Mr Morrison why the man had behaved so strangely. Mr Morrison laughed and said the man had not expected to see such a sophisticated woman from Indonesia. I was far from sophisticated and felt even less so but, compared to the poor man's image of the Indonesian savage, I must have looked sophisticated.

A visit to a Girl Guides' camp was more enjoyable and afterwards one of the girls invited Jo to visit her home, warning her that 'they were poor because her father was a simple labourer'. Jo commented that 'their house was simple and small but quite comfortable. They had a refrigerator and the children each had their own bicycle. According to Indonesian standards they were very well-off'.

Other gatherings were less friendly. She was invited to the United Nations anniversary, where she was the only Asian present. When Indonesia was discussed

> the speaker eyed me accusingly and asked why Indonesia had to resort to arms and could not settle things through arbitration...and I failed to convince them that we were forced to take up arms. None of the younger people came up to talk to me; I was rather left alone. This was really unlike the spirit of a United Nations as I imagined it. Only some said, while passing me, that I should not take everything so much to heart.
>
> Nor was she particularly impressed on the occasion when, buying a return ticket to Canberra and asked her name, the response to 'Kurnianingrat' was 'Don't you have another name? Mary, or Elsa, or Topsy?' I was annoyed with the man but I couldn't help laughing at his impudence.

On the whole people were friendly and hospitable so that her overall impression of Australia was positive.

The scholarship provided opportunities for travel. In Canberra she visited Pak Usman, who presented her with 'a tennis racquet for old times sake'. She found an atmosphere of formality there which was totally lacking in Sydney. She also visited Melbourne—where she was shown around a frosty, wintry city by some Indonesian students—and Tasmania. There a long trip had been organised for her to visit rural schools, which she found were centres of activity in rather isolated areas and she also saw her first snow. What she most enjoyed during her year in Australia was 'the safe feeling that you could go out unescorted at any time of the day and night'. Reflecting on the whole experience she found

> It had been a happy year for me, coming straight from the revolution. I remember vividly how, one day, when I was sitting at the station waiting for a train, I felt a deep joy and peace within my heart, for no apparent reason. Never again in my later life did I experience the same feeling. I shall always remember the scholarship with gratitude

because it gave me the opportunity to learn to appreciate
Indonesia's nearest neighbours.

Indonesia's First Foreign Language

Jo returned to Indonesia in late December 1950. Most of her
Yogya friends had moved to Jakarta with the central
government and she was offered a room by one of them.[55] She
was warmly welcomed at the Ministry of Education and 'every
inspectorate there wanted me. I don't know why. Maybe at that
time I was young and full of enthusiasm. First they didn't know
what to do with me and I was sent to several places to give talks
about my experiences in Australia'.[56]

Her father was 'rather annoyed that I did not get a job at
once; he did not think much of my travelling and giving talks'.

Then she was appointed head of a Teacher Training School
(SGA) in Jakarta 'based on the same principles as the teacher
training schools during the Dutch colonial period' with a Dutch
director and mainly Dutch teachers. Her job was to 'take over
and make it a Republican institution', rather a heavy
responsibility to be placed on the shoulders of someone so much
younger than her staff but at least her father had the satisfaction
of knowing she had a proper job.[57] Later she reflected that

> as an Indonesian who took over from the Dutch it was
> easy to be popular with the students. The Ministry of
> Education was always ready to help me and I knew many
> influential people in the Ministry personally from my Yogya
> days. I should have been able to make something of the
> school,

but she felt that she did not achieve this, commenting that 'If
I were to be appointed again I would do it quite differently'.[58]
Therefore when, in 1953, she heard that an Inspectorate for the

---

55   Cing's sister, Titi, whose husband was Samsudin.
56   Interview 3 February, 1992
57   On 21 June 1951, when over 80, he died after suffering a stroke 'and was
      buried on the same day in Purwakata where the heads of our family have
      a special burial place'.
58   Interview 3 February, 1992

teaching of English (IPBI) was to be set up under Mr Wachendorff, whom she had met in his capacity as head of a Senior Secondary School, she applied and was accepted. She had initially got to know the third member of the Inspectorate, Nini Rudoph, through Nini's husband, Chris, head of a Junior Secondary School when she returned from Australia, because he was very interested in some of the material she had brought back with her on role playing for teaching spoken English.

Accommodation was at a premium in Jakarta in the 50s but the three sisters were fortunate to obtain the front half of a house.

> Bibib looked after the accounts, Yetty's responsibility was to make the home cosy and I had to see to it that we had sufficient money to keep the household going. Strangely enough at that time a teacher earned enough to live on. We could afford to go to the cinema regularly...from time to time we could treat ourselves to a meal in a restaurant, we could buy magazines and books, and we could keep ourselves dressed to our liking. The Indonesian currency was stable. From time to time we bartered newspapers for a chicken but it was a golden age compared with the Japanese occupation period.

Jo described IPBI as 'a small but active inspectorate', which it certainly was during its brief existence from 1953–56 and told me later that she was 'very eager to welcome (the Volunteer Graduates) because I had had such a nice time there (in Australia)'.[59] Mr Wachendorff had a coherent and well thought out program based on a thorough study of the problems involved in the teaching of English. While Indonesian continued to replace both Dutch and regional languages as the medium of instruction in schools from primary to tertiary level, he emphasised that

> English is not and will not ever be a social language in the Indonesian community. Neither is it nor will it be the second official language in the administration of this

---

59   Interview 3 February, 1992

country. These negatives lead us to the exact position of English in Indonesia. It is no more and no less than the 'first foreign language'.[60]

The secondary schools should therefore be equipping the pupils 'with a "working knowledge" of English and not just with a smattering of the language plus a lot of useless theory about it'.

One of the first programs of IPBI was setting up a syllabus for secondary schools which would emphasise a practical knowledge of the language. Here IPBI had the help of two British Council members—Professor Hill, who also taught English at the Faculty of Arts (*Fakultas Sastra*) at the University of Indonesia (UI), and Mr Bailey[61]—and Bryce van Syoc, leader of the Ford Foundation teaching group.[62] They met at least once a week, working out the details of the syllabus and, when Betty Feith and I arrived, we were peripherally involved in this activity. I wrote in April 1955 that I had been 'semi-co-opted to this committee because they have entrusted me with the task of writing the reading exercises' using only 'vocabulary and grammatical structures already familiar to the pupils...a sort of jigsaw element about wresting my stories from the material available' which I quite enjoyed. Occasionally too, as the 'many fascinating discussions on the use of the English language' took place they

---

60   'Pendjelasan Ketua Konperensi tentang tudjuan Peladjaran Bahasa Inggeris di Indonesia'. Konperensi Pemimpin2 B.I.: Bah Inggeris, Djakarta 8–11 Pebruari 1955. (Clarification by the Conference Chair (Mr Wachendorff) concerning the direction of English language teaching in Indonesia. Conference of Heads of B I English language courses, Jakarta 8–11 February 1955) p.1 Typescript in my possession.

61   Hill I perceived as 'a brisk and frightfully English (and rather supercilious) professor, who is nice but nubbly' and Bailey as 'a jolly old bachelor, with a rather pontifical style of address and a fund of ponderously funny anecdotes'. (Bulletin New Series (B. N/S-i.e. circular letters from Tommy to family and friends, the new series of which began after 10/12/54) No. 10. 14/2/1955

62   About a dozen young enthusiastic people to help with the teaching of English. They were salaried by the Foundation while the Indonesian government was required to provide comfortable accommodation for them, including appropriate buildings for the classes. Both 'comfortable' and 'appropriate' were defined by American rather than Indonesian standards which to us seemed a waste of.resources.

would refer to us regarding Australian usage. I found the English language typing of syllabus material, especially drills, less enjoyable but reflected that 'at least it is a good preliminary canter among my jigsaw pieces before I start to fit them together'. Betty concentrated on the library and the distribution of English language books, ordered through the British Council and distributed by IPBI to the schools which had ordered them.[63]

Another IPBI activity in which we were soon involved was the conference for the heads of the English B I courses, two year courses established in 1950, which trained teachers in individual syllabus subjects to qualify them for teaching that subject at secondary school level. IPBI gradually took over the management of the courses, though not without some friction with the *Inspeksi Kursus-Kursus* (Inspectorate of Courses). These courses were still mostly conducted by Dutch teachers and, under the terms of the agreement Indonesia was forced to make with the Netherlands, these teachers were guaranteed employment until their contracts expired. Nini already had an BI diploma for English but Jo had to sit for a BI examination before taking part in running the courses.

In February 1955 at the *Gedung Merdeka*[64] IPBI held a four-day conference to introduce the new syllabus to the heads of the BI courses but, as most of those who attended were almost at the end of their contracts, I noted that IPBI 'wasn't very hopeful that much would be achieved in the way of conversion'. Still a great deal of preparation went into 'stencil upon stencil' of syllabus outlines, book lists, outlines of demonstration lessons and a book display, the latter arranged by Betty.

> It was provided in the Rules of Order that, if requested, English could be used as the working language of the conference ...because some of the Dutch teachers who had been in the country for over twenty years, still couldn't speak a word of Indonesian!

---

63   B. N/S No. 15. 25/3/1955
64   Site of the proclamation of independence (see footnote 37), a symbolic place to hold such a conference. By 1955 it was a conference centre with several conference rooms and a large courtyard-hall.

The overwhelming majority voted for English. The IPBI heads were so sure of this outcome that they had asked me to be official note taker to the secretary, Jo, which would not have been possible had it been Indonesian.

> We all dressed carefully for the occasion. All the women had their best dresses—I'd worn my blue linen suit in an attempt to look the part of the efficient secretary—and Nini wore *kain* and *kebaya* (she usually wears Western dress to the office) and was receiving a certain amount of teasing. Poor Mr Wachendorff was sadly clutching a coat in case, as indeed happened, his superiors from the Ministry should be wearing coats. And, true to type (the Chief Inspector could be transplanted to the Victorian Education Department without the wilting of a single leaf!) they came in coats and ties.

The conference was not deliberative but consultative and I reported that 'not everybody was as hostile to the new syllabus as we had originally feared'. For Betty and me the conference marked the point at which we really felt ourselves fully accepted as part of the IPBI team, involved in 'the sharing of hopes and fears and the general team work'.

A month later I described our colleagues and office in more detail for friends back home.

> When you enter the Inner Office you pass through a female guard of honour—two Indonesians on the left and two Australians on the right. Jo…wears the traditional *kain* and *kebaya* and always with exquisite taste. Her long black hair is fastened in a large bun at the nape of the neck. She has a poise and dignity which make her seem much taller than she really is…She is seldom moved to anger but she can be very Crushing when necessary.
>
> With her is Nini, or Mrs Rudolph, a slight, merry Javanese, with thick wavy hair worn clipped back from her face but long enough to be worn traditional style when she wears *kain* and *kebaya*. For office wear she has the most amazing array of blouses and skirts, which make me green

with envy. Many of them she acquired when she was in the States.[65]

All I said of Mr Wachendorff, in the centre of this guard of honour, was that we were still a bit in awe of him as 'for one thing he is the only one who continues to address us formally... intimidating for Australians', although I concluded by writing:

> The English Language Inspectorate is under the guidance of a man with very definite ideas as to how English should be taught and why. English is the first foreign language here and people are anxious to learn it but he wants to produce quality rather than mere quantity and he wants the language to be of use to Indonesians. Sometimes he gets depressed, as well he may, that he has to spend so much time on administrative details...but here one really feels that great things are being done, plans are being laid for even greater things and the education of a new nation is being guided by a team of people, not the least of whose qualities is their ability to incorporate two Australians into their team so smoothly and harmoniously that we feel we've been part of it all our lives and would like to be part of it all the rest of our lives. Are we happy in our work? Too right![66]

Our only problem was that quite often Jo, Nini and Wachendorff would unwittingly switch into Dutch, thus unintentionally excluding us from the discussion. Years later, when I said 'I think we missed a lot of what was going on because we didn't speak Dutch...I can distinctly remember one occasion when Wachendorff said, "We were talking about that yesterday and we had to say 'Ya, but you were talking in Dutch'", Jo was quite contrite.

'Oh my goodness!' she exclaimed, 'I didn't realise that! I thought you really knew everything, that we involved you in everything!'

---

65   B. N/S No. 15
66   B. N/S No. 15

I suggested, 'We probably didn't have enough background for some of it', but she replied: 'No, I think we just plainly forgot that you couldn't follow us in Dutch'.[67]

Our next conference was the Standard Training Working Conference held at Puncak in April 1955 for the Ford Foundation teachers. As we were driven up there to prepare for the opening, we saw many of the official delegations returning from the first Asian-African Conference in Bandung which had just concluded.[68] Ours was a residential conference. Jo, recalling it, asked

> Do you remember they wanted the conference in Bali, in fact? The government didn't have enough money and decided to have it in Puncak and there were a few among them who agitated about it. I took the trouble to get angry with them. I couldn't understand—they wanted to go to Bali but it wasn't possible.[69]

Jo also commented to me on

> that great difference between the American graduates and the Volunteer Graduates. You were paid too little like Indonesians and the Americans had all kinds of facilities... And their holidays also had to be paid. I remember that. Everything went to the benefit of those graduates in fact.[70]

---

67   Interview 3 February 1992
68   Herb Feith was busy writing an information book for the Conference, while Din and I, with Jo and Nini, combined to provide a translation of *Indonesia Raya* for the benefit of the Asia-Africa Conference delegates. B. N/S No. 19, 16/4/1955. We also met Professor and Mrs Burton and Professor Fitzgerald, the observers from Australia, in Jakarta after the Conference.
69   Interview 3 February, 1992 This was hardly surprising considering that the Bandung Conference had just involved so much expense (Sastroamijoyo, 1979: 286–87).
70   Interview 3 February, 1992. In writing about the coming conference I noted the 'quite fabulous salaries (approx. £A75 a week!)' of many foreign experts and commented that 'even when they want to identify themselves with their fellow workers, their wealth becomes a barrier'. B.N/S No. 20, 23/4/55. In preparing for the conference I was asked to translate the songs which were sung on the final night, published later

There were then two Standard Training Courses for English language teachers, one at Yogya with 55 students and the other at Bukittinggi with 25, staffed partly by the Ford Foundation linguisticians 'with the usual fabulous foreign expert salary' and partly by Indonesians, who would ultimately replace the foreigners.[71] I was quite tart in writing home about the conference. 'Undoubtedly these people are doing a very good job. (Apart from anything else they have told us so themselves!)' I added equally tartly that

> What we can't understand is why these 'linguisticians', with their infallible technique, don't apply themselves rather more rapidly to the study of Indonesian...some of them are learning but they don't seem so markedly superior to us. (Our) few months start should be nothing in comparison with their superior technique.[72]

After typing up the 35 pages of Conference notes I realised that 'at least everybody now knows what everybody else has been doing'. I also noted that the Yogya centre was relatively well equipped and had a teaching staff of seven and administrative staff of eleven while IPBI, responsible for all English teaching programs in Indonesia, had a technical staff of five and an administrative staff of five. Still we returned from Puncak to find we had a new, larger and better appointed office where 'there are new worlds for Jo's interior decorating genius to conquer'.[73]

The next IPBI project was the *Kursus Persiapan Mengajar Guru² B I Bahasa Inggeris* (Course of Training for Teachers of

---

as *Lagu lagu Indonesia/Songs of Indonesia*, Heinemann Australia, 1969.

71   Later there were others opened in Makassar (Ujung Pandang), Semarang, Padang and elsewhere which involved a lot of travelling for IPBI members who had to ensure that the teachers 'had comfortable accommodation and were introduced properly to the local government'.

72   B. N/S No. 21, 27/4/55 This was my first experience of so large a group of young Americans whom I found 'friendly but lacking in sensitivity' while acknowledging that it was perhaps easier to see their blunders than to recognise our own.

73   B. N/S No. 22, 13/5/1955

B I English) a full time, intensive course for ten students, each with a B I certificate and at least ten years teaching experience. The majority of students lived in at a new printing school, whose second year accommodation was not yet in use. Betty and Herb also lived on the premises and Jo was the non-resident principal. She and Mr Wachendorff taught the theory and the practice of language teaching respectively. Betty was responsible for conversation and reading. I gave the first half of the lectures on modern literature and Ann Macdonald, a more recently arrived Volunteer Graduate at IBPI, gave the second half.

Betty wrote in April 1956 to tell me that the *Kursus Persiapan* had closed the previous day, Herb added the news that she had chaired the closing session in Indonesian 'which evoked a lengthy eulogy of the PPK (Ministry of Education) Australians'. She reported that the students had left joyfully while the Boss (Mr Wachendorff) said gloomily 'It was a wonderful experience; but can IPBI do it again?'[74] The opportunity did not arise. Jo recorded that

> Nini was the first one to leave because she had to look after her first baby. Not long after that Tommy, her husband and her first daughter returned to Australia and Betty and Herb Feith followed soon after. Mr Wachendorff decided to accept a teaching post at the Faculty of Letters at U.I. and so I was left to hold the fort but, in September 1956, I left to study English Literature and Linguistics at Cornell University on a Ford Foundation Scholarship.

*****

This is where Jo ended her reminiscences. She returned to Indonesia after enjoying two years of study and independent life in America and joined Mr Wachendorff at the Faculty of Letters. In 1961 she became head of the English Language Department, not an easy task.[75] She was also, with Molly

---

74   Bett to Tommy 5 April, 1956. We had returned to Australia in March 1956.

75   Nini to Tommy 27 June, 1961 'quite an honour for her, but I think she deserves it for I think nobody works as hard as she does for the English

Bondan, Ali Alatas and others, writing *Indonesia 20 Tahun Merdeka* (Twenty Years of Independence) which, although almost completed, 'has never been published because of the changed political situation after 1965'.[76] In 1970 she and Pak Ali Sastroamijoyo, widowed former Prime Minister and Nationalist Party leader, married. She wrote that 'I never planned to give up my life as I had shaped it, but you see that things always turn out quite different from what we expect',[77] as was also true when, five years later, he died. Then she wrote, 'Now that I belong to the older generation I'm expected to pay more attention to all family events and affairs'. Although persuaded to write her memoirs, after failing eyesight made reading impossible and her English language classes increasingly difficult, she insisted that she was 'just an ordinary woman with no outstanding achievements at all', entrusting the manuscript to me only on condition that I kept that clearly in mind. When Jo wrote to me, that she had 'learned to appreciate Kartini much more through your writings. Do you see the irony of it?' I replied that there was much of Jo Kurnianingrat in my image of Kartini.[78] She was as surprised by this as I was by her modest self estimate.

Nini, when writing to tell us of Jo's death, said

> During the first *tahlian* (prayers for the dead on the day that she passed away) and on the day of the funeral I realised that she had been a special person for so many, many people. Some ex-students had taken the night-express from Yogya to be at her funeral and these people were only a few years younger than Jo! Then I also knew, Herb, that no one

Language Department. I'm sorry for Mr Wachendorff for he was the other candidate. His health was an important factor'.

76 Jo, 'Memories of Molly' (Bondan) Typescript in possession of writer.

77 Jo to Tommy 4 February, 1970

78 Jo to Tommy 14 December, 1987; Tommy to Jo 26 December, 1987. I am strongly convinced, as I conclude this article that, whatever motives Abendanon may have had in publishing Kartini's letters, Rosa Abendanon-Mandri, when re-reading the letters to translate them into Spanish, would again have communed with the Kartini she had known as if she were still alive (Abendanon, 1976: xxvii).

would be able to finish the book she was writing, there were too many facets of her life for one person to write about.[79]

In a letter she wrote to me in 1988, shortly after the death of Pak Ali's eldest son, Jo told me that she had a strange dream about me before his death.

> We met, and we sat together and we had a conversation without words, but I fully understood you and felt very close to you. In the end you confessed to the same thoughts and feelings I had, and wondered about it. I was surprised that you wondered about it because to me everything seemed quite natural.[80]

This article has been for me a continuation of that conversation without words. While still wondering about it I can only hope that our joint authorship would also have seemed quite natural to her. She was one of many 'ordinary women' living in extraordinary times and building the future independent Republic of Indonesia which their grandchildren have inherited.

References

Abendanon, J. H. 1976, (ed.), *Door Duisternis tot Licht: Gedachten over en voor het Javaanse Volk* (Through Darkness to Light: Thoughts about and for the Javanese people), Gé Nabrink & Zn, Amsterdam.

Abeyasekere, Susan, 1987, *Jakarta A History*, Oxford University Press, Melbourne.

Belben, Gillian, 1995, 'Harumani Rudolph-Sudirdjo: "Learning and Teaching through Changing Times"', *Network*, 2(1), July.

Benda, Harry J., 1958, *The Crescent and the Rising Sun*, Van Hoeve, The Hague.

Bondan, Molly, 1992, *Spanning a Revolution: The Story of Mohamad Bondan and the Indonesian Nationalist Movement*, Pustaka Sinar Harapan, Jakarta.

---

79   Nini to Tommy/Din, Betty/Herb and Ann 7 November, 1993
80   Jo to Tommy 16 October, 1988

Coté, Joost (trans.) 1992, *Letters from Kartini: An Indonesian Feminist, 1900–1904*, Monash Asia Institute in association with Hyland House, Melbourne.

—— (trans.) 1995, *On Feminism and Nationalism: Kartini's Letters to Stella Zeehandelaar 1899–1903*, Monash Asia Institute, Melbourne.

Dobbin, Christine, 1980, 'The Search for Women in Indonesian History', in A. Thomson Zainu'ddin (ed.), *Kartini Centenary, Indonesian Women then and now*, Annual Indonesia Lecture Series no. 15, CSEAS, Monash University, Melbourne.

Kahin, George McT., 1952, *Nationalism and Revolution in Indonesia*, Cornell University Press.

Kurnianingrat, 1959, 'An Indonesian Opinion on the V.G.S.', *Djembatan*, II(4), September.

Reid, Anthony, 1974, *Indonesian National Revolution 1945–50*, Longman, Melbourne.

Ricklefs, M. C., 1981, *A History of Modern Indonesia*, Macmillan.

Sastroamijoyo, Ali, 1979, *Milestones on my Journey*, (C.L.M. Penders), University of Queensland Press, St Lucia.

Soedarpo, Mien, 1994, *Reminiscences of the Past*, SEJATI Foundation, Jakarta.

Suleiman, Satyawati, 1979 'The Last Days of Batavia', *Indonesia*, 28, October.

Sutherland, Heather, 1973, 'Notes on Java's Regent Families' Part 1, *Indonesia*, 16, October.

—— 1974, 'Notes on Java's Regent Families' Part 2, *Indonesia*, 17, April.

—— 1979, *The Making of a Bureaucratic Elite: The Colonial Transformation of the Javanese Priyayi*, ASAA Heinemann Educational Books (Asia).

Varma, Ravindra, 1974, *Australia and Southeast Asia: The Crystallisation of a Relationship*, Abhinav, New Delhi.

Vreede-de Stuers, Cora, 1960, *The Indonesian Woman: Struggles and Achievements*, Mouton & Co.

Zainu'ddin, Ailsa, 1969, *Lagu lagu Indonesia/Songs of Indonesia*, Heinemann Australia.

—— 1970, 'Education in the Netherlands East Indies and the Republic of Indonesia' in R. J. W. Selleck (ed.) *Melbourne Studies in Education 1970*, Melbourne University Press.

Index